DREAMING COWS

The Paintings,
Murals and Drawings of

Betty LaDuke

Celebrating Heifer International

by Susan Jo Bumagin

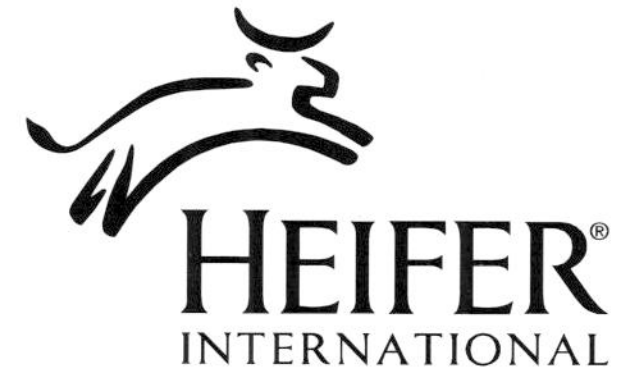

Heifer International
1 World Avenue
LittleRock, AR 72205
www.Heifer.org

The mission of Heifer International is to work with communities to end hunger and poverty and care for the Earth. Since 1944, Heifer has helped 10.5 million families in more than 125 countries move toward greater self-reliance through the gifts of livestock and training in environmentally sound agriculture. The impact of each initial gift is multiplied as recipients commit to Pass on the Gift by giving one or more of their animal's offspring, or the equivalent, to another in need. Visit Heifer.org to learn more about ways your family can help end hunger and poverty. And visit Heifer Village at Heifer's World Headquarters to see the *Dreaming Cows* mural panels and paintings.

Designed and produced by
Verve Marketing & Design,™
Chadds Ford, PA 19317 USA

Hardcover ISBN 978-0-9798439-8-3
Softcover ISBN 978-0-9819788-0-2

Description of the Work:
Betty LaDuke and Heifer International are kindred spirits. She is an artist and world citizen deeply concerned with the issues of poverty, hunger, social justice, sustainability and the environment. Heifer International has been working in just those areas since Betty was a young girl. Through her Heifer Study Tours, Betty has seen Heifer's work up close and created works that express the hope, dignity and self-reliance that the Heifer model has created in more than 125 countries around the world. *Dreaming Cows* documents the paintings and mural installation Betty created for Heifer International's Heifer Village at their World Headquarters in Little Rock, Arkansas. The book is not only a documentary of her creative process, but also a testament to the strong, resilient and hopeful people around the globe who have benefitted from Heifer's work.

Text is set in Adobe Caslon, display type is Bitstream Humanist 521.

Printed on 10% post-consumer paper, using lead-free, soy ink: 20% soy or vegetable content.

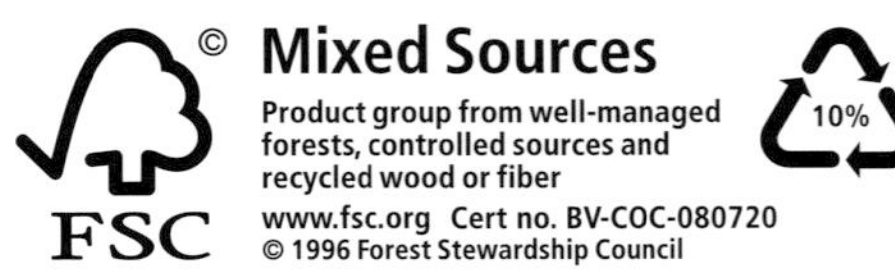

Artist's Acknowledgements

Presenting a five-year collection of joyous work—drawings, paintings and mural panels inspired by Heifer International projects around the world—has been a wonderful challenge and collaborative process. Susan Jo Bumagin caringly looked, listened and wrote the stories behind each image. She also told of my longer life journey that led to crossing paths, in 2003, with Heifer. This first experience in Rwanda and Uganda inspired *Dreaming Cows*, an artist's version of hope, social change and environmental sustainability.

It was Tom Peterson's idea to include my paintings in 2004 when Heifer International received the Conrad N. Hilton Humanitarian Prize and the United Nations sponsored an exhibit celebrating sixty years of effective work by Heifer. Select *Dreaming Cows* paintings were displayed near the deep magical colors of the Mexican muralist Rufino Tamayo, a mentor when I lived in Mexico more than fifty years ago. Two years later, Tom invited me to create a mural of Heifer's work around the world in what would be a permanent exhibit in the newly built Heifer Village.

The list of old and new friends who supported various phases of this work is long. Early encouragement came from Isaak Egge, Carla Bonetti and Becke Corkern. Thanks to Barney Johnson, my technical assistant, who spent many hours cutting and routing plywood panels for the mural project. I am deeply grateful to Robert Jaffe, a truly skilled photographer who I have worked with for many years. Many others supported my work on the *Dreaming Cows* project. Thank you to Heifer staff members who wrote about my sketchbook habit and art in *World Ark*, published notecards, encouraged me to paint and then displayed my paintings and the mural project. Thanks to Tom Peterson, Ann Harper and Peggy Scherer for making me feel that art can make a difference by opening people's eyes and hearts to sustainable solutions. I wish my parents were still here to witness this incredible affirmation but I am pleased to celebrate with my husband, Peter Westigard, and my children, Winona LaDuke and Jason Westigard, and their children.

Betty LaDuke, 2009

Author's Acknowledgements

First, I would like to express my deep appreciation to Betty LaDuke—gifted artist, woman extraordinaire and collaborator par excellence. Betty devoted many hours to discussing her work, values, philosophy and life. She was a joy to work with and a total inspiration. The Heifer and Verve Marketing & Design Team that supported us were responsive, timely, enthusiastic and helpful. Many thanks to Tom Peterson for bringing me into the Heifer fold to work on this wonderful project and to Bill Fitzgerald, who served as a great sounding board and who wrote the chapter on Heifer International. Thanks also to Peggy Scherer, Kathy Ouellette, Sue Malikowski and Diane Lemonides. Heartfelt appreciation is extended to Frankie Lappé and Susan Kanaan for many years of friendship and support. Finally, I am profoundly grateful to my husband, Paul Korn, who always hears me out with wisdom, patience and good humor.

Susan Jo Bumagin, 2009

CONTENTS

Preface . . . 8
"Betty LaDuke: The Power of Art and the Art of Power" by Frances Moore Lappé . . . 10
"Go in Hope" by Bruce Guenther . . . 12
Betty LaDuke's Story . . . 15
Symbolic and Spiritual Imagery . . . 23
The Story of Heifer International . . . 29
Special Foldout Section: Heifer Village, Dreaming Cows Mural Sequence . . . 33
Mural Project . . . 36
Introduction to "Dreaming Cows" Exhibit, Paintings, and Mural Project . . . 45

Africa: Rwanda, Uganda and Tanzania . . . 49

AFRICA PAINTINGS

Rwanda Sunrise . . . 53
Uganda: Dreaming Cows . . . 55
Rwanda: Passing on the Gift . . . 56
Rwanda: Celebrating the Gift of the Heifer 'Consolation' . . . 58
Uganda: Mrs. Nanfuka Teopista's Goats . . . 61
Tanzania: Masoud Joseph, Farmer . . . 62
Green Bananas and Ankole Cows . . . 63
Rwanda: Coffee Harvest . . . 64
Rwanda: Reconciliation . . . 67

AFRICA MURAL PANELS

Africa: Reconciliation . . . 71
Africa: Dreaming Cows . . . 73
Africa: Planning for the Future . . . 75
Africa: Beneath the Sun . . . 76
Africa: Returning From School . . . 77
Cow Landscape with Rain Birds . . . 79
Africa: Celebrating the Gift . . . 81
Africa: Goat Pride . . . 82

Asia: Cambodia, Vietnam, Thailand and Myanmar . . . 85

ASIA PAINTINGS

Cambodia: Rice Harvest . . . 90
Cambodia: Mrs. Sim Roen's Ducks . . . 91
Cambodia: Building Community Leaders . . . 93
Vietnam: Dragon Fruit Dreams . . . 96
Vietnam: Mekong River Market . . . 97

ASIA MURAL PANELS

Asia: Rice Harvest . . . 98
Asia: Building Community Leaders . . . 99
Asia: Village Market . . . 100
Asia: Mekong River Market . . . 101

Eastern Europe: Poland, Kosovo and Albania 103
EASTERN EUROPE PAINTINGS
Poland: Barka Project, Organic Farmer, Cherry Tree and Rabbits 109
Poland: Brzezowka Village Hen Project 111
Poland: Wola Galezowska Orphanage Pig Production Project 112
Poland: Red Cow Family 114
Poland: Tree of Life 117
Albania: We may be Poor but our Culture is Rich 120
Kosovo: War Widows Project 122
Kosovo: The Cow's Name is Nora 125
Kosovo: Romani Goat Project 127
EASTERN EUROPE MURAL PANELS
Eastern Europe: Hen Project 129
Eastern Europe: We may be Poor but our Culture is Rich 130
Eastern Europe: The Cow's Name is Nora 131
The Americas: Equador, Peru and United States 133
LATIN AMERICA PAINTINGS
Ecuador: Spinning Dreams 138
Ecuador: Riobamba Market Day 141
Ecuador: Riobamba, Three Pigs 142
Ecuador: Seeds of Hope 143
Ecuador: Riobamba Welcoming 145
Peru: Passing on the Gift 147
Peru: Andean Tree of Life 149
Peru: Pachamama Awakening 151
Peru: Cuchuma Women's Poultry Collective 152
LATIN AMERICA MURAL PANELS
Latin America: Tree of Life 153
Latin America Market Day Landscape 154
Latin America: Pachamama 155
UNITED STATES MURAL PANELS
USA: Saving Rural America 160
USA: Gibbs Elementary School: The Worm Story 163
USA: White Earth Reservation Wild Rice Harvest 167
Celebrating Women's Creative Hands and Spirits 170

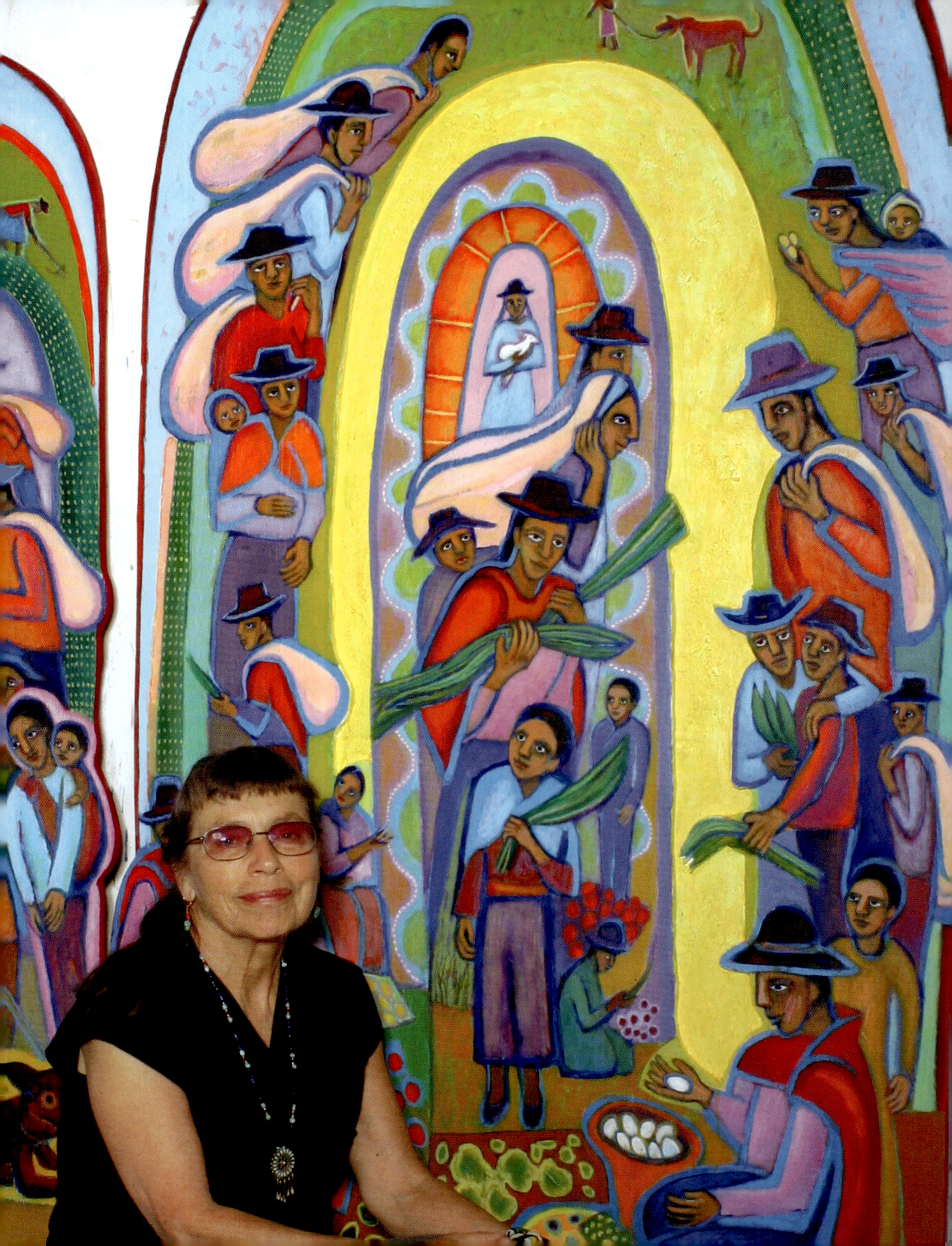

To Heifer families the world over

—Betty LaDuke and Susan Jo Bumagin

Betty LaDuke, Studio, Ashland, Oregon

photo by Helga Motley

PREFACE

Dreaming Cows conveys much about Betty LaDuke's art and her life. Here, I want to talk about Betty, the person. At seventy-five years, she moves through the world with the ease of a much younger person, drinking in whatever environment she inhabits with intense curiosity and deep respect. A strong Bronx dialect (a carry-over from her childhood) belies a worldliness that stems from countless meaningful encounters with people in more than fifty countries, most often in the developing world.

Betty's generosity is ever-present. When in 2003 she discovered Heifer International, she was delighted to find an organization whose mission and values so matched her own. A few years and eight Heifer educational tours later, Betty has donated many sketches, original prints, paintings, and now, a 100-foot long mural that illuminates Heifer's work around the world. A walk through Heifer International in Little Rock, Arkansas, is a walk through LaDuke country: her work can be seen everywhere, lighting up small office spaces and large conference rooms alike.

Betty is always pleased when people like her work but she finds real joy in heartfelt thanks from families she draws in the field and from such comments as those of Elizabeth Olowu of the Oba Akenzua II Art Foundation in Nigeria:

"At last, in the midst of a turbulent Nigerian situation, I have found the time to write to you and say I love you, Betty, for all you have done to let the outside world know something about my research, which has been decaying here in my country. *Africa Through the Eyes of Women Artists* is a marvelous piece of work, which will forever be a pride to Africans in general and to the particular. Some of these women, no doubt, would perhaps have died with their significant contributions to art unknown and lost except to themselves. I congratulate you heartily for your courage, hard work and the resultant success. Since I received that book last year, it has been passing from the hands of one historian or artist to the other; I got it back only today and the comments of the readers have gladdened my heart. More grease to your elbow, Betty."

As the book will make abundantly clear, Betty aligns with and supports women and women artists from every corner of the universe. She was thrilled when a women's weaving collective in Harare, Zimbabwe, adopted her designs to create weavings that are sold to support the Collective and the women's families. And one day, to my shock, I received two amazing prints of an original painting and mural panel that I had admired, as a gift. Why? Because this is what Betty LaDuke does. She shares her blessings.

Forever a teacher, Betty encourages people to consider their past while focusing on the present and a hopeful future. In a letter, Katarzyna Malec (Heifer's Poland director) wrote:

"I am learning from you to approach things in a different way. For example, I would never think of similarities between the disaster made by Katrina in New Orleans to the disaster of World War II, since one resulted from the phenomenon of nature and the second one unfortunately from purposeful action of human beings, but you are right that the final destructions can be compared." Betty's clearest message is that we all benefit from taking care of each other and the Earth.

Betty LaDuke is not afraid to buck the status quo. Proud of her activist role, some of her art includes astute political commentary. Though she can appear somewhat tenuous in person, she is tenacious under the surface and unwilling to compromise on the core values that she holds dear. That those values make a positive contribution in a visually stunning way is her gift to all of us.

SJB, 2009

Betty LaDuke: The Power of Art and the Art of Power

By Frances Moore Lappé

What an honor to help introduce you to Betty LaDuke.

How often over my lifetime have I heard doyens of the art world remind us of the power of art to touch our hearts. I always imagine they're speaking especially to people like me, who no doubt live way too much in our analytical left brains. I listen and have felt encouraged to open up to the feelings that art evokes, allowing art to release not only awe and pleasure but the full gamut of human emotion.

I've been surprised to find Betty LaDuke's life and work open me to yet an even wider vista, one I'd never fully registered. She reveals, as vividly as perhaps any artist, the power of art to empower.

I believe that human beings—all of us—are creative by nature. As such, a basic human need is to experience ourselves as doers, as creatures with power to shape our world. Here I use power to mean our capacity to act—not simply to get by, but to act in ways that give meaning to our lives. I also believe that today's unprecedented global crises—from climate chaos to grotesque and worsening inequality of life opportunity—can be resolved only as more and more of us experience ourselves as powerful, as doers, not mere observers. Our planetary challenges are simply too deep and pervasive to be solved from the top downward.

Thus, empowering "regular" people is in my view the primary calling of the 21st century. How do I see LaDuke empowering those who are her subjects as well as those who simply experience her art, as you are about to?

Consider where power originates: certainly, for most of us, it requires a sound base. In LaDuke's extraordinary gift for capturing specific place, family and community, she reinforces our capacity to appreciate the primary sources of power in many of our lives.

And, as Bumagin so appropriately emphasizes in this beautiful collection, LaDuke's art "can create bridges"—a metaphor capturing another dimension of power. Surely we find strength in realizing those "bridges," in knowing that we are never isolated but deeply connected beyond our communities, even across oceans and cultures. LaDuke's work fortifies us in sensing our emotional relationship with people whose lives on the surface appear utterly unlike ours but whose joys and sorrow are our own.

Throughout her work, LaDuke makes plentiful use of the sun. Its light "stirs you to move, to engage—you can't hide from the sun. It awakens and beckons you to move forward," she says. In other words, LaDuke's sun imagery reminds us that, no matter how dim our prospect of success, we can still act; even if it is in a word, a glance, a touch, a stance. This, I believe, is our ultimate power, for every act moves energy around us, creating new openings, often unforeseen.

While LaDuke's work empowers others, it also surely empowers her, as this book makes clear. "These women are my new role models," LaDuke has said of her subjects, "who teach me about life and the creative spirit. They have inspired my books and canvasses."

Betty LaDuke's extraordinary life, and her continuing acts of creation appear to me an unending spiral of empowerment through beauty. May you be swept up, too.

Go in Hope

By Bruce Guenther
Portland Art Museum, Oregon

Forty years on, and Betty LaDuke still travels in search of personal connection and authenticity. Starting innocently enough as a sabbatical exercise, her sketching trips out of Oregon and into the world have become the vehicle for LaDuke to generate new images for her paintings, meet other women artists, and to form an international web of connection for political and aesthetic advocacy. She has filled sketchbook after sketchbook in all four corners of the world with the faces of people—and women more specifically—leading their lives, eking out an existence beyond the post-consumer societies of the West, and making their own art in all its guises, from high to low. Her artwork, seen as a response to the world and the human condition, has found a dedicated following over the years among feminists, academic and humanitarian communities, and her subjects themselves. It is an art willfully outside of the mainstream art world's aesthetic concerns and firmly inside the heart.

Setting her course early in her career, LaDuke has chosen to remain a narrative, image-based artist, whose aesthetic vocabulary is grounded in the expressive figuration of mid-twentieth century modernism. Standing against fashion and the art marketplace, she has stayed true to the social imperatives of the mentors and influences that shaped her training and worldview. Artists such as Charles White, Elizabeth Catlett, Rico Lebrun, and the Mexican muralists who brought art and political advocacy into dialogue were LaDuke's teachers and role models. The perspective she has evolved concerning the function of art in society and the role of the artist underlies all the assumptions that drive LaDuke's aesthetic choices and social engagement. Her work is an art of community, a catalyst for reconciliation.

Invigorated and challenged by each successive travel experience, Betty LaDuke has spent most of her career as an artist dedicated to exploring and sketching world culture—physically, emotionally and intellectually. Programs such as Heifer International, Freedom from Hunger and Credit with Education, which have provided support and opportunities for LaDuke to travel and observe indigenous communities, have also given her venues in which the art can be a catalyst for action. The paintings and prints that have evolved from those travels embody the artist's continuing effort to give voice to the complex emotional realities of her own family, women's spiritual identity and humanity's relationship to the earth. As the photographer Robert Frank once observed about his process: "You have to find your way by intuition, not by intelligence, but intuition." It is much the same for LaDuke as she has intuitively found her way to an artistic practice that is both synthetic and authentic. Her best work contains the seed of life wrapped in the conventions of art.

LaDuke has claimed for her practice the freedom to invent and reinvent from across all manner of reference and methods of making, uniting intention, content and style free of any conflict or irony that may have marked her earlier work of the 1950s and 1960s. The bold simplicity of LaDuke's imagery, with its totemic personages, stylized patterning and rich coloration, belies the often-complex overlays and cross-referencing of cultural, mythic and spiritual symbolism she constructs on her canvasses. Resituating her painting as an intercultural dialogue in order to bridge the chasm of class and expectations, LaDuke inadvertently underlines the middle-class optimism that colors her perspective and defines her values.

Questioning the Western concept of cultural divisions between high and low, ancient and modern, LaDuke has moved easily to the integration of folkloric forms and patterns into the formal vocabulary of her work. The dense overlay of cultural mythology on the domestic narratives in her work serves to express LaDuke's deep sense of womanhood and the universal importance of family to her. The last decade of work, and certainly the celebratory Heifer International multi-component Mural Project, has been characterized formally by the use of a strong outline of color around all the figures, which serves both to isolate them in the composition and to enrich the patterning of the whole. It is always a sunny day in LaDuke's paintings—high noon and happy—rich with their bright, complementary and contrasting hues that define the celebratory imagery.

Betty LaDuke has been a firsthand participant in the cultural decentralization of the contemporary art dialogue. In her sketchbook tours and subsequent publications, she has broadened awareness of artists outside the art centers of the West by gathering and publishing data on women artists and women's lives from different geographical and political contexts. She has sharpened her own practice through her interaction with this global community. Seeking in the lives and art of non-Western women a mirror of her own experiences and a source for symbols of a larger, universal truth, LaDuke remains true to the heritage and spirit of the socially engaged artist. Her focus on personal growth and self-definition in the 1970s, and her celebration of cultural diversity from the 1980s into the present Mural Project, has kept her work vibrant and urgently current.

In an age when the mainstream art world celebrates the cool detachment of post-modern simulacra and object as image, LaDuke forges ahead to "tell the story," in traditional charcoal and paint, in works that arise from the center of her experiences as a witness, a voyeur and woman. Mindful of Paul Klee's observation that "art does not reproduce the visible, but makes visible," she fills her works with signs and symbols to maximize the potential to connect and communicate with the viewer. The world she has first recorded in her sketchpads and subsequently reinvents in paintings is alive with color and pattern, joy and hopefulness. It is not as it was on that dirt path in Africa or Asia, but as it became in Betty LaDuke's mind and heart—color, not dust; hope, not hunger.

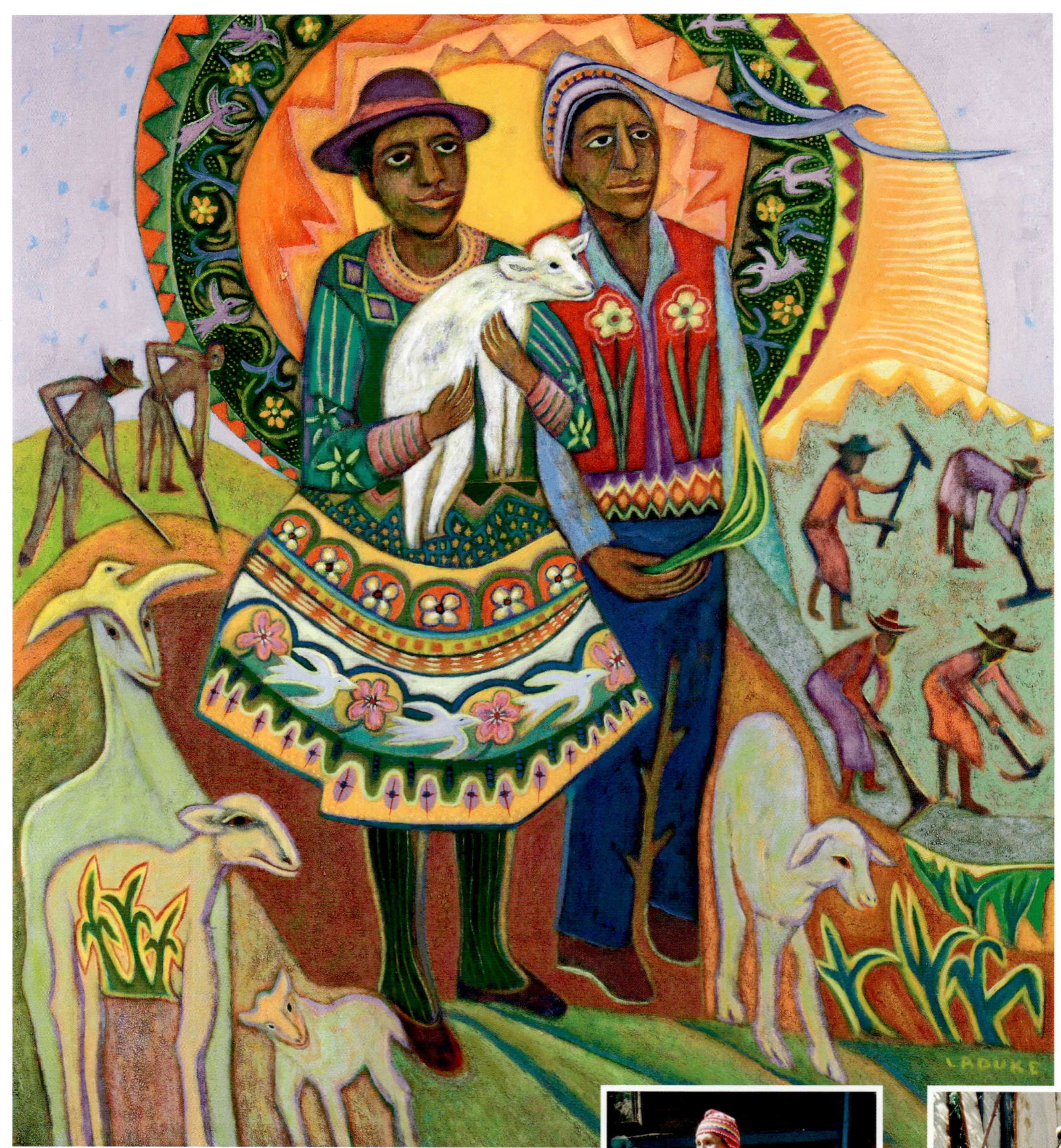

Above: *Peru: Andean Tree of Life*, 60" x 54" acrylic, 2004;
Right: Aurelio and Paolina, Cuchuma, Peru

Betty LaDuke's Story

"Art can create bridges between people and continents by sharpening our sensitivity to life's diversity. The earth is our shared home. What I do in Ashland, Oregon, can make a difference in Africa, and even a very small difference is important. I believe there is no other way." [1]

—Betty LaDuke

Introduction

Like many of the images in her etchings and paintings that evolve from the literal to universal symbols, Betty LaDuke has grown from a girl born and raised in the Bronx, New York, into a woman of the world. After more than seven decades, Betty never forgets where she came from, while at the same time, her vision has been profoundly affected by journeys to almost fifty countries in Africa, Asia, Europe and the Americas. Her luminous and richly colored works reflect a spirituality and deep respect for cultural diversity, communities working together, gender equality and "Pachamama" or Mother Earth. The author of six books and four videos about her experiences and those of other women artists throughout the world, Betty has exhibited her paintings, sketches and mural panels in more than 300 one-person shows.

At the core of her being is a lifelong belief that everyone is entitled to respect, dignity and basic human rights: human beings must connect to each other and to the Earth with understanding and compassion. Since her days as an art student in Mexico in the 1950s, Betty has traveled to parts unknown to record the tribulations and triumphs of women and their families whose remarkable resilience has overpowered great odds. Her books describe women who "are my heroines.[2] They are our contemporary goddesses. Survivors of malnutrition, political oppression, even massacres, they block the movement of armed military personnel with sticks, stones and their bodies to protect children. I have seen their faces…"[3]

Recurrent themes of identity, community, spirituality and locality (that which connects people to their families, extended families and communities) are found within vividly

---

[1] *Women Artists of the American West*, edited by Susan R. Ressler, Chapter 15, "An Artist's Journey;" p. 298; 2003.

[2] *Compañeras: Women, Art, and Social Change in Latin America* (1985); *Africa Through the Eyes of Women Artists* (1991); *Women Artists: Multicultural Visions* (1992); *Africa: Women's Art, Women's Lives* (1996).

[3] Ressler, p. 281.

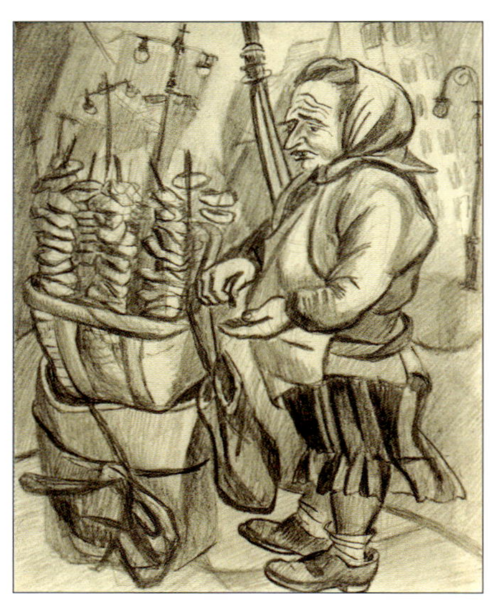

Bagel Lady, pencil drawing, 1950

textured forms and patterns that distinguish one cultural heritage from another. As a professor emeritus who taught art at Southern Oregon University for 32 years, Betty values education. Her etchings, paintings and murals teach us about the human condition as they captivate us with their earthiness, symbolic reach and heart-wrenching beauty.

Early Years

Born in 1933, Betty Bernstein was the only child of Jewish parents who had escaped war and hardship by immigrating to the United States from villages in Ukraine and Poland in the 1920s. Her father worked as a house painter in the Bronx and her mother worked as a seamstress in a pocketbook factory. The family lived in a tenement apartment within an integrated neighborhood of Italian, Irish and Jewish families whose children played together on the streets. Betty grew up to the smells of chicken soup, borscht, pickled herring, cabbage and spaghetti.

A seminal experience for her future life as an artist occurred at the age of nine when she attended Wo-Chi-Ca, a Worker's Children's Camp in New Jersey. There, professional artists and art counselors Charles White and Elizabeth Catlett encouraged Betty to express herself freely. They shared their own art, including "Images of Dignity," a series that had been shaped by their experience as African Americans. It was here that Betty was first introduced to Mexican mural painting and other art forms that would influence her future choices.

Student Years and Beyond

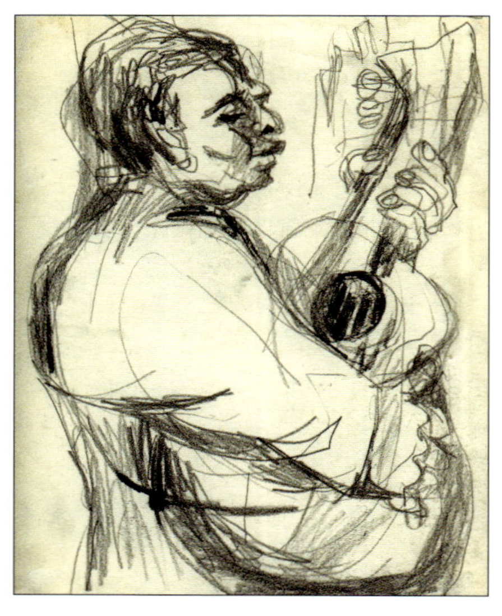

Rampart Street Blues, pencil drawing, 1951

Betty was accepted into the prestigious High School of Music and Art in Harlem, New York. When assigned to sketch life in the city, she began with neighborhoods in the Bronx, Harlem and New York's Lower East Side.

She won a scholarship to the University of Denver where her college years began and then to the Cleveland Institute of Art where she continued her studies from 1951-1952. An adventuress ahead of her time, Betty hitchhiked solo to St. Louis in 1951, took a Mississippi riverboat to Cairo, Illinois; and then traveled to Memphis, Tennessee, where she worked in nearby cotton fields. During her travels, this spunky young woman sat at the back of the bus and used 'colored only' restrooms and water fountains. Reacting to the injustice of segregation, Betty made a spur-of-the-moment decision when she arrived in New Orleans: "I altered only one fact to coincide with my new identity: I told my employer my mother was black. Black is many tones, many shades, and with my suntan, I qualified."[4] So, at the age of eighteen, Betty Bernstein, who had grown up with the songs of Paul Robeson and Pete Seeger and the poems of Countee Cullen and Langston Hughes, experienced what it was like to be a black person in America. An awareness of oppression would follow Betty over the course of her life to every continent.

[4] *Women Artists of the American West*, edited by Susan R. Ressler, Chapter 15, "An Artist's Journey;" p. 284; 2003.

While in New Orleans, Betty waitressed at the Dew Drop Inn at Rampart Street, where she sketched life around her including Big Joe Turner singing the blues in *Rampart Street Blues* (1951).

Upon her return to Cleveland, Betty's first exhibit was held at an African American cultural center called Karamu House in 1952. Mixed media portraits of neighborhood people illustrated heartfelt connections that set the stage for a lifetime of give-and-take between artist and subjects that would enrich her work: "My new friends introduced me to new foods: sweet potato pie, collards and pig knuckles. Pickled pig knuckles! I loved chewing gristle around bones. After all, I had grown up with chicken's feet in my mother's soup."[5]

In 1953, Betty won a scholarship to study art in Mexico at the Instituto Allende in San Miguel. Life in the small rural town—the daily and seasonal rituals of caring for family, farming, cooking, selling, working and praying—mesmerized her:

"I sketched women before sunrise: grinding, kneading and then slapping small balls of corn *masa* or dough, to form tortillas that they cooked on a flat clay dish over an open fire. At the market, the women patiently sat beside their tortilla-filled baskets, waiting for customers, so they could earn enough to begin the process all over again."[6]

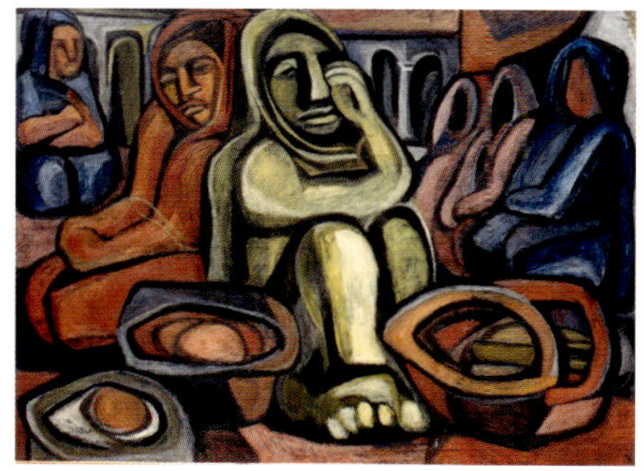
Market Women with Tortilla Baskets, oil on masonite, 32" x 48", 1953

During this period, Betty learned about murals by observing well-respected painters Diego Rivera, David Siquieros and Rufino Tamayo at work. She especially appreciated the pride of these artists for their country's indigenous cultures, which had previously been marginalized during colonization. Aztec and Mayan archaeological sites provided additional inspiration. Betty valued the beauty and utility of local crafts such as baskets (made with the fiber of local plants) that served many purposes in daily life and became an additional source of income on market day.

Betty remained in Mexico beyond her student years. In 1954, five exhibits of her paintings and drawings were sponsored by the Mexican government. Two years later, an organization sponsored by the United Nations and the Mexican government, Patrimonio Indigenista del Vallédе Mesquital (PIVM), invited her to paint murals on the patio walls of one-room schoolhouses that would reflect Otomi Indian culture in the Ixmiquilpan region. The traditions and struggles of the Otomi, which left a deep impression, were a precursor to later encounters with indigenous cultures struggling for survival throughout the world.

Return to the United States in Search of Family and Community

When Betty returned to New York in 1956, her first full-time job was as the art program director at the Grand Street Settlement House in the Lower East Side. It was here that she met her future husband. Sun Bear (Vincent LaDuke) had been traveling the country

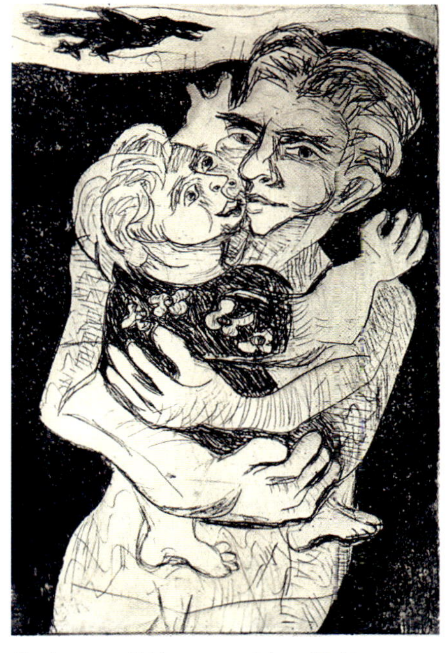
Sunbear and Winona, etching, 1960

[5] *Women Artists of the American West*, edited by Susan R. Ressler, Chapter 15, "An Artist's Journey;" p. 284; 2003.

[6] Ibid.

to raise consciousness about conditions on Native American reservations and to raise money for better housing. Betty moved with Sun Bear to White Earth Reservation in Minnesota where she learned how to hunt and trap animals. Despite an appetite for venison stew and wild rice harvested from nearby lakes, she could not commit to the tough existence on the Reservation. The couple moved to Los Angeles, where Sun Bear worked sporadically as a movie extra in stereotypic roles. In 1959, their daughter Winona was born.

Not long after, Betty completed her undergraduate degree and secondary teaching credential in art. She taught art at an East Los Angeles junior high school while working on her Master's degree in printmaking. In their free time, the couple often attended pow wows and visited reservations in the West and Northwest.

While Ashland was "home," the activist in Betty felt somewhat out of place in this small homogeneous and predominantly white community. She describes a series of thirteen box paintings called *Love Totems* that highlighted major events of 1968 to include portraits of Martin Luther King, the Pope and the Pill, Khrushchev, President Johnson, the Beatles and flower children, and scenes from the Vietnam War and the Detroit riots. Another series of images, entitled *No Exit*, (which portrayed three symbolic nude figures harking back to Jean Paul Sartre's existential play) grabbed front page headlines of the local paper *Daily Tidings* (February 14, 1968): "Ashland Artist Stirs A Ruckus."

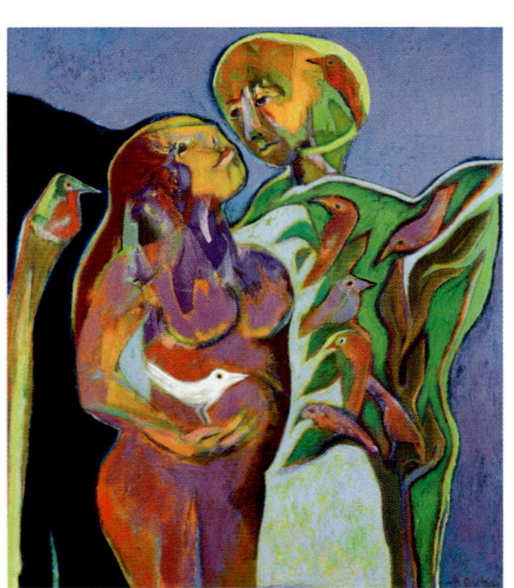

Summer Joy, acrylic on canvas, 56" x 50", 1972

Evolution of Themes in Art and Life

While Betty's family was often the subject of her sketches, she began to explore religious and historical themes in the early 1960s, including her own Jewish heritage. *Los Marranos* (1961), for example, told the story of Jews who converted to Catholicism during the Spanish Inquisition but who secretly continued to practice Judaism. During this period, Sun Bear and Betty parted ways. Betty and Winona headed north after six years in Los Angeles to settle in Ashland, Oregon where she still lives with her husband, Peter Westigard.

In 1964, Betty began teaching at Southern Oregon State College (SOSC). It is here that she met Peter, an agricultural scientist who became her second husband in 1965. Of the early years of marriage, she said, "The first decade of our marriage was a challenge! Bagels are tough and chewy; pears are sweet and mellow. Big adjustments! Talking and listening; listening and talking. My Bronx style was emphatic, while Peter's California voice was a whisper by comparison, but his message was clear and strong. Camping trips, hiking and exploring mountain lakes and Oregon's wild ocean beaches offered space for our varied moods as we were nourished by the magnificence of nature."[7]

Peter's research benefitted the local pear industry and reduced grower dependence on chemicals (via integrated pest management [IPM], which uses predator insects and hormone traps for male insect sterilization). Betty's ongoing interest in food production and her later work with Heifer International benefitted greatly from Peter's interests and knowledge.

During this period and into the 1970s, Betty painted large mythical landscapes:

"I entered into each form—the earth, trees, rocks and water—letting them possess me so that I, too, became the huge wave rising and falling in *Ocean Sunrise*; a tree approaching winter in *Redwood Silence*, or a bird within a mountain as in *Summer's End*. Sometimes Peter and I embraced within a rock form as in *Whale's Head*, or became filled with the energy of flowers, birds and sunshine, as in *Summer Joy*."[8]

---

[7] *Women Artists of the American West,* edited by Susan R. Ressler, Chapter 15, "An Artist's Journey;" p. 287; 2003.

[8] Ibid., p. 288.

For the first eighteen years of her employment at SOSC, Betty was the only woman teaching full-time in an art department that expanded from five to eleven faculty members. Discovering the Women's Caucus for Art (WCA) within the College Art Association and the National Art Education Association in 1977 was a "turning point" in her professional career. Not only was she exposed to a wide range of women artists but also to art historians and critics. In 1978, she initiated a course entitled "Women and Art," which she continued to teach until her retirement in 1996. The strength and accomplishments of women became an ongoing and significant theme in Betty's subsequent work.

The Acorn Doesn't Fall Far From the Tree

Winona was a frequent subject during her growing up years and again, years later, harvesting rice with her son as part of the large mural created for Heifer International's Heifer Village. Betty describes the *Merry-Go-Round* (1969), painted when her daughter was ten: "She is firmly seated on a galloping wooden horse. Was I foretelling the future? In 1996, she appeared on a real horse on the cover of *Sierra Magazine* along with the announcement of her vice-presidential candidacy for the Green Party with Ralph Nader as president." After graduating from Harvard University, Winona began her life's work to preserve and restore traditional Native American ways and environmentally sound practices. In 1989, she founded the White Earth Land Recovery Project in Minnesota, whose mission is to "facilitate the recovery of the original land base of the White Earth Indian Reservation, while preserving and restoring traditional practices of sound land stewardship, language fluency, community development, and strengthening our spiritual and cultural heritage."[9]

In 1970, Betty and Peter's son, Jason, was born. He, too, appeared in many of Betty's paintings and prints including *Terrible Two's* (1971) and *Summer Play* (1971), *Jason's Journeys* (1972), and *Jason Climbing* (1973). Years later, Jason would become the editor of Betty's book *Women Against Hunger, A Sketchbook Journey* and a graphic designer for the book *Africa, Women's Art, Women's Lives.*

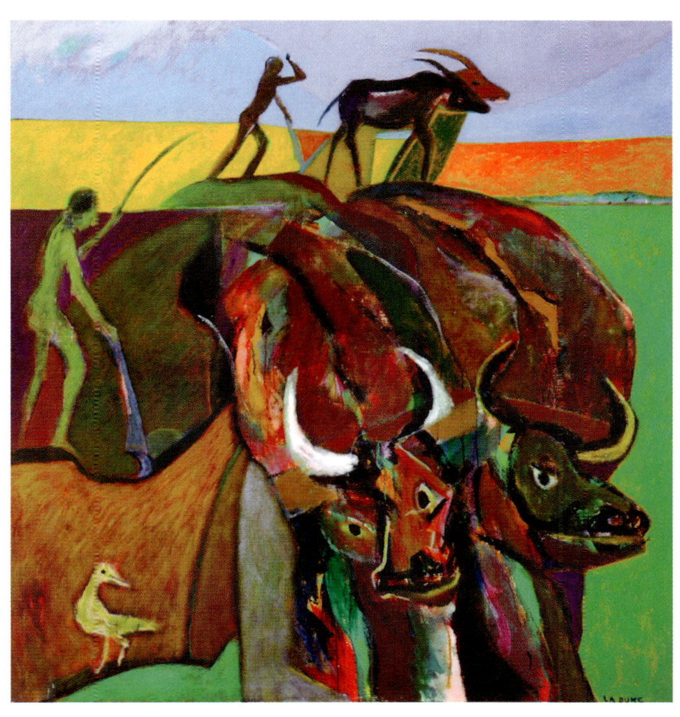
India: Spring Ritual, acrylic on canvas, 72" x 68", 1972

Exploring a Multicultural World

In the 1970s, Betty's world and work expanded as a result of a 1972 sabbatical to India. This trip became the first of many annual pilgrimages to non-Western cultures. Armed with a sketchbook, camera and notebook, Betty documented the work of many women artists on these journeys while experiencing a taste of life vastly different from her own.

"Red, burgundy red, cherry red, orange red, hot red, spices of cumin, coriander, turmeric, cayenne to create delicious meat, fish, vegetables, curry sauces tempered by cool white yogurt. Conflicting sensations.

[9] NATIVE HARVEST BROCHURE *Native Harvest*, created in 1995 as an outlet for the Land Recovery Project's products, has become a thriving catalogue mail order and internet business that generates a steady income for the White Earth Reservation community.

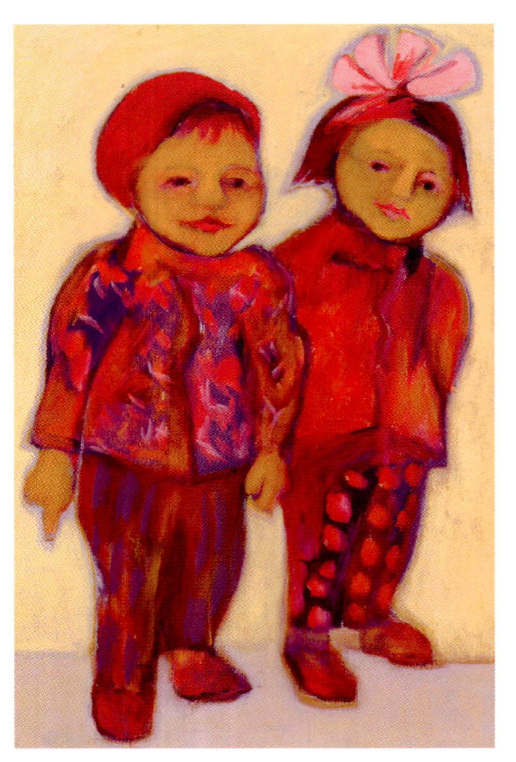
Chinese Children, acrylic on canvas, 38" x 32", 1976

Many new foods to taste, coupled with an awareness of insufficient food for many, and the justification by people with full stomachs that it is Ananda or Karma. Accept your fate." [10]

When she returned home, she began teaching "Art in the Third World" at SOSC. Betty's work from India later became a traveling exhibit entitled *"Impressions of India."* With the support of her family as well as various grants and fellowships, she traveled to India two more times between 1972–1980 and also visited Australia, Papua New Guinea, the People's Republic of China, Sri Lanka, Thailand, Indonesia and Borneo. During this fruitful period, another traveling exhibit entitled *"China, an Outsider's Inside View"* was developed that symbolically illustrated socialist progress in a country whose people were intimately familiar with harsh living conditions.

In Australia, Betty was struck by similarities between the history of oppression of Aboriginals by English colonists to that of Native American Indians. In Papua New Guinea where she traveled along the Sepik River by houseboat, the focus was on spirits, ancestral images and stories of creation. In the painting *Borneo: Iban Birth Rite* (1981), the depiction of "puas" or blankets used to receive newborn babies, affirmed an oft-made symbolic connection between weaving and the life cycle. In each locale, Betty embraced the fabric of life as she assimilated each culture's rituals, belief systems and ways of living. These meaningful encounters were integrated first into her heart and soul and then, into her art.

Latin America

From 1980—1985, Betty visited thirteen Latin American countries, focusing mainly on social and political issues that embodied the lives of women and women artists. *Compañeras: Women, Art, and Social Change in Latin America* was published in 1985. Paintings during this period reflected the disappeared of Chile during the reign of Pinochet (*Chile: Children of the Disappeared* [1982]); the untimely death of children (*Bolivia: Pachamama and El Tío* [1983]); past, present and future in *Peru: Earth Mother* (1983); and a host of others. The imagery of *Peru: Mother Earth* helped shape the concept of metamorphosis, which began to permeate more and more of her work. Visually, the corn and the women become one: "The women's bodies become corn-filled. The painting illustrates the integration of people with the land and with the food they are growing."

A visit to Edna Manley, sculptress and wife of Jamaica's first prime minister after British rule, was an additional source of encouragement in 1986. Manley's sculpture *Ghetto Mother* inspired the creation of *Jamaica: Tomorrow* (*Homage to Edna Manley*) [1986].

[10] *Women Artists of the American West*, edited by Susan R. Ressler, Chapter 15, "An Artist's Journey;" p. 290; 2003.

Africa

From 1986–2007, Betty generated more than 200 paintings that convey themes and daily life within many African nations. From 1986–1990, she visited women artists in Senegal, Mali, Nigeria, the Ivory Coast, Kenya, Egypt and Morocco, which led to the publication of *Africa Through the Eyes of Women Artists* (1991). A new series of paintings emerged entitled *Africa: Between Myth and Reality:* "These paintings are my praise song to Africa, especially the women, bringing forth, nurturing and sustaining all life forms: cultural guardians and healers, mythical goddesses and sexual beings." [11]

The Africa paintings tell stories about the continuity of life. Survival rhythms of growing, tending, harvesting and eating food; creation myths and fertility; the role of women; marketplaces; celebrations; war and peace; and honoring the Earth are but a few basic themes that carry over to her later work with Heifer International. While these concepts overlap from country to country, each geographic location is unique. Kenya, for example, conveys an interweaving of all sizes and shapes of animal in lush natural habitats (captured, for example, in *Kenya: The Zebra Tree of Life* [1998] and *Kenya: Masai Spirit Quest* [1989]). In contrast, Eritrea (which Betty visited for eight consecutive years in the midst of its thirty year war with Ethiopia) is a hot desert country "where for the first time, I am painting camels."

Examples abound of paintings that connect to the processes of food production and consumption—that which Betty calls "survival rhythms." Creation myths and fertility take center stage in many other images. The role of women in society remains a constant central theme, as represented by *Nigeria: Bird Women, Keepers of the Peace* (1986). This painting portrays a group of women whose headdresses become mythical spirit birds and guardians of the peace. A group of women weavers at Cold Comfort Farm Weaving Collective in Harare, Zimbabwe, later wove the images of this painting into tapestries entitled "Rainbird Women." These tapestries have been sold in commercial art galleries in Europe and the United States.

Marketplaces are another hallmark of Betty's work. How she loves them! *Burkina Faso: Women on the Move* (1993) is one of many works that shows women at market—buying, selling and socializing—as they manage children, animals and produce. Likewise, LaDuke paintings are replete with celebrations of all kinds, as seen in: *Ghana: Spirits Rising* (1993), which celebrates the end of a loan cycle and the women's sense of accomplishment; and in *Eritrea: Women Celebrate* (1997), where before an Eritrean wedding, women prepare *suwa*, a fermented beverage made from dried *injera* (a pancake-like bread made from teff flour).

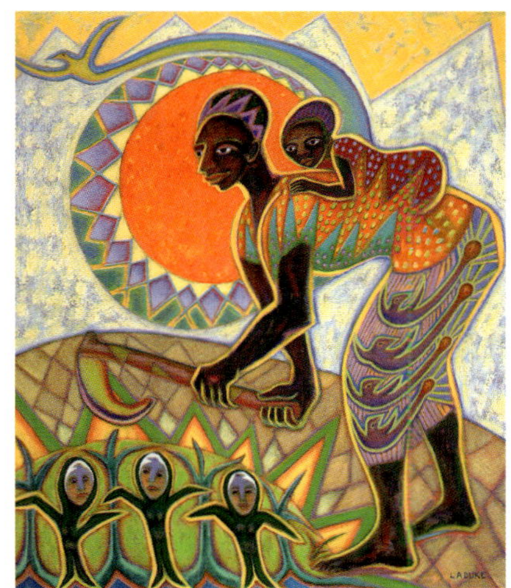

SURVIVAL RHYTHMS

- *Burkina Faso: Pounding Millet, Sharing Dreams* (1993) shows women talking together as they share bowls to pound grain.
- *Cameroon: Millet Rhythms* (1994) illustrates the backbreaking work of weeding millet plants. This painting has since become the cover of a textbook on Africa Studies entitled *Understanding Contemporary Africa* (1996).
- *Cameroon Fish* (1994) reminisces about a delightful meal shared with Peace Corps volunteers.
- *Eritrea: Chicken Vendors* (1996) melds the forms of women and chickens at a market in Asmara.
- *Eritrea: Sifting Grain, Sharing Dreams* (1995): Women spend hours cleaning grain before it is pounded into flour. The grain kernels are filled with "women's dreams of love and fulfillment." (BLD)
- *Eritrea: Reshaping the Land* (1995): During the war between Eritrea and Ethiopia, the land was stripped of trees. To make the land useful again, the steep mountain slopes were terraced to improve productivity and prevent erosion.

Eritrea: Reshaping the Land, acrylic on canvas, 60" x 54", 1995

[11] *Women Artists of the American West*, edited by Susan R. Ressler, Chapter 15, "An Artist's Journey;" p. 294; 2003.

CREATION MYTHS

- *Senegal: The Creation Myth* (1987); fish represent the woman fish vendor's children.

- *Nigeria: Osun's Children* (1987) shows the beneficent River Goddess Osun reaching out to support infertile women and providing treatment and comfort to people who suffer.

- *Mali: Dogon Rain Chant* (1988): A mother's prayer for rain reaches across cultures to represent a Dogon woman as well as Betty's daughter Winona, who nurses her children.

- *Africa: Mandala* (1987): Birds holding male and female figures within them fly above three lizards chasing each other. They carry seeds of new life.

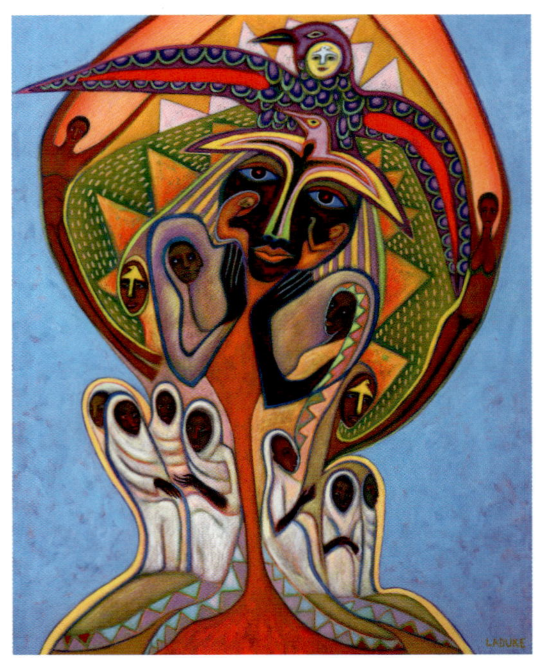

Eritrea: Tree of Life, acrylic on canvas, 60" x 54", 1996

War and Peace

War and peace constitute significant areas of focus, beautifully represented by work from eight years of visits to Eritrea between 1994–2002. Three years after the thirty year war between Ethiopia and Eritrea ended, Betty went to Eritrea to interview artists for a book about women's art in Africa and subsequently, to present workshops at the Asmara School of Art. During earlier visits, she painted scenes of daily village life, reshaping the land and rebuilding communities.

In 1998, the Ethiopian government initiated a program of ethnic cleansing during which families were separated and longstanding Eritrean residents were deported or killed without warning. These terrible events, known as the Border War, moved Betty to paint life within refugee and relocation camps. This led to a series of paintings that articulated dislocation and loss, to include: *Refugee Camp* (1999); *Mandala for Peace* (1999); *Grandmothers Dreaming Peace* (1999); *Saho Family Dreaming Home* (2000); and *Eritrea-Ethiopia: Where Have All the Fathers Gone?* (2000). Several circulating exhibitions, including "*Africa: From Eritrea with Love*" (paintings and drawings) and "*Eritrea-Ethiopia, Prayers for Peace*" (paintings), also came out of these sobering trips. [12]

In addition to Eritrea, Betty's journeys from 1991–1997 took her to Ghana, Burkina Faso, Benin, Togo, Cameroon, Mali and Zimbabwe. Interviews from this period resulted in *Africa: Women's Art, Women's Lives* (1997) and *Women Against Hunger, A Sketchbook Journey* (1997), whose cover featured a copy of the painting *Women's Solidarity, Spirit of Credit with Education* (1997). The painting demonstrates the success of a micro-lending program. Women meet weekly under a cottonwood tree to pay back loans of $30 to $50 to the non-profit organization Freedom from Hunger (FFH) for self-initiated projects. They learn about good fiscal practices and even about how to improve family health.

[12] *Sojourners Magazine*, March/April 2001; Vol. 30, No. 2.

Symbolic and Spiritual Imagery

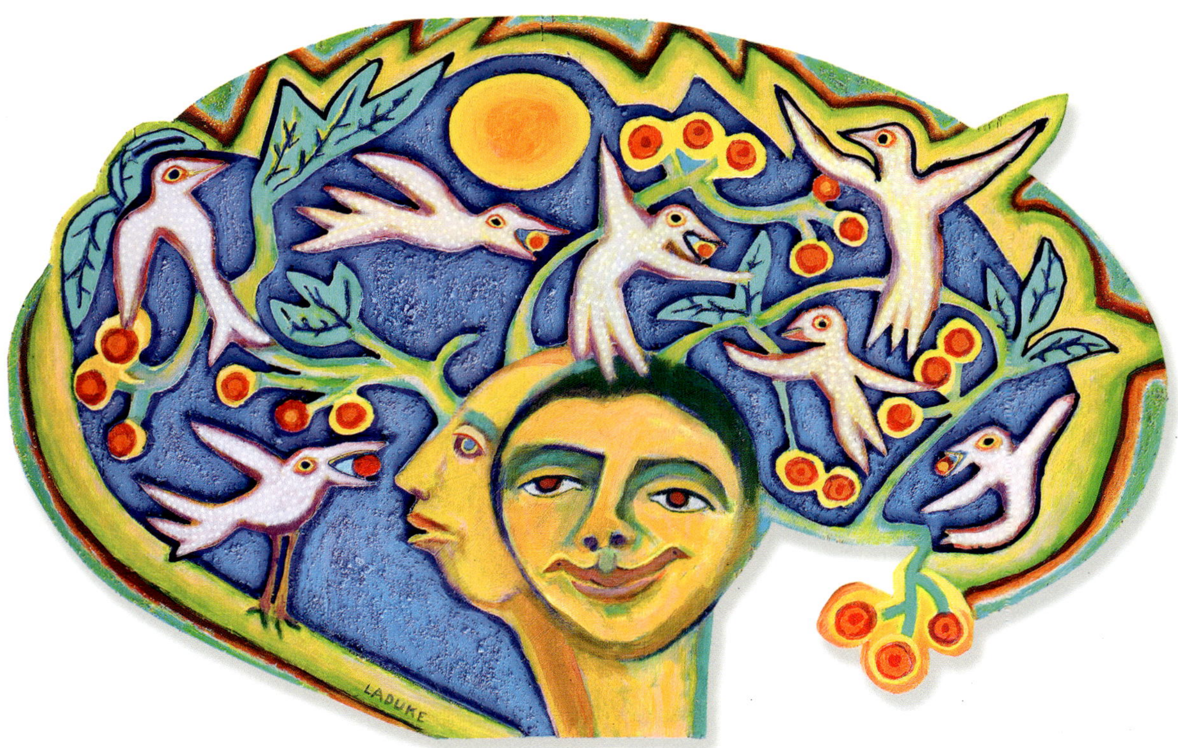

Oregon Cherry Harvest, 24" x 37," acrylic on wood panel, 2008

"LaDuke is the storyteller of the spiritual and ecological values and practices of indigenous peoples around the world."[13]

—Gloria Feman Orenstein

In 1976, Betty's visit to China left a deep impression, especially the belief that humankind is very small within the magnitude of nature. Manifested through art, literature and other cultural outlets, this philosophy changed her approach: "I saw a non-Western sense of form that was lyrical. It moved differently and transformed my way of painting."

Much of Betty's work is imbued with a sense of timelessness that moves to natural rhythms of the land, the seasons, the cultures she inhabits and the people. She entices viewers with imaginative play—the beatific face of the sun, a cow that grows plants within it or a bird

[13] Orenstein, Gloria Feman, *Multi-cultural Celebrations, the Paintings of Betty LaDuke 1972-1992*; Pomegranate ArtBooks, San Francisco CA; 1993; p. ix.

"O the joy of my spirit! It is uncaged! It darts like lightning! It is not enough to have this globe, or a certain time—I will have thousands of globes, and all time!"

—Walt Whitman, "Poem of Joys," Leaves of Grass[14]

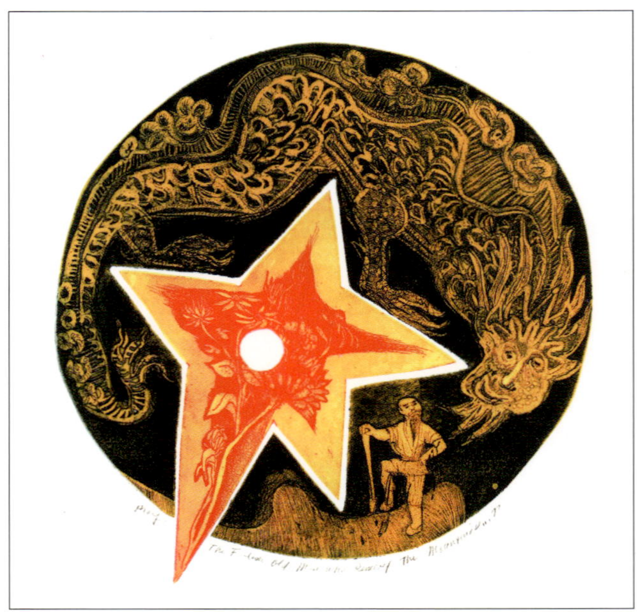

The Foolish Man Who Moved the Mountains, etching, 18" x 18", 1976

that constitutes part of a human face. Betty challenges her audience to move beyond literal or photographic representation to engage with the mythical and spiritual imagery that permeates her work.

Spirituality

In Betty's universe, spirituality transcends specific religious experience, embracing an "awareness of a tremendous energy that keeps us all connected and going, a timeless kind of energy and the importance of just honoring life." [15]

The poetry of Walt Whitman, Carl Sandberg, Pablo Neruda, Langston Hughes and Countee Cullen has influenced Betty's sensibilities in profound ways. In their own distinct styles, each poet wrote about becoming "one" with the land. Betty has visually built upon this idea by fusing human and animal bodies with nature in her work. In *Peru: Pachamama Awakening* (2005), for example, the face of Mother Earth is contained within the lower part of a woman's body; and in *Rwanda: Reconciliation* (2003), the fingertips of joined hands morph into birds. All this ties into her notion of spirituality: "We are just a tiny speck within the chain of life. Going outside of oneself—seeing the bigger energy connections that take in life outside of one's immediate body—allows us to join with them. When one is not bound by the moment, it is possible to see a continuity of all life forms and to experience limitlessness."

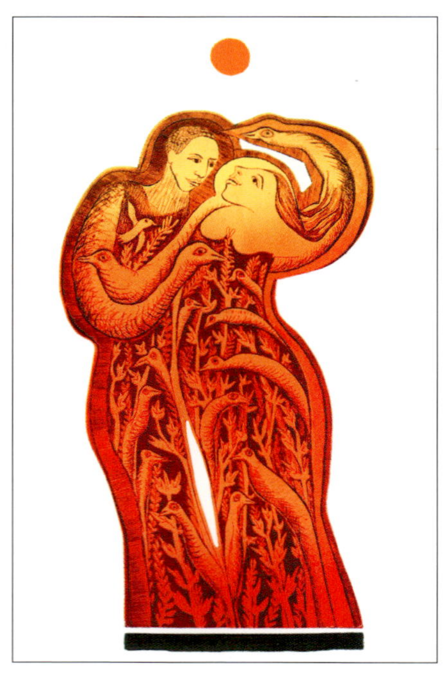

Granada: Brief Flowering, 18" x 18", etching, 1985

Because life is always in flux, the potential for transformation is everywhere. Even when we are not aware of change taking place, it is happening, as Betty suggests, sometimes in the form of arms turning into birds or human bodies becoming lizards as in *Africa Night Journey* (1986). "Life," says Betty, "is bigger than the material moment."

Storytelling

Stories were an intrinsic part of Betty's childhood. She loved to hear about the lives of her family in the old country. The storyteller would sometimes poke fun and, at other times, impart lessons and values that remain with Betty to this day. She learned about independence, resourcefulness and community-mindedness from her Polish grandmother. Bela was a self-educated woman who drove a horse and buggy to neighboring towns to

[14] www.bartleby.com/142/196.html.

[15] Betty LaDuke quoted in Arbogast, Marianne, *"Probing Global Richness and Diversity;"* The Witness; June 2000; p. 31.

deliver home-ground flour at a time when most women stayed at home. She placed a bench by her house to encourage news-sharing with passers-by; and she conveyed the importance of learning to her children by always taking an interest in learning and by sending as many of her children to school as possible. Years later, Bela's daughter, Helen, shared her creativity with her only child. A favorite story describes Helen's attempt to contain pigeons nesting on the balcony of a twelfth floor Bronx apartment. Hoping to frighten them away, she salvaged and wove together a collage of plastic Christmas trees and flowers. Although she did not succeed in scaring away the birds, Helen's imaginative spirit obviously took hold in her daughter.

"Stories give you a sense of who you are that helps you to move beyond the past. They pass down important messages about how individuals and communities evolve within specific timeframes."

—Betty LaDuke

Betty has continued the family tradition of storytelling through her art, much of which relates to Native American culture. In *The Telling of the World, Native American Stories and Art*, W.S. Penn says, "Storytelling for Indians is not something that happens in the past, though stories may tell about the past; it is a process that continues—its meaning and importance are present and even future. Above all, then, stories integrate; they put the 'I' into the context of the 'We,' connect one person to another—whether that other be animal, mineral, or vegetable." [16] LaDuke stories often refer to the struggles of the past while focusing on bounties of the present and hopes for the future. Whimsy, folklore, singing and dancing accompany messages of peace, harmony, community building and reconciliation.

Beauty

Throughout her career, Betty has honored outward beauty found in nature and inward beauty, which she defines as a sense of inner peace and harmony. This concept of beauty has been greatly influenced by her experiences in other cultures, and especially by the concept of bambolse, derived from the Gurensi wall painters of Ghana. In the article, *Gurensi Wall Painting*, Fred T. Smith describes its meaning:

"When we walk on the Path of Beauty, beauty comes from within us, for to walk this path is to understand and acknowledge the essence of beauty in all other forms of life as well."

—Gabriel Horn[17]

"Like many other African peoples, the Gurensi do not have a word that translates as 'art.' However, they do recognize a concept, bambolse, that means 'embellished,' 'decorated,' or 'made more attractive.' . . . The intention is that action must have been primarily to increase the aesthetic merit of the form if the decoration is to be bambolse." [18]

To live in beauty is spiritual. Decorated earthenware, baskets and boats seen in such paintings as *Ecuador: Riobamba Market Day* (2004) and *Vietnam: Mekong River Floating Market* (2006) represent the artist's interpretation of bambolse. Betty explains, "When people who struggle with basic survival create significant and pleasing patterns and designs in their environment, even in everyday objects, they are surrounded by grace. Otherwise, why decorate pots, baskets or boats?"

[16] W.S. Penn, Editor, *The Telling of the World, Native American Stories and Art*; Stewart, Tabori & Chang; New York; 1984; p. 6.

[17] Horn, Gabriel; *The Book of Ceremonies: A Native Way of Honoring and Living the Sacred;* New World Library; 2000; p. 41.

[18] Smith, Fred T., "Gurensi Wall Painting;" JSTOR: *African Arts*, Vol. 11, No. 4 (July, 1978); p. 36; links.jstor.org.

LaDuke Symbols

Oft-used symbols, described below, send powerful messages: Mother Earth signifies fertility and the strength of women; the ever-present sun provides warmth and energy while corn and other plants flourish within the "inner landscape" of cows and people. The Tree of Life, an age-old universal symbol, incorporates people, animals, plants, decorative patterns and the sun in paintings of Africa, South America and Eastern Europe. Birds reflect hope and possibility; flowers integrate beauty into daily life; spirals convey timelessness; and hands join people and communities together.

THE SUN

> "...Help me to shatter this darkness,
> To smash this night,
> To break this shadow
> Into a thousand lights of sun,
> Into a thousand whirling dreams
> Of sun!"
>
> *Langston Hughes, Excerpt from "As I Grew Older"* [19]

In addition to warmth and energy, the sun reflects unity as it encompasses all that exists beneath it. In many LaDuke paintings and mural panels, the sun is portrayed as a mandala within the landscape and also as a bright border embracing creatures and plants that bask within its glow. To Betty, this source of light "stirs you to move, to engage—you can't hide from the sun. It awakens and beckons you to move forward." In *Africa: Sunrise* (1989) and *Rwanda Sunrise* (2003), the sun is both a life force and an observer of life that is witness to the past, present and future. In the mural panel *Africa: Beneath the Sun* (2007), the sun asserts itself after the rains as a key force within the seasonal cycle of growth.

MOTHER EARTH

Mother Earth nourishes the people who populate Betty's work and in a broader sense, represents fertility. Through her, Betty tells a story of reciprocity: when people care for the Earth, the Earth, in turn, provides for the people. When one is endangered, so is the other. Earlier Africa paintings emphasize symbols of the Earth, often in the form of pregnant women. For example, in the painting *Africa: Osun's Children* (1990), the central female figure is filled with plant forms and children. The woman has no feet because "her body flows into the Earth, rises from the Earth and becomes one with it." In *Africa: Rain Chant, Dawn* (1988), the Mother Earth figure nurses one child, holds another and carries two more within her legs. Symbolically, "mother" and "Mother Earth" are inextricably connected.

Mother Earth is a powerful symbol that takes many forms: it can be a big curve forming the underbelly of a cow, as in *Rwanda: Reconciliation* (2003) or a circle within

[19] www.squidoo.com/poetry-by-langston-hughes.

a circle that holds a group of women, as in *Vietnam: Dragon Fruit Dreams* (2006). She can be seen more literally in the paintings, *Peru: Earth Mother* (1983) and *Peru: Pachamama Awakening* (2005). Mother Earth is the ultimate female icon whose radiance envelopes all living beings and whose warmth and nurturing spirit encourages growth, human and otherwise.

TREE OF LIFE

Throughout time, the Tree of Life has been recognized as an important symbol in many cultures and religions. The future Buddha, Prince Siddhartha, is said to have attained enlightenment at the center of the world under a sacred tree.[21] Adonis, the Greek God of vegetation, was born in a tree trunk.[22] The Hindu God, Krishna, was known to stand "under the Kadamba Tree sacred to him. . . at the center of the world."[23] Psychologist Carl Jung described the tree as a symbol of the psyche or the self in the process of maturing.[24]

The Tree of Life is a recurrent image in Betty's work, as seen in *Africa: Zebra Tree of Life* (1988); *Africa: Masai Tree of Life* (1988); *Eritrea: Tree of Life* (1996); *Poland: Tree of Life* (2005); and *Peru: Andean Tree of Life* (2005). The artist appreciates the interconnection between all parts of the tree. Its roots derive nourishment from the Earth, which sustains its trunk. The strength and solidity of the trunk support branches that reach toward the sky, suggesting growth and expansion. The tree's cycle of life is a metaphor for the cycle of all life: it approximates death as it loses leaves in winter, sprouts new growth in spring and regenerates continually through seeds and fruits.

"...on either side of the river, was...the tree of life, which bare twelve manner of fruits, and yielded her fruits every month; and the leaves of the tree were for the healing of the nations."

—Black Elk, of the Oglala Sioux Nation[20]

Africa: Mandala, acrylic on canvas, 72" x 68", 1986

BIRDS

A signature LaDuke symbol is the bird, which appears in many forms and hovers protectively over people, plants and animals across the universe. Integral to many of Betty's internal and external landscapes, birds often inhabit faces and appear in hats and traditional designs. They represent possibility, freedom and imagination. These creatures partner with the sun and sing to the Earth. They join with and often become part of other animals. In *Rwanda: Reconciliation* (2003), they fly toward justice and harmony and in *Nigeria; Bird Women, Keepers of*

[20] Cook, Roger, *The Tree of Life, Image for the Cosmos*; Avon Publishers; 1974; p. 8.

[21] Ibid., p. 39.

[22] Ibid., p. 47.

[23] Ibid., p. 50.

[24] Ibid., p. 32.

"A spiral has no beginning and no end—it propels us forward."

—Betty LaDuke

the Peace (1986), they function as guardians of the peace. Sometimes whimsical and at other times watchful, they communicate openly. Always, LaDuke birds send a message of hope.

Birds first appeared in Betty's work during the period in the 1950s spent with the Otomi people of Mexico. On a practical level, farming communities depend on them for information about when the rains will come and when it is time to plant. But to Betty, the bird's most powerful message is spiritual.

HANDS

Hands are another powerful cross-cultural symbol. In Morocco, for example, the symbolic hand of Fatima (daughter of the Prophet Mohammed) is superstitiously used for protection throughout the Middle East and in parts of Africa. In Betty's work, hands clasp together to signify unity and connection. They might transform into birds or reach toward the sun from inside of a cow. In the painting *Rwanda: Reconciliation* (2003) and the mural panel *Africa: Reconciliation* (2007), joined hands are a key symbol used to convey the concept of reconciliation in a country devastated by civil war and genocide. In the painting *Ecuador: Riobamba, Welcoming* (2004), a pair of hands lovingly tends food in the fire, symbolizing a warm welcome to guests from a woman of little means.

FLOWERS

As a child of the Bronx, Betty did not grow up with flowers: "There was only one snake plant in the house but I began to look at neighborhood flower shops. I gravitated toward the colors, the joy of flowers. I loved them."

Floral designs, which vary from culture to culture, are prevalent throughout Betty's art. They decorate clothes and brighten the landscape, as illustrated by the mural panel *USA: Saving Rural America* (2008) and much of her work about Eastern Europe. They help people celebrate life's forward movement. Flowers remind us that beauty can be found anywhere.

SPIRALS

Betty has followed women weavers throughout her journeys. The symbolic act of weaving speaks of women whose lives are inextricably connected to those around them in much the same way the yarn is interwoven to create cloth. In the mural panel *Celebrating Women's Creative Hands and Spirits* (2008), the spiral is a prominent symbol. "Women who weave," Betty tells us, "specifically do something to make the pattern imperfect because they don't want to challenge the Creator spirit. You don't want the ego to get too big." A spiral, she continues, offers a way to understand how things grow by reflecting the continuity of life.

FULL CIRCLE

Betty's art weaves all of these symbolic elements together into a larger story of humankind. In doing so, she helps us to experience the struggles, accomplishments and dreams of people she portrays throughout the world.

The Story of Heifer International

Long before the term "NGO" (non-governmental organization) was common in international news, an organization dedicated to alleviating hunger was created by a man who saw a need. While its idea was simple, its effect has been profound. The first "Heifers for Relief" Committee was started in Goshen, Indiana, in 1939 at the Church of the Brethren, one of the country's historic peace churches. Now a respected international development organization, Heifer International has helped more than 10 million people in more than 125 countries through gifts of livestock and training.

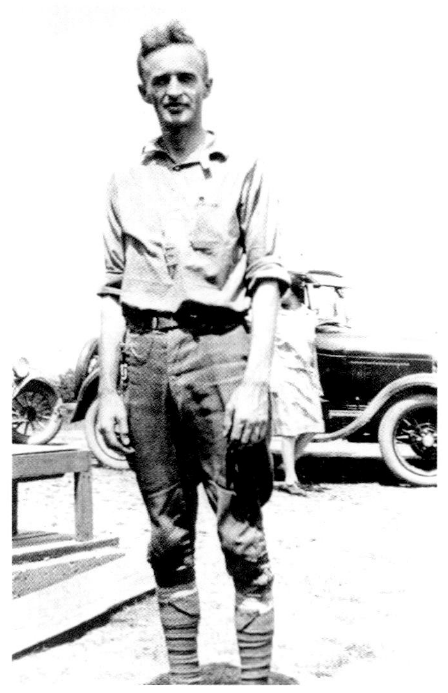

Dan West, founder of Heifer International, in his role as a camp counselor in the 1920s.

Heifer International began as the innovative idea of Dan West (1893-1971), an educator, farmer and Church of the Brethren staff member who did relief work during the Spanish Civil War in 1937–1938. While there, Dan saw first-hand the disastrous effects of hunger and poverty on people who were caught up in situations beyond their control. He knew that those who lined up to receive cups of powdered milk would be back the next day because they lacked the means and opportunities to do anything else. There was no way for them to pull themselves out of a desperate situation. He realized that they didn't want to stand in a relief line any more than he wanted to offer them powdered milk as a way to address their needs.

Day after day, week after week, as West and his compatriots delivered food and supplies in the war-torn Spanish countryside, he kept thinking, "There's got to be a better way." Back home in Indiana, families provided for themselves by working the land and raising livestock. It dawned upon him that what the people of Spain needed was "not a cup, but a cow." If they had a renewable, sustainable way to provide for themselves rather than a temporary handout, they might not only survive, but thrive.

In 1939 on the eve of World War II, Dan West returned home from Spain determined that this bold idea was not just a good thing to do, but the *right* thing to do. After consulting with church members, farmers, government officials and educators at some of the most prestigious universities in the country, he developed a practical plan to deliver immediate and renewable aid: they would send heifers (young cows that have not yet given birth).

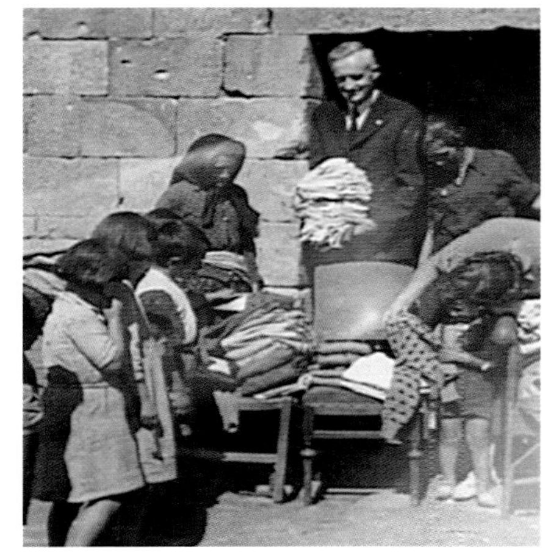

WW II showed Dan West—and the world—that hunger and need knew no boundaries or borderlines.

The following year, Dan's idea took hold. Excitement built and the concept spread to other congregations. But with war raging overseas, there was no possibility of shipping heifers to Europe for some time. So on July 13, 1944, the liberty ship William D. Bloxham left the port of Mobile, Alabama, bound for Puerto Rico, a territory with a serious milk shortage. They carried a load of 17 heifers (bred before their departure), two weeks worth of alfalfa and hay and a full crew of sailors and "seagoing cowboys" to tend the herd. With a war on, the Bloxham was accompanied by four well-armed U.S. Navy ships. Nine days later, they arrived in San Juan with an additional calf that had been born in transit.

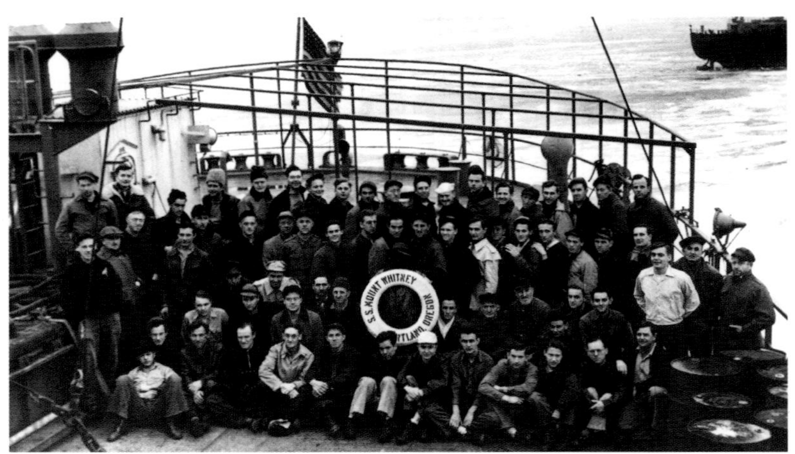

Hundreds of "Seagoing Cowboys" helped ferry livestock across oceans to help fight hunger and poverty, first for the UNRRA, and then for Heifer.

The first heifer delivered on the island was named "Faith." An appropriate name, as the Committee was going on faith that their program would succeed, be maintained for the long-term and make a difference in the lives of many. More than six decades later, the concept has been proven sound time and again.

Heifer and UNRRA

By the end of World War II, little agricultural activity existed in Europe. Livestock had been slaughtered, and for six years, no effort had been made to replenish farmlands. Funded by donations from more than 50 nations, the United Nations Relief and Rehabilitation Administration (UNRRA) was established. One of its first orders of business was to work with Heifer to transport "relief heifers" to Europe.

Heifer and UNRRA shipped thousands of head of livestock overseas on converted liberty ships. To tend the livestock, thousands of seagoing cowboys were recruited at a wage of about $150 per 4-6 week trip. The large majority of these men came from the Church of the Brethren, where the Heifer concept had been nurtured and widely accepted.

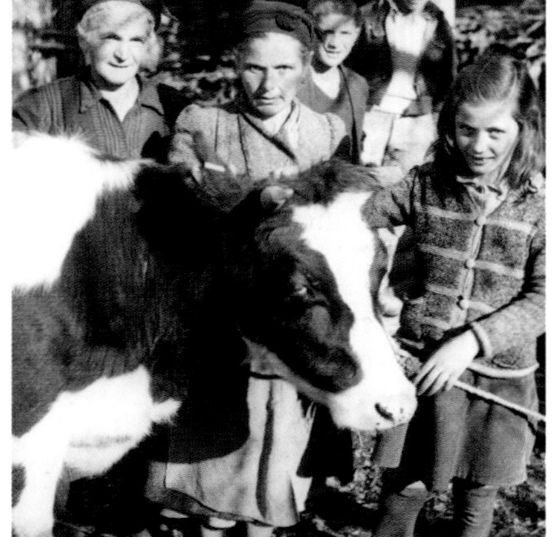

A healthy, productive cow could mean the difference between life and death in a country devastated by war's destruction.

UNRRA ultimately became responsible for some $4 billion in development aid and the relocation of millions of displaced persons in Europe and China. It developed a livestock program of its own, borrowing heavily from Heifer's model and successes. When the Marshall Plan was developed in 1947, UNRRA evolved into what we know today as the United Nations High Commissioner for Refugees (UNHCR) and the United Nation's Children's Fund, or UNICEF.

Without UNRRA, the ability to transport donated livestock was greatly diminished. But as Heifer continued its work, church and civic groups joined them, thus enlivening a grassroots spirit. Under Dan West's continued guidance, the Brethren's efforts gathered strength from the participation of Baptists, Lutherans, Mennonites, Catholics, the Evangelical and Reformed Church (later the United Church of Christ), the Rural Life Association and other non-church related service agencies. Through the end of the 1940s, funding from other sources enabled shipments to continue.

Heifer Grows

By 1947, almost 5,000 cattle donated from 39 states had been sent to Europe. But early on, Heifer realized that cows weren't going to be the answer to every hunger situation. In 1947, the first shipments of dairy goats went to Japan and Okinawa, where grazing space was a pricy commodity and most families didn't own enough land to support a heifer. The U.S. Army provided transport for that goat project, which grew from 530 to 5,000 by 1950. In

1952, planeloads of hatching eggs and chicks were sent to Korea. It's believed that of Korea's present chicken population, some 50–80% are descended from those first "Heifer chicks." Two years later, a "Noah's Ark" shipment of sheep, pigs, rabbits and bees sailed for Korea.

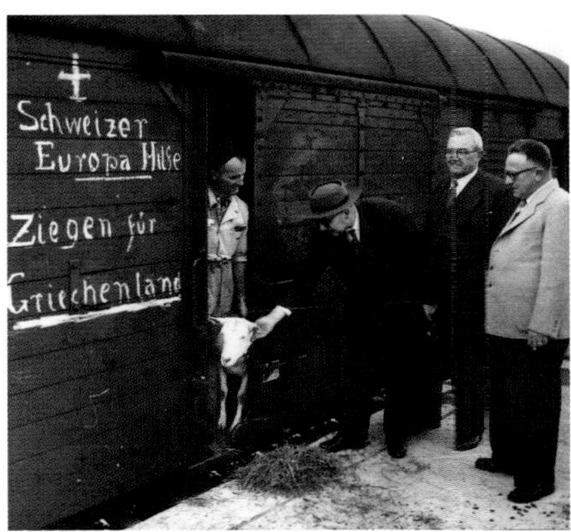

Heifers were the first livestock used by the non-profit; later came goats, sheep, pigs, chickens, fish, camels, bees, llamas rabbits and many more species. All help lift people out of poverty and into self-reliance.

This move toward diversifying livestock set the stage for Heifer's shift from relief to development work in the coming years. As the organization grew, it saw that hunger affected more than just far-off lands: the first shipment of livestock within the United States was sent to Cotton Plant, Arkansas, in 1947.

In 1951, Heifer hired its first full-time Executive Director/Program Director, Thurl Metzger, a former UNRRA liaison officer and seagoing cowboy. Early in Metzger's tenure, the Heifer Project began to reach still more countries. The first shipment of bulls went to India in 1955 to upgrade native cattle. This experiment led the government of India to adopt crossbreeding of Heifer and native animals to improve productivity and disease resistance. At the height of the Cold War in 1956, Heifer negotiated with the Soviet Union to supply livestock for cross breeding. Fifty-two heifers and three bulls were shipped from Houston, Texas, to Odessa in the fall of that year. It was Dan West's strong belief that hunger doesn't distinguish between the cries of communist and capitalist babies. Two years, later, celebrations were held—briefly—as the 10,000th heifer was shipped to Germany. The work continued.

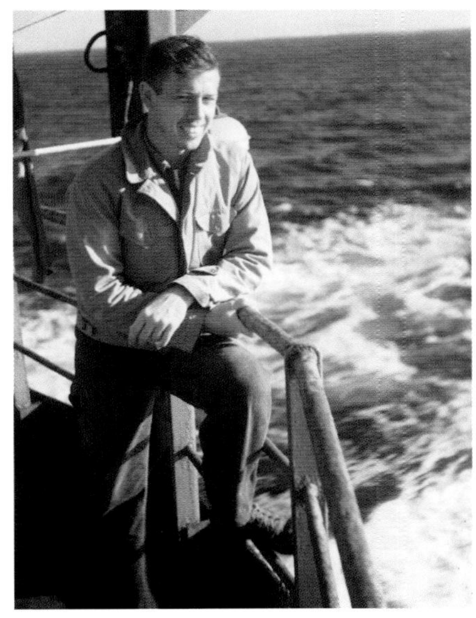

Former "Seagoing Cowboy" Thurl Metzger on a voyage to Poland, 1947. He became Heifer's first full-time Executive Director/Program Director and served until 1981.

The "Modern" Period

Today, Heifer International is a large, sophisticated multi-national organization with all the organizational charts, marketing plans, information technology and strategic alliances of a large business. One of the earliest of those strategic alliances was made in 1961 with the Peace Corps. The two groups developed joint programs in St. Lucia, West Indies and Ecuador. Subsequent contracts resulted in joint programs in Bolivia, Iran and other areas of need.

In 1969, Dan West was honored at "25 Years of Giving Life," an ox roast at the organization's birthplace in Goshen, Indiana, for 2,000 guests. He died two years later on January 7, 1971. While it is hard to express the profound impact of his legacy, the late Andrew Cordier (then Dean of the School of International Affairs at Columbia University and trusted aide to UN Secretary-General Dag Hammerskjold) came close: "Few men have left behind them such a rich legacy of faith, conviction, and good works. The Christian principles for which he stood would, if applied, put an end to the major disturbances of today's world. His influence was deeply felt by many people in and outside the church. The extraordinary character of his life and the clearness and depth of his convictions mean his influence will be felt in the lives of people for decades and generations to come."

Continuing the work of the enormous project Dan West started, that same year Heifer purchased a large working ranch near Perryville, Arkansas, where it gathered a herd of 700

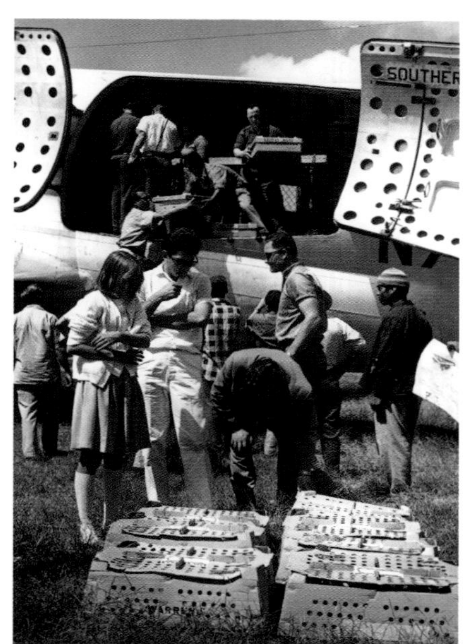

Heifer staff and volunteers unload live chicks in Ecuador in the 1960s.

beef cattle for future programs. At the same time, some 2,000 registered Black Angus cattle helped fulfill programs in Mississippi, Arizona, Guatemala and Israel. Soon after, cattle were shipped to Cameroon and Tanzania, marking the beginning of dairy development and research programs, as well as the Africa Program. Shortly thereafter, the first Heifer Learning Center, established in Ceres, California, began a public outreach and education program.

Little Rock, Arkansas, became home of Heifer's International Headquarters in 1986. The 40th anniversary of Heifer's first livestock shipment was marked in 1983 and in 1986, Ronald Reagan presented Heifer with the President's Award for Volunteerism. Dan West's widow, Lucy West Rupel, accepted the award at the White House. Two years later, partnerships were forged as *Send a Cow* in England and *Bothar* in Ireland were created to support and assist Heifer projects.

Heifer China opened in 1989. Throughout the late 1980s and early 1990s, programs expanded in Russia, Poland, Romania and Bosnia in Central and Eastern Europe. Recognizing that natural disasters often disrupt already precarious food systems, Heifer established a Disaster Fund in 1998 to respond to Hurricane Mitch, which devastated Honduras. This fund facilitates rapid response to worldwide emergencies.

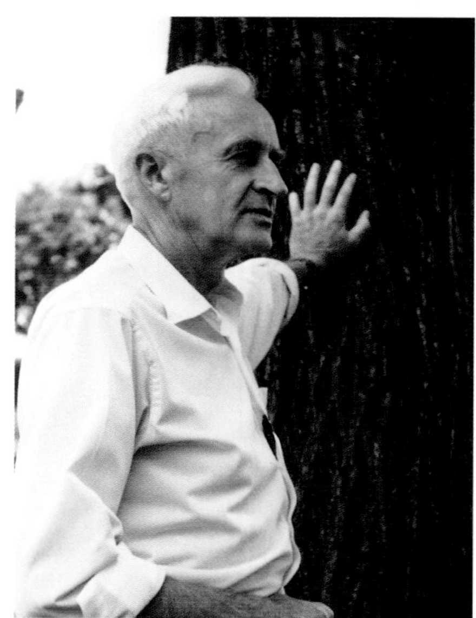

Dan West (1893-1971) Made the idea of "not a cup, but a cow" a reality. His legacy lives on to this day.

Remembering Dan West's observations about hungry people's reluctance to seek help, Heifer formalized some major tenets that remain central to its operation today. Though people may feel humbled by a Heifer gift, if they are asked to pass on that gift, they, too, become donors, a role that bestows a greater sense of dignity, pride and self-reliance. The 1960s and beyond saw a growing global awareness of the connection between survival and care of the Earth. As populations grew, Heifer recognized that it couldn't just feed people; it had to be a good steward of natural resources and make its efforts sustainable in the long run. Equally central is the notion that caring for the Earth goes hand in hand with caring for the animals. Integrated farming techniques benefit both: manure, for example, fertilizes crops that increase nutrition while replenishing depleted soils. Animals, fodder grasses and trees replenish nitrogen and other nutrients in the soil. By-products such as milk, wool and eggs represent sustainable sources of income and nutrition. Heifer's mission statement sums it all up: To work with communities to end hunger and poverty and to care for the Earth. Its vision is a world of communities living together in peace and equitably sharing the resources of a healthy planet.

With increased donor support, the organization grew rapidly during the 1990s and beyond. The one-millionth animal was passed on in China in 1999. Just three short years later, China also saw the three-millionth Heifer animal passed on. By the end of the 1990s, Heifer's web site was educating the public and raising funds for the organization's work. In 2000, the organization's name was officially changed to Heifer International (HI), to better characterize the true nature of its scope and work. Soon after, the present "jumping cow" logo was created to brand this growing international humanitarian organization.

Mural Sequence

AFRICA: BENEATH THE SUN / PLANNING FOR THE FUTURE

AFRICA: CELEBRATING THE GIFT

AFRICA: RETURNING TO SCHOOL

AFRICA: DREAMING COWS

AFRICA: RECONCILIATION

ASIA: MEKONG RIVER MARKET

ASIA: VILLAGE MARKET DAY

ASIA: BUILDING COMMUNITY LEADERS (DIPTYCH)

ASIA: RICE HARVEST (DIPTYCH)

EASTERN EUROPE: WE MAY BE POOR BUT OUR CULTURE IS RICH

EASTERN EUROPE: THE COW'S NAME IS NORA

EASTERN EUROPE: HEN PROJECT

LATIN AMERICA: MARKET DAY (TRIPTYCH)

LATIN AMERICA: TREE OF LIFE

UNITED STATES: SAVING RURAL AMERICA

UNITED STATES: GIBBS ELEMENTARY SCHOOL: THE WORM STORY

UNITED STATES: WHITE EARTH INDIAN RESERVATION, WILD RICE HARVEST

DREAMING COWS MURAL PROJECT AT

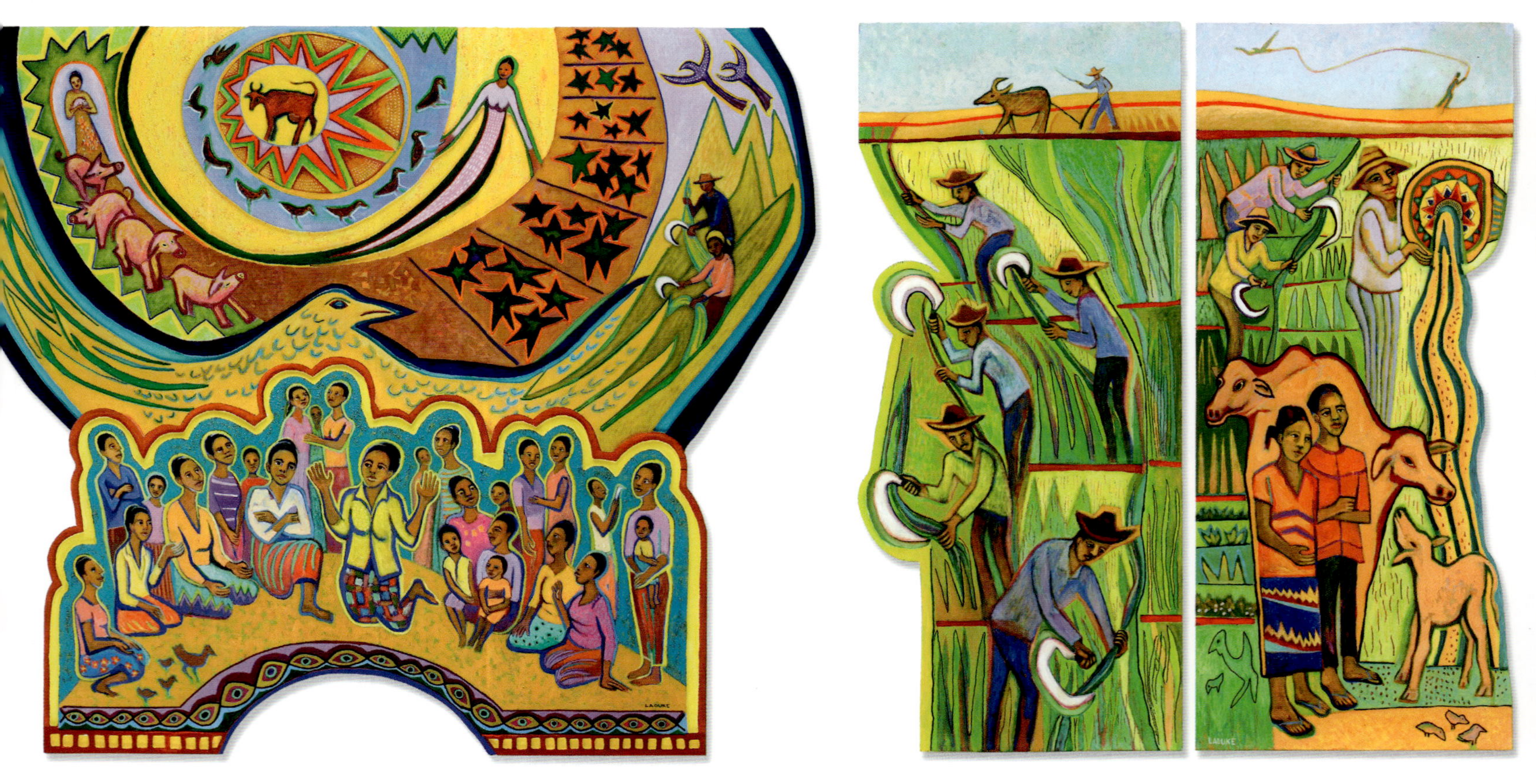

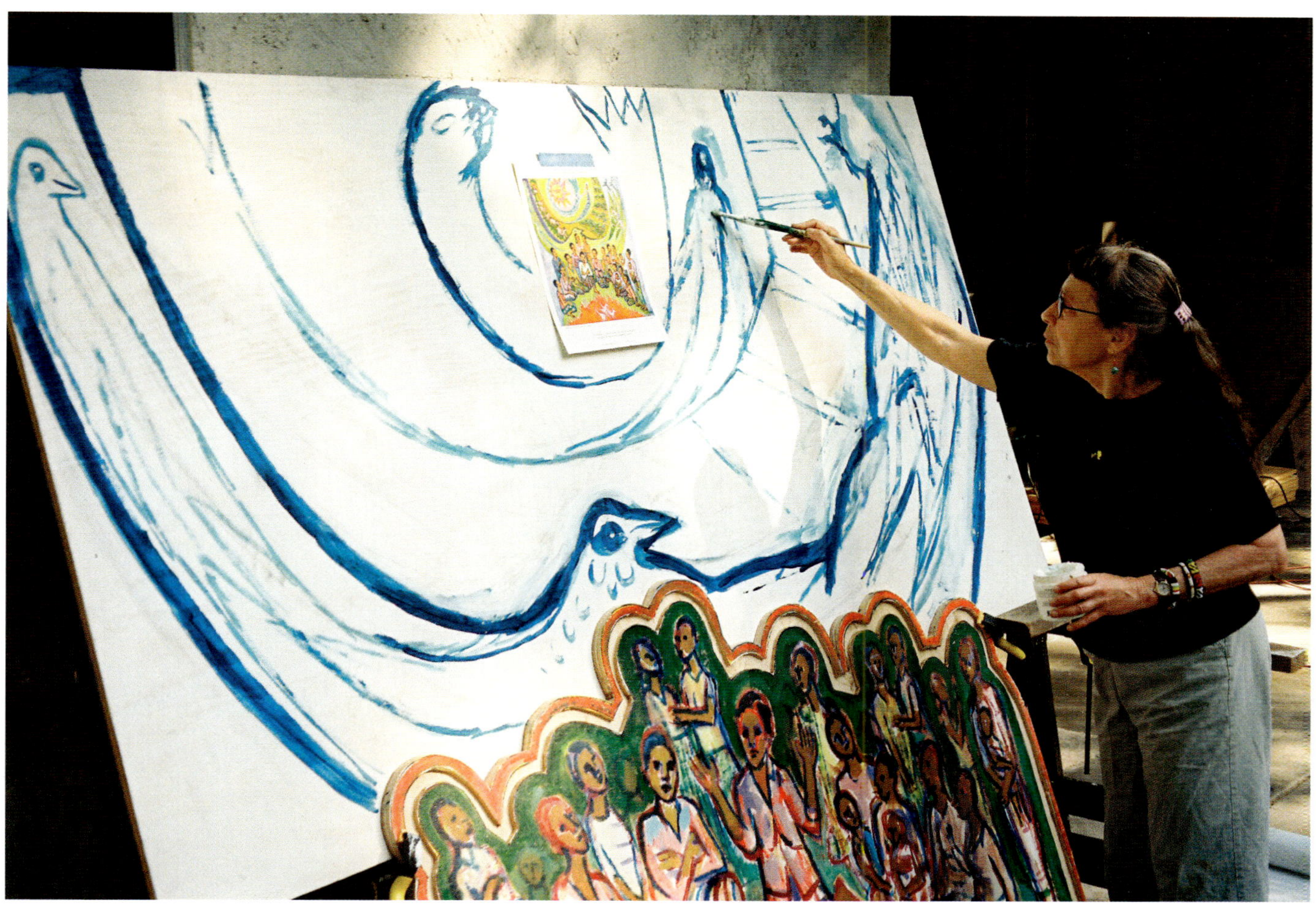

Asia Mural Panel, top section, in process.

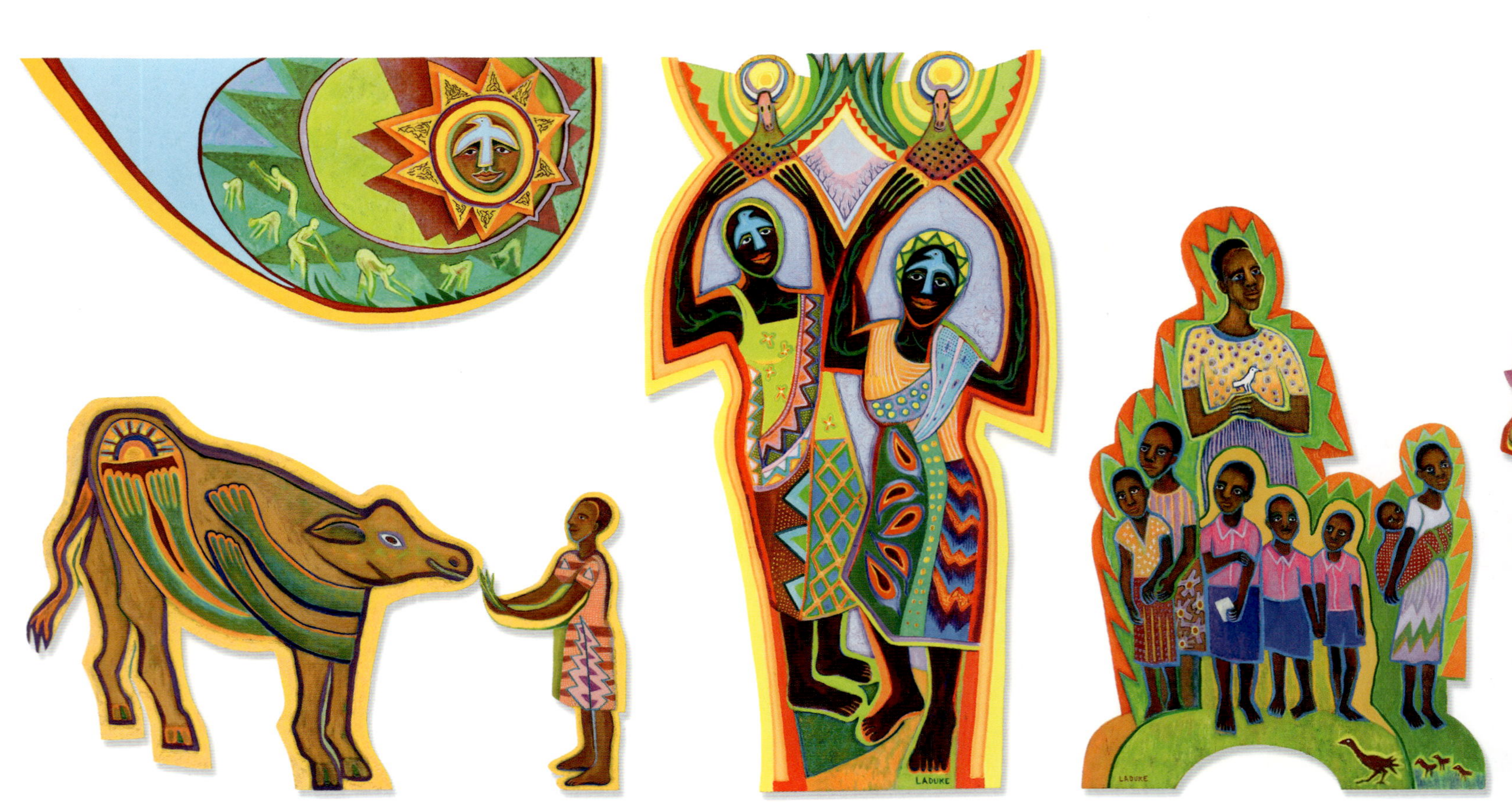
LADUKE
LADUKE

T H

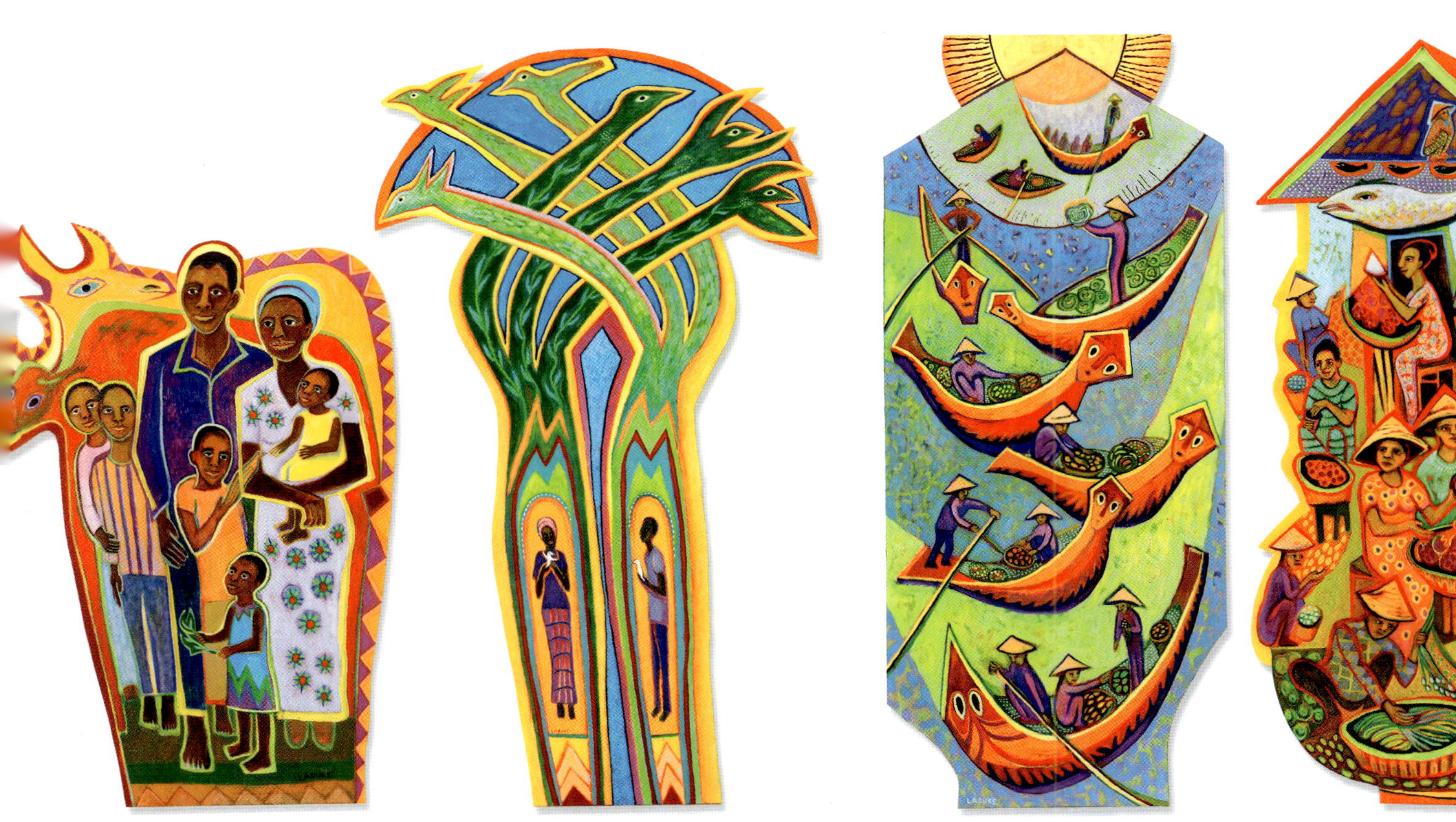

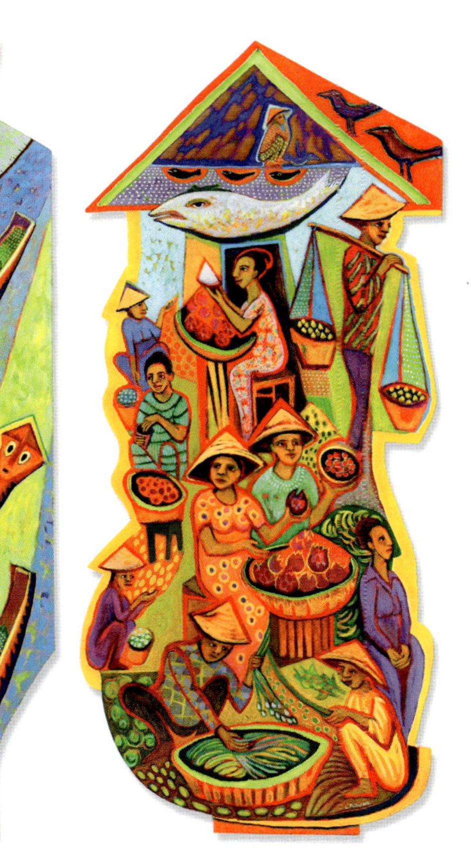

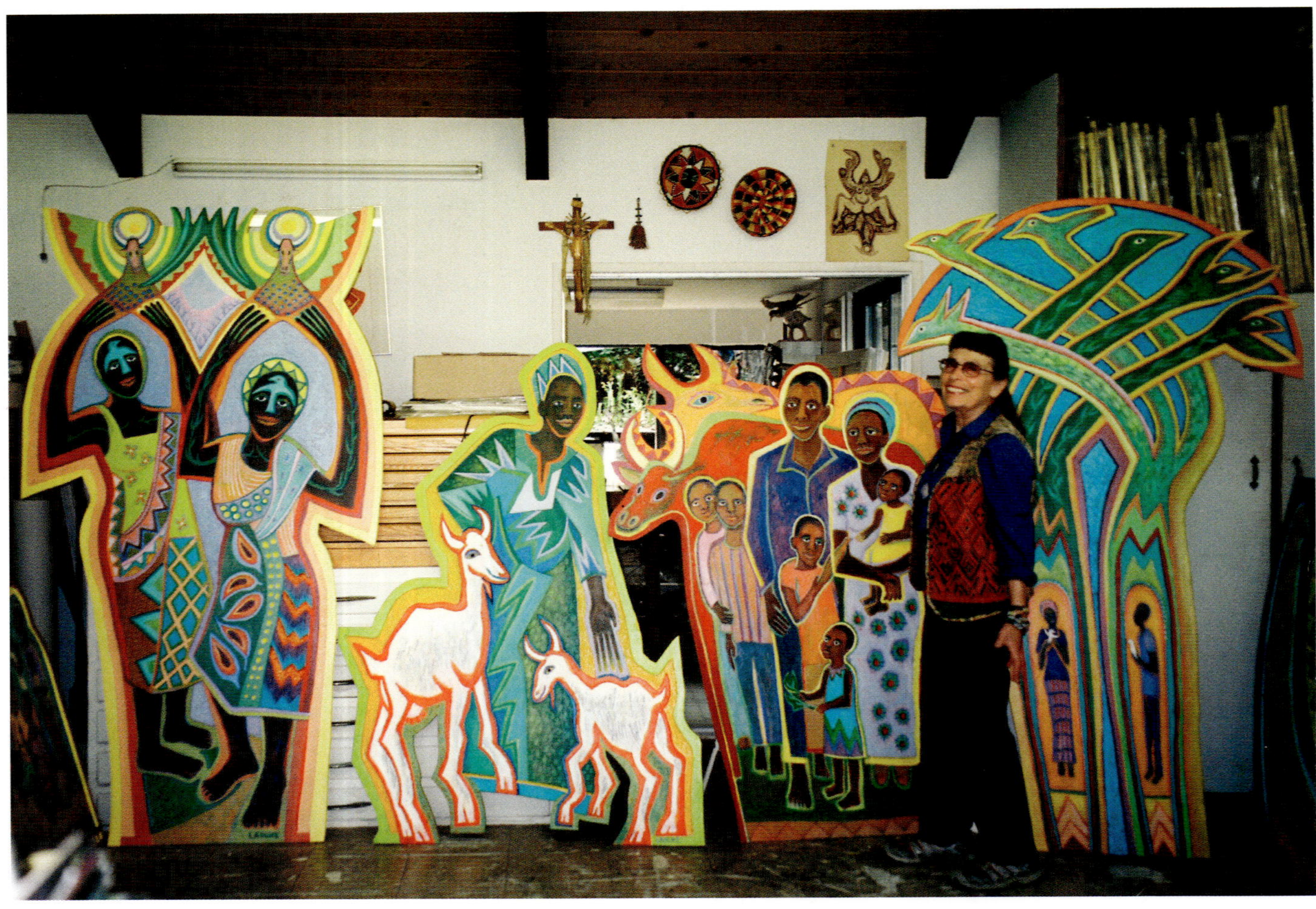

Betty in her Ashland Studio, at the beginning of the Africa Mural Project.

Artist's Statement

"Painting a vision of renewed hope began with my "Dreaming Cows" paintings and continued into the Mural Project. Gradually, forms reemerged from the confines of the canvas rectangle to stand six and seven feet tall as cut and shaped plywood panels. Individuals with their animals, families and communities—all sharing, caring and planning for the future—became a part of my studio environment and my family, too.

I made new friends while visiting Heifer projects in the United States. Worms, wild rice and rural Americans became part of the Heifer story. Significant universal themes were reinforced, namely reconciliation; what it means to be human; the need to work through conflicts with dialogue rather than war; and celebration—an expression of gratitude and joy for dreams made real."

G E

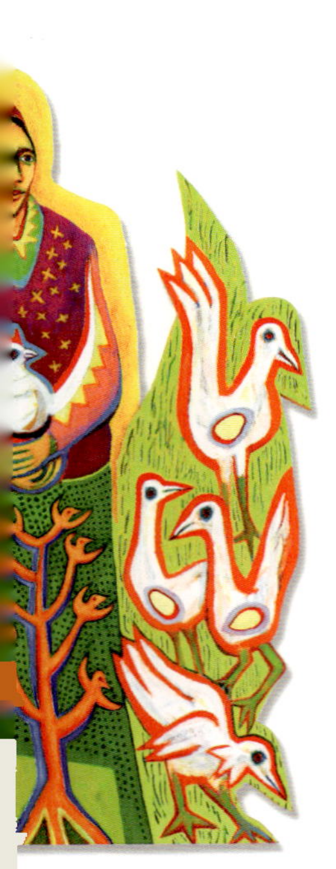

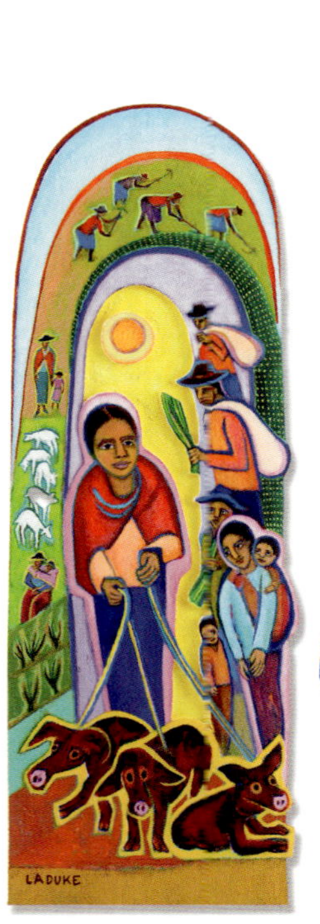

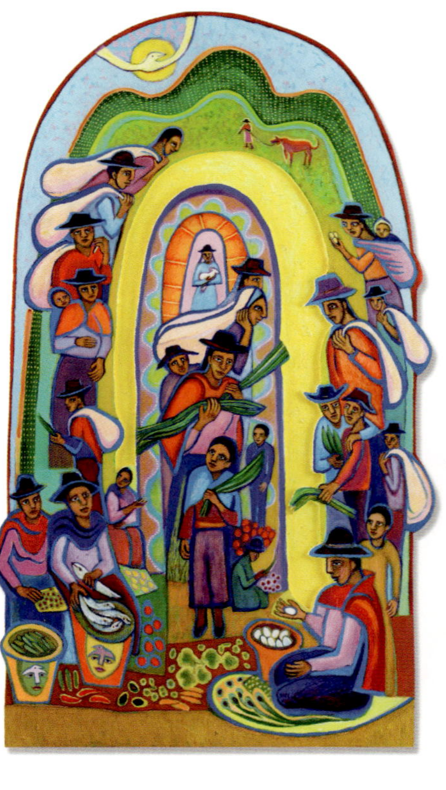

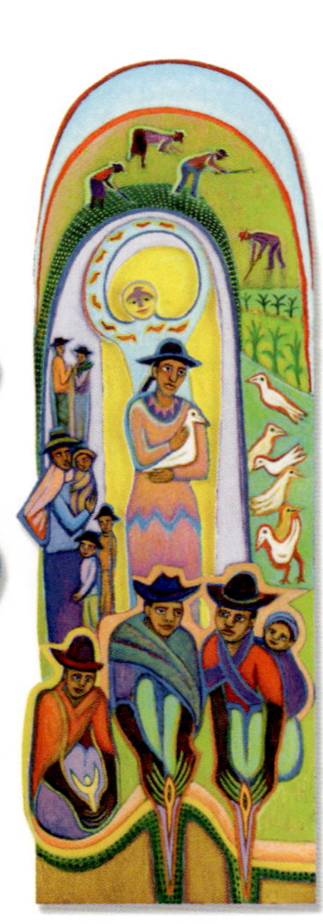

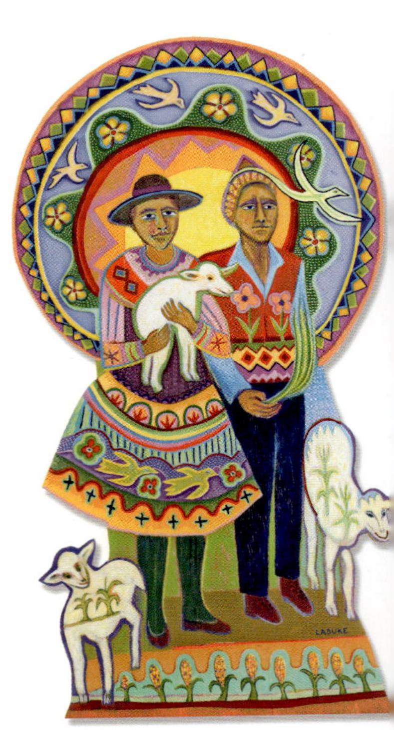

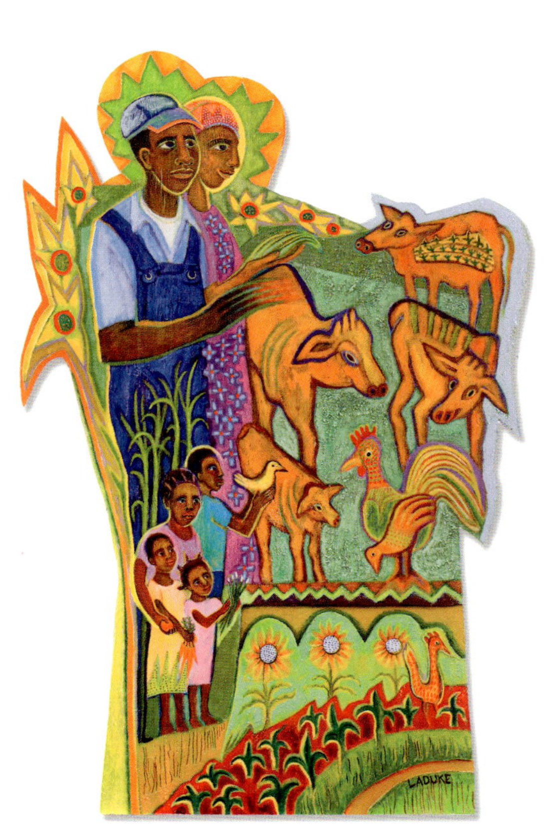
LADUKE

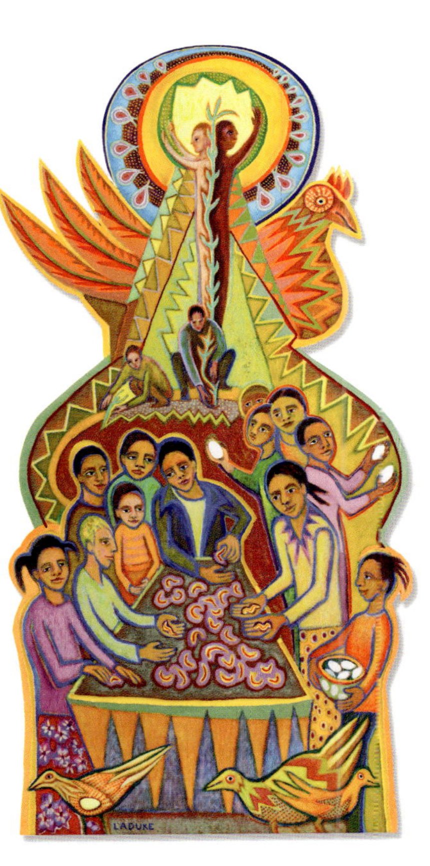
LADUKE

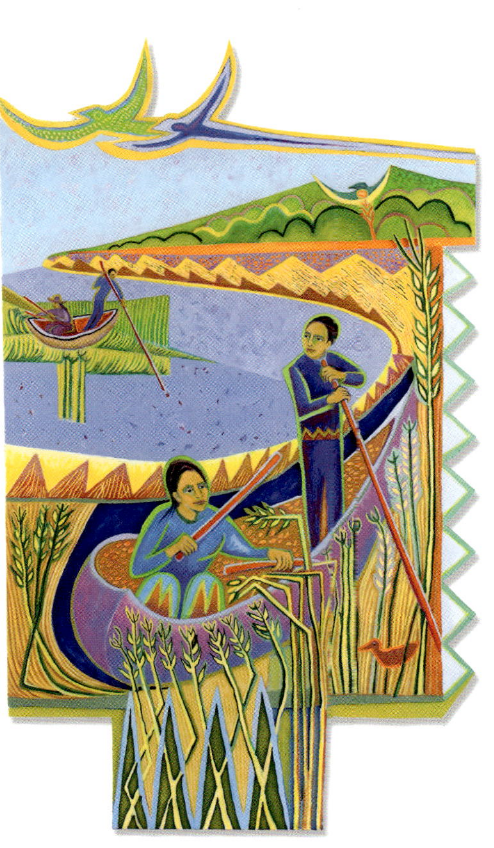

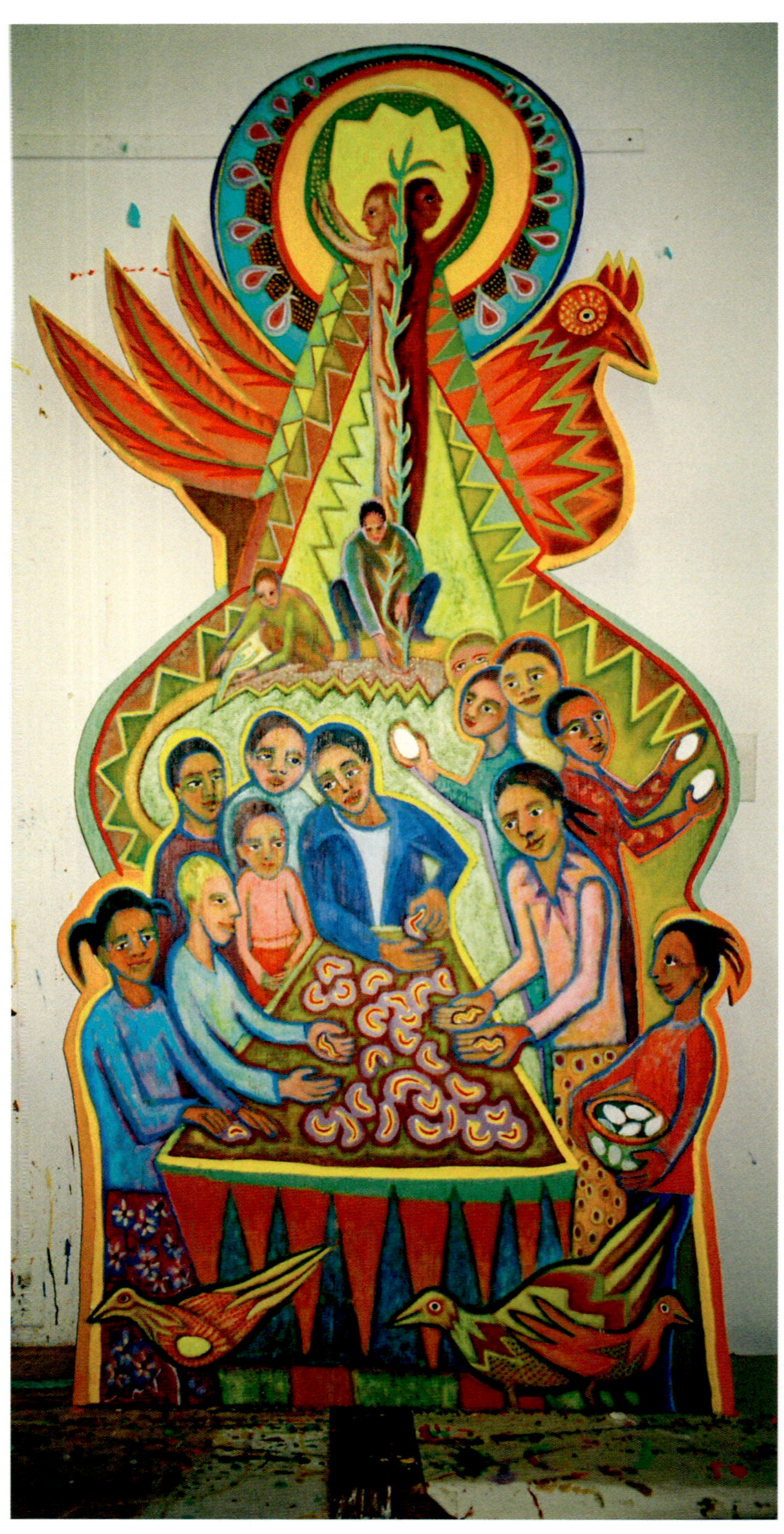

Worm Story Mural Panel in process with the basic composition established.

HEIFER INTERNATIONAL'S HEIFER VILL

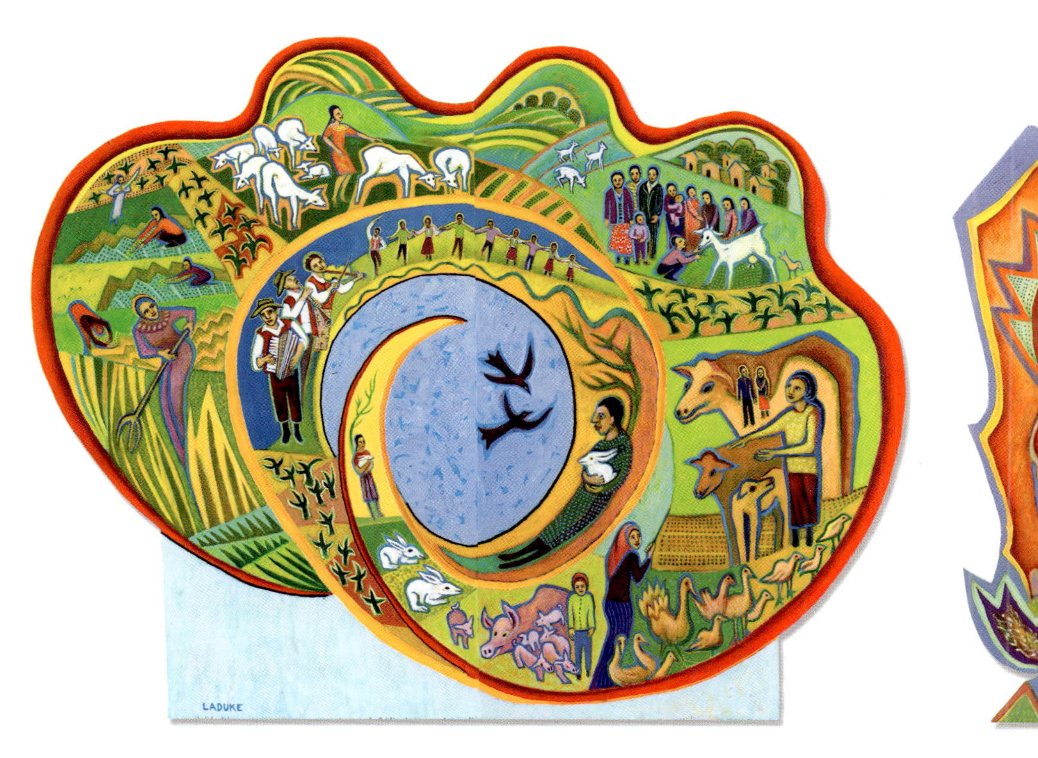

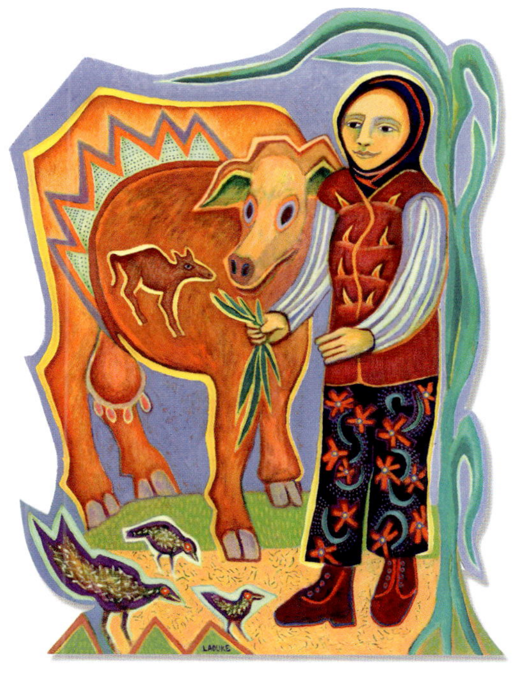

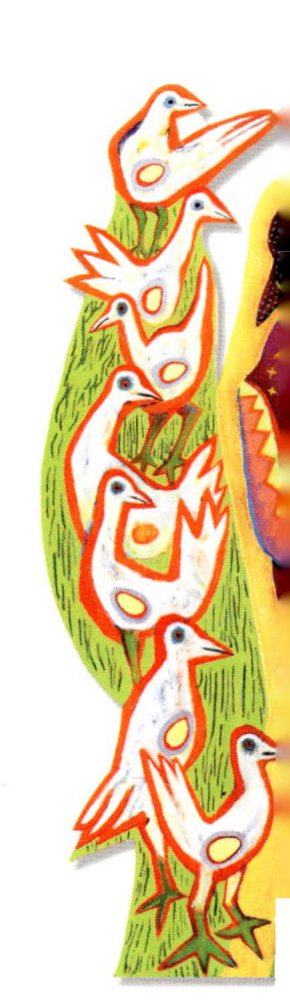

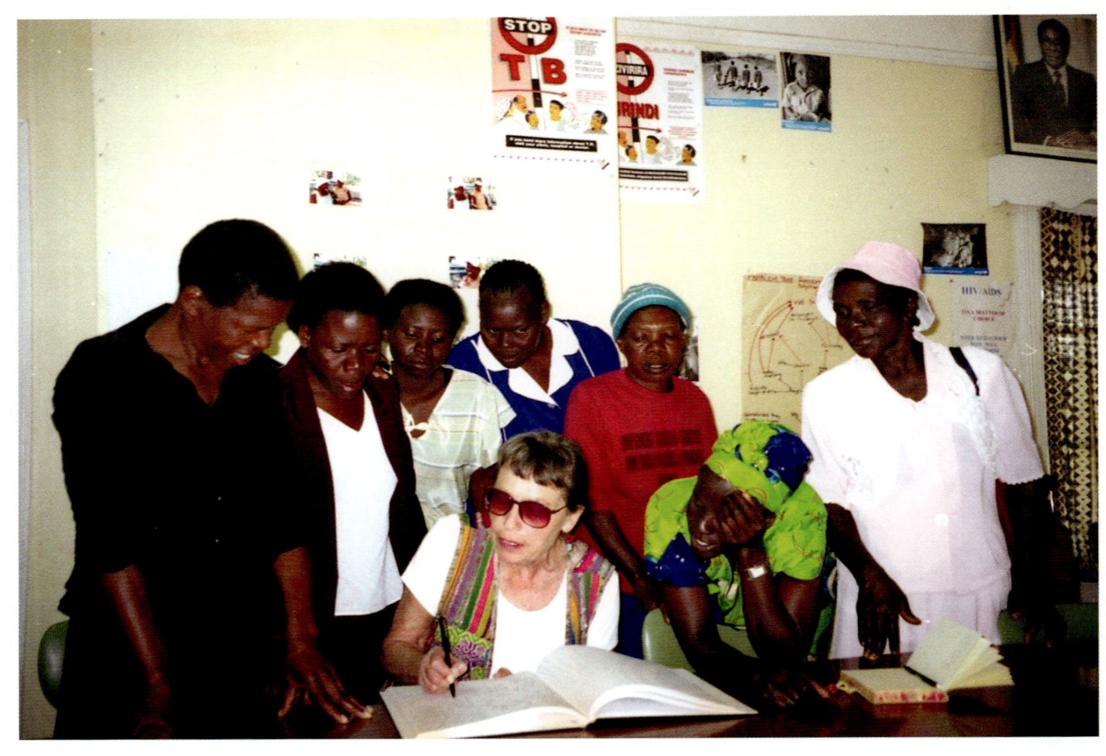

"LaDuke is the storyteller of the spiritual and ecological values and practices of indigenous peoples around the world."[13]

—Gloria Feman Orenstein

[13] Orenstein, Gloria Feman, *Multi-cultural Celebrations, the Paintings of Betty LaDuke 1972-1992*; Pomegranate Artbooks, San Francisco CA; 1993; p. ix.

Introduction to "Dreaming Cows" Exhibit and "Dreaming Cows" Mural Project

"During these years of transcending borders, I have found that a Northwest artist can enjoy painting the cows of village people around the world as they love and care for them in peace and war. These experiences are personal as well as political as the Earth is our common home. Sharing the joy, sharing the pain—that is what artists do."[25]

—Betty LaDuke

Beginning with her first Heifer Educational Study Tour to Uganda and Rwanda in 2003, Betty LaDuke has sketched her way through twelve countries in Africa, Asia, Eastern Europe and the Americas on Heifer International tours. Thirty-three of the acrylic paintings that emerged from these sketches have become her "Dreaming Cows" series and circulating exhibit. Each lively painting draws the viewer in with its dazzling colors, shapes and textures. Intricate landscapes and striking patterns blend seamlessly to tell the story of Heifer's work in diverse cultures around the world. While many images carry the pain of scarcity and loss, a prevailing sense of hope shines through.

In 2007, Betty was invited to create a mural for the new Heifer Village at Heifer International Headquarters in Little Rock, Arkansas, where several of her canvasses are on permanent display. This large-scale work would depict Heifer's humanitarian efforts to build self-reliance, shared resources and sustainable development in communities throughout the world. The "Dreaming Cows" Mural Project incorporates an amalgam

[25] *Jefferson Monthly*, The Members' Magazine of Jefferson Public Radio, August 2001, p. 17.

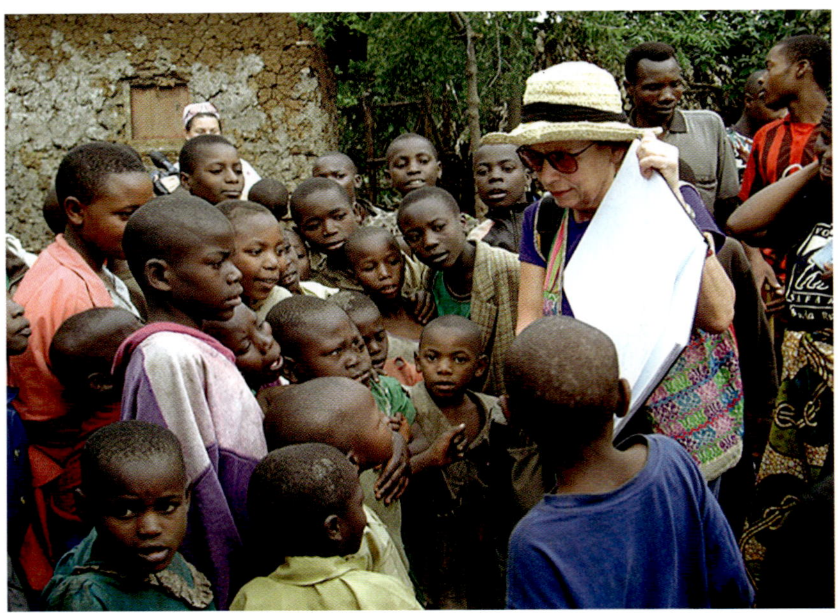

Betty with people of Rwanda sharing drawings, 2006.

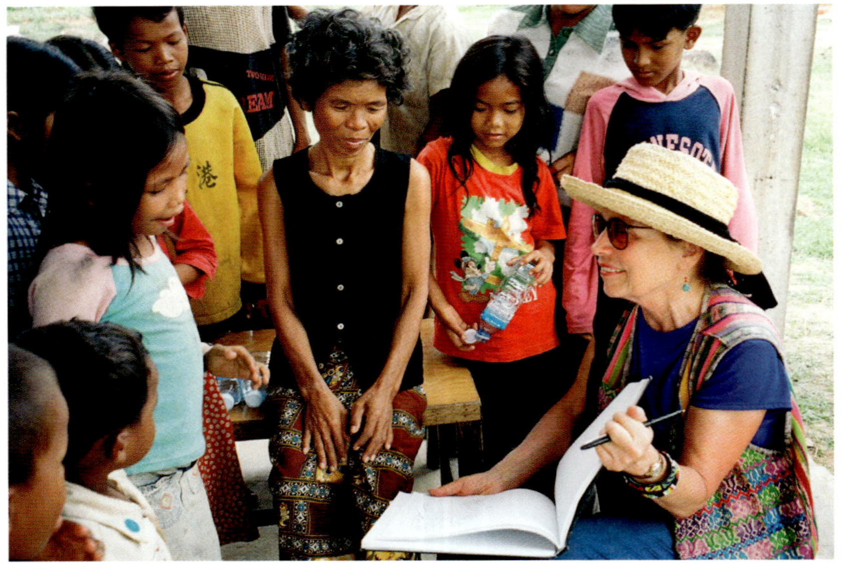

Betty with people of Vietnam sharing drawings, 2005

of images that evolved from the "Dreaming Cows" paintings. Its twenty-one plywood mural panels (each up to 7' x 4') are individually cut and shaped. The panels have also been reproduced in a museum-quality (giclée) print format, which allows for a circulating exhibit.

In every piece, whether painting or mural panel, Betty's very human encounters are portrayed by a symbolism and spirituality that honors people's connection to the Earth—what she calls their "universal and basic survival link to the environment." Basic themes of her work, expressed in fresh and remarkably vibrant tones, speak of cultural diversity and the interconnection between people, land, water and animals. The centrality of people's relationships to their families and communities is highlighted along with her subjects' strong sense of pride and renewed hope for the future. Bold colors portray families who now practice sustainable agriculture and integrated livestock farming. They reap tremendous rewards from such practices as does the environment, which benefits from soil and water conservation and tree plantings.

Why "Dreaming Cows?" Cows hold an important place in the worlds of Betty LaDuke and Heifer International. These animals represent food, fertility, improved health, earned income and community connections to thousands of Heifer recipients. "A good milk cow," says Betty, "can give as much as four gallons of milk a day." Cows often connect to women's bodies in her work, connoting "good" mothers who sustain and nourish and a deep respect for Mother Earth. In comparing cows to artists, other similarities are noted: "We both need to be fed in order to produce nourishment for others. My food for inspiration continues to be the Heifer International program of helping people to help themselves. I am impressed by how diverse communities, with the guidance of Heifer veterinarians, agronomists and community organizers, work together to make barren land fertile, maintain healthy animals and respect the environment as renewable sources of food, energy and life. Visually expressing these ongoing experiences from 2003 – 2008 has been both a challenge and a joy."

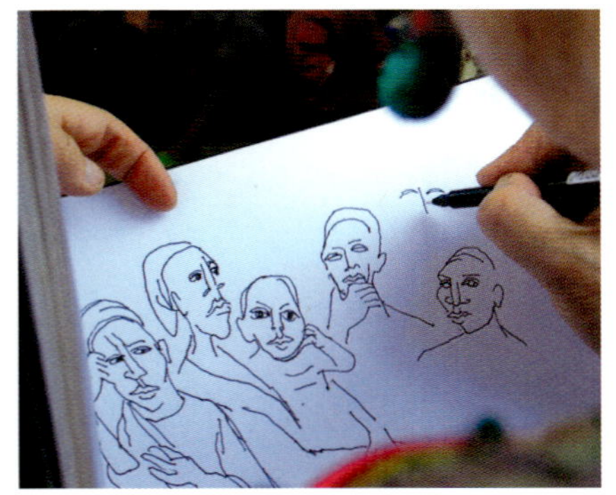

In all of her work, Betty encourages the viewer to move beyond literal images to a more imaginative place. What begins as an "ordinary" likeness (of an arm or a bird, for example)

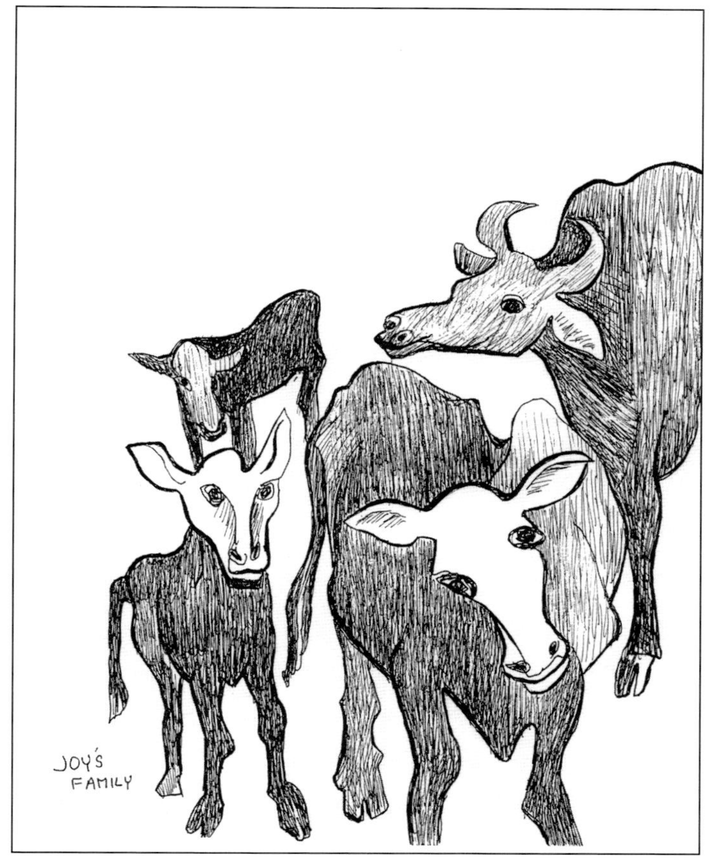

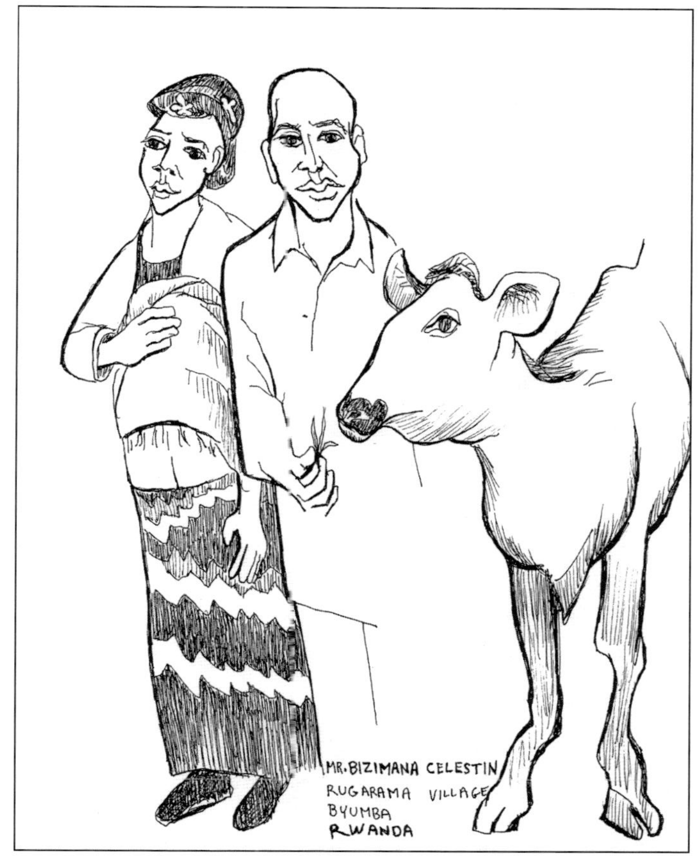

becomes an "extraordinary" or almost mythical rendering. Her work moves beyond the moment to reflect universal meaning. Spontaneity plays a major role in the process. Most often, Betty does not begin with a clear idea of the final product. Rather, it evolves as she works. "My 'Dreaming Cows' paintings and mural panels are symbolic stories that invite you to meet the eyes of the people who inhabit them. We are global neighbors and our future survival depends on our greeting each other with mutual respect."

Left: *Joy's Family*, 2003
Right: *Mr. Bizimana Celestin, Rugarama Village, Byumba, Rwanda*. Black and white drawings appearing throughout *Dreaming Cows* are Pen and Ink, 11" x 14"

AFRICA

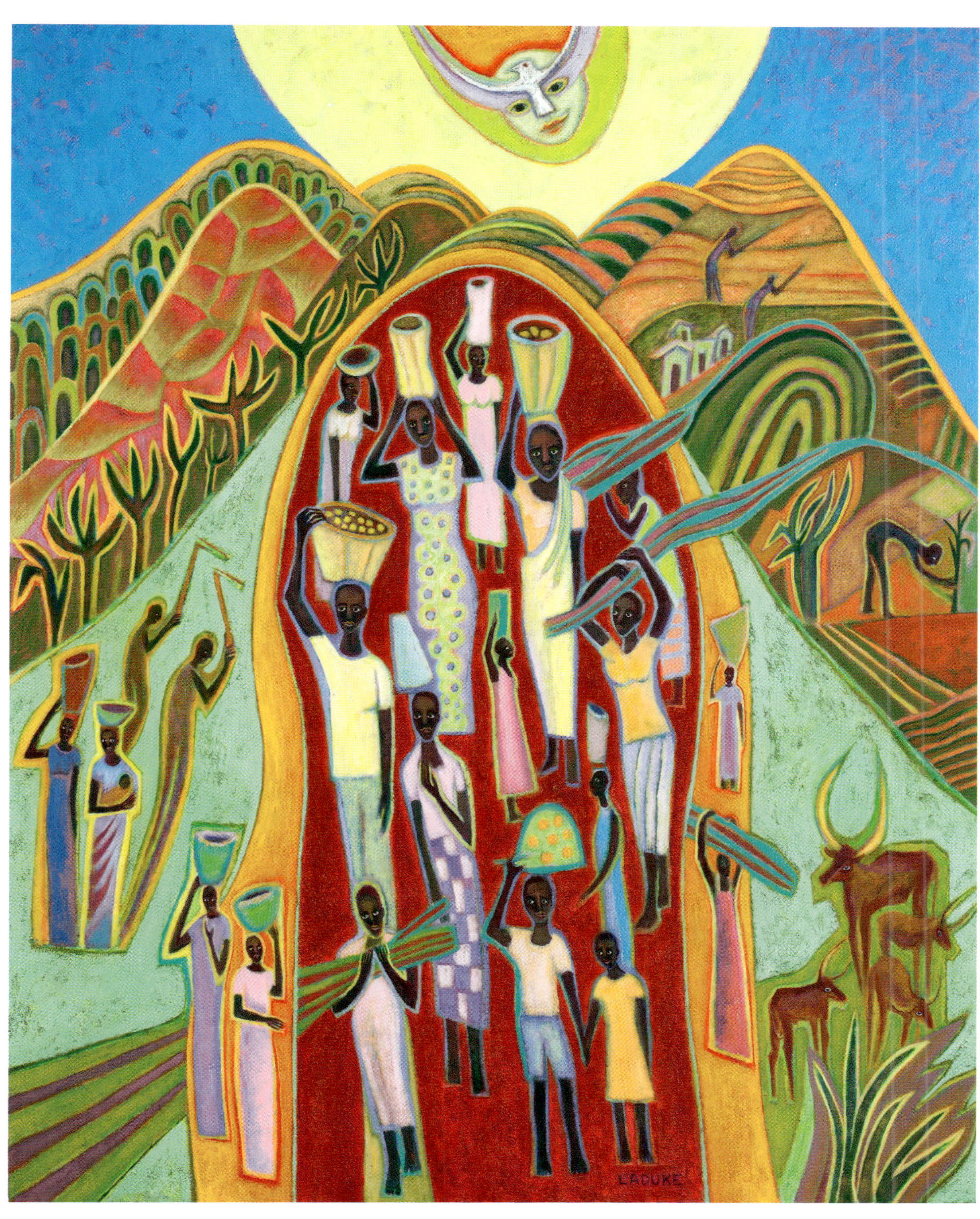

RWANDA

UGANDA

TANZANIA

The Africa Murals

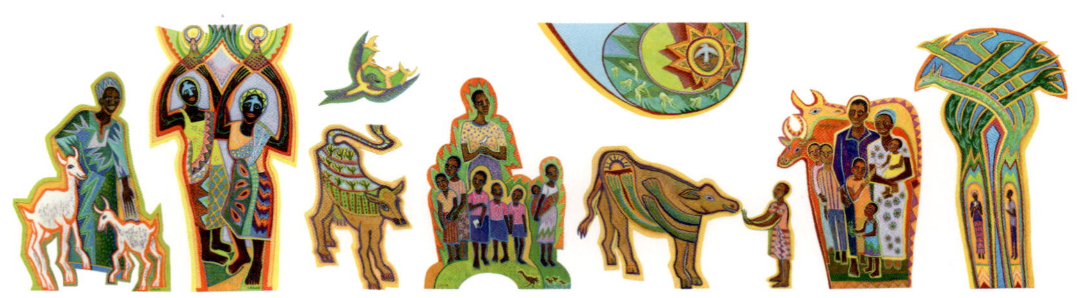

"I have a tremendous appreciation for the local cultures and the marvelous diversity . . . Africa is so rich in that sense, and much of the culture is still intact, through language, through village life, through traditions that are centuries old. I find a great deal of beauty in these day-to-day traditions that people share and I want to catch that . . . "[1]

—Betty LaDuke

[1] Arbogast, Marianne, "Probing Global Richness and Diversity;" The Witness; June 2000; p. 30.

Rwanda, Uganda and Tanzania

While Rwanda, Uganda and Tanzania have separate histories and cultures, Heifer International's consistent approach to working with survival issues in these countries is seen throughout Betty's work. The Africa paintings highlight the energy and life flow of rural communities.

Betty's paintings from Rwanda also reflect her questions about how people cope with the aftermath of genocide. Reconciliation is a key concept. In 1994, over the course of 100 days, it is estimated that between 500,000 – 1,000,000 members of the Tutsi minority and thousands of moderate Hutus were slaughtered by extremist Hutu militia groups in Rwanda.[2] Village after village was destroyed during the bloodiest period of the Rwandan Civil War, now often referred to as one of the worst genocides of the 1990s. Victims were often killed in their villages or towns by neighbors and fellow villagers.[3]

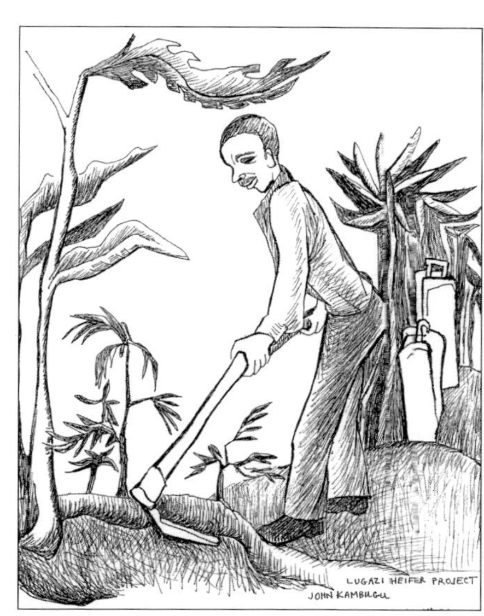

Lugazi Heifer Project: John Kambilgul,
Pen and Ink drawing, 2003

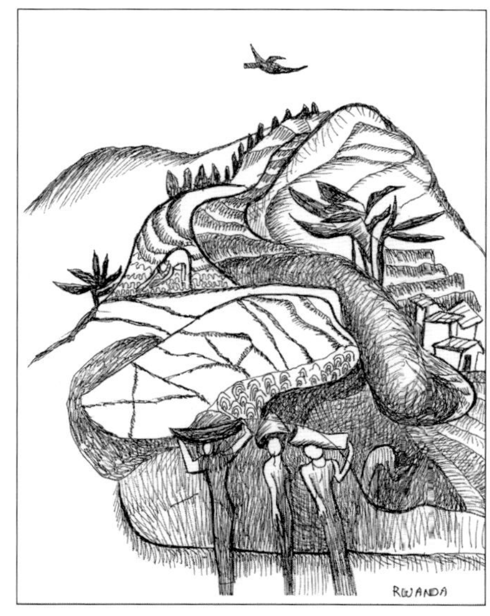

Uganda women working the land,
Pen and Ink drawing, 2003

---

[2] *Africa Recovery*, Vol. 12 1#1 (August 1998), page 4.

[3] Human Rights Watch website: www.hrw.org/reports/1999/rwanda/Genol-3-02.htm#P21_7273.

Not long after Betty discovered Heifer International, she participated in a 2003 Educational Study Tour to Rwanda and Uganda. "I was curious about how Heifer could make a difference after the terrible tragedy that Rwandans had endured only nine years earlier." In Uganda, too, with its own tumultuous history of dictatorships, military coups, corruption and years of civil war, she wondered how people could pick themselves up after such devastating loss. And really, how much could a cow or a goat help them to get on with their lives? Further, Betty was struck by Rwanda's population density—the highest on the African continent.[4] She observed that families in Rwanda and Uganda live primarily on small self-contained farm plots in mountainous terrain. Under these conditions, could hardworking families do more than just survive?

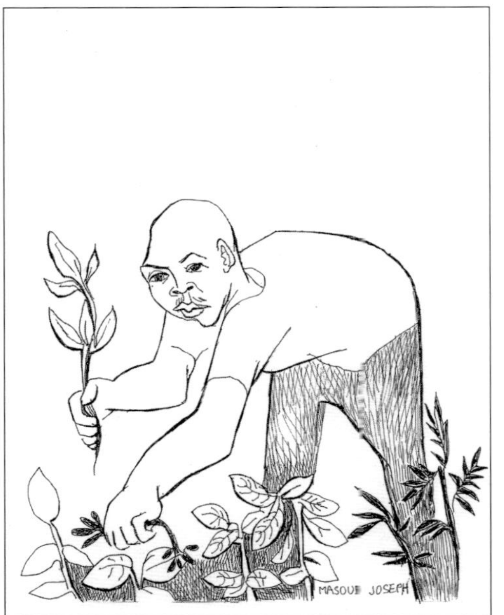

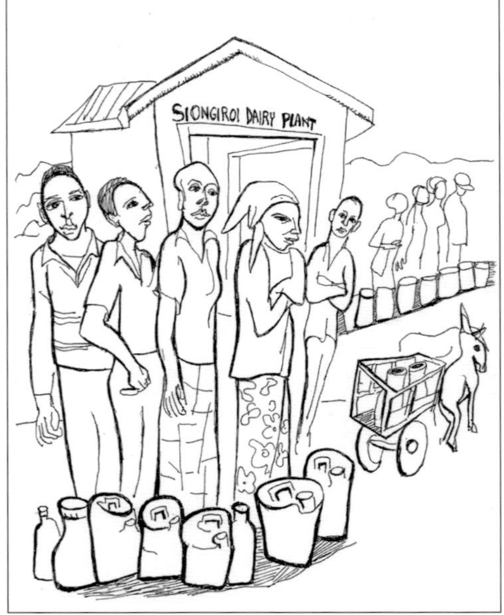

Left: Masoud Joseph, Tanzania, 2006;
Right: Tanzania, Siongiroi Dairy Plant, 2006

By the end of the trip, Betty had some answers. During the tour, she visited proud owners and happy new recipients of cows, goats and other animals. She learned more about Heifer's sustainable approach to alleviating malnutrition and hunger as well as its work to improve health, initiate micro-enterprise and encourage integrated farming. She resonated with Heifer's tradition of "Passing on the Gift" and supported their efforts to educate and build self-reliance as well as interdependence. She supported its commitment to partner with local organizations such as churches, social groups and non-profit organizations.

Rwanda Sunrise p. 53

This painting is filled with movement as villagers carry produce, wood, bamboo and water in their arms and in calabashes and baskets on their heads en route to market, work and school. They are walking on a road of deep red that reminds us of blood and the many lives lost to the genocide of 1994. The past and the present are symbolically intertwined. In the background, others work their small plots as the mountainous landscape spreads like angel wings. The land is precious. Cows are contained within a small but fertile area because Heifer has taught the villagers how to sustain the Earth by curbing the animals' tendency to roam freely.

Overhead, the sun's face reflects an awareness of the past as it looks down upon a flow of life that has moved on. Transition is also reflected in the upward wingspread of the bird within the sun and in the panorama of land, banana and bamboo trees, homes, animals and people below.

[4] *Encyclopedia of the Nations*: Africa: Rwanda: According to the UN, the annual population growth rate for 2000–2005 is 2.16%, with the projected population for the year 2015 at 10,565,000. Rwanda is the most densely populated country on the African continent.

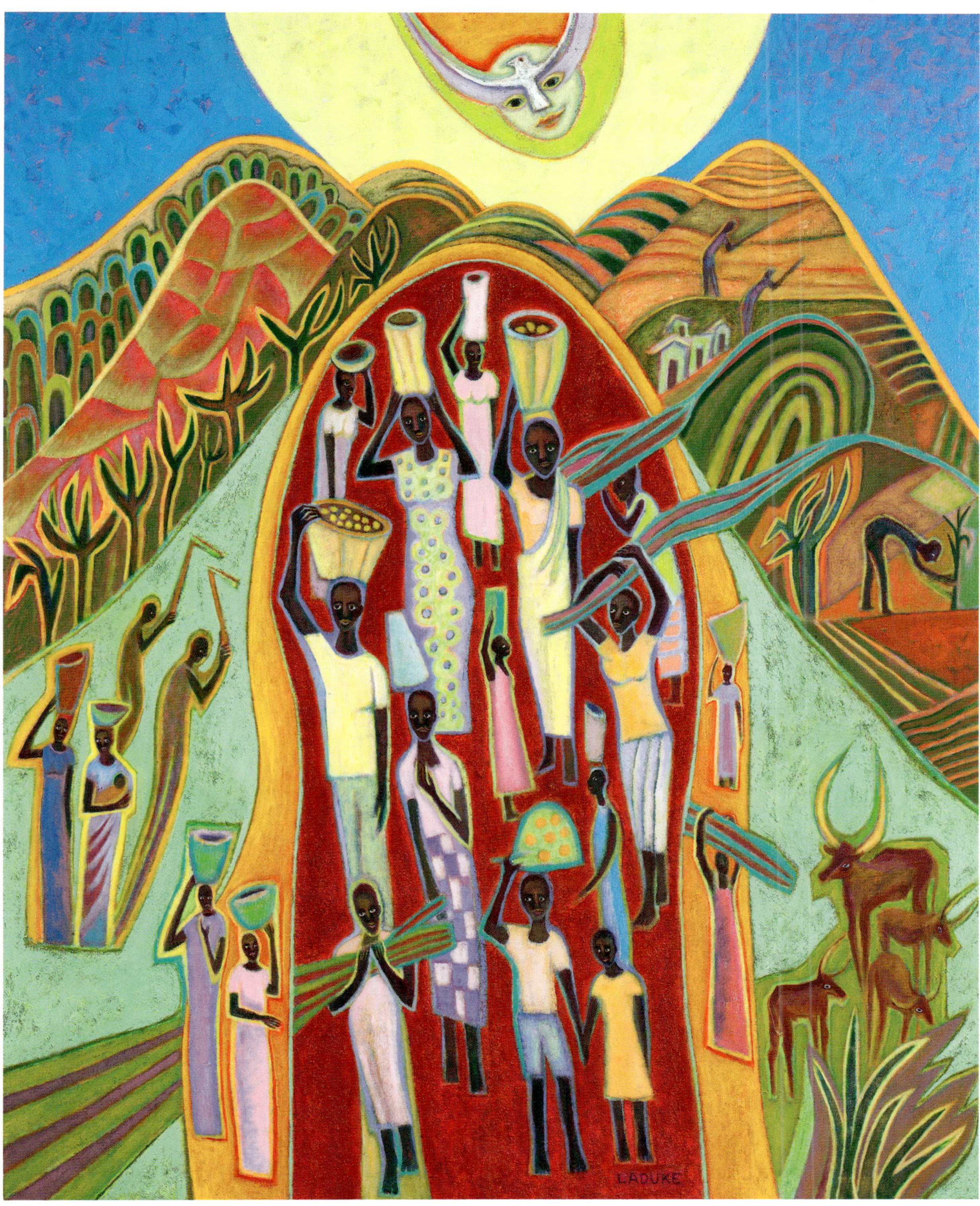

Rwanda: Sunrise • 68"x44" • 2003

While Ankole cows have traditionally been part of the bride price in Rwandan culture, they have not been bred to be milk producers. Heifer has brought the best milk-producing cows that survive in hot climates to Rwanda, thereby increasing the cow's contribution to the family. Life is slowly reviving from the ashes of genocide.

All paintings in "Dreaming Cows" series are acrylic on canvas.

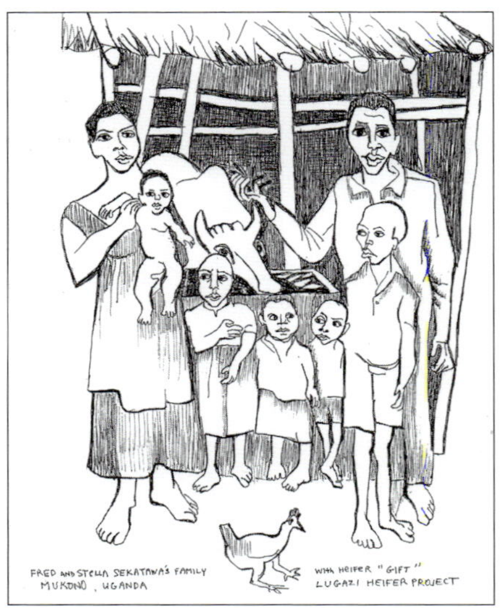

Sekatawa family in Mukono, 2003

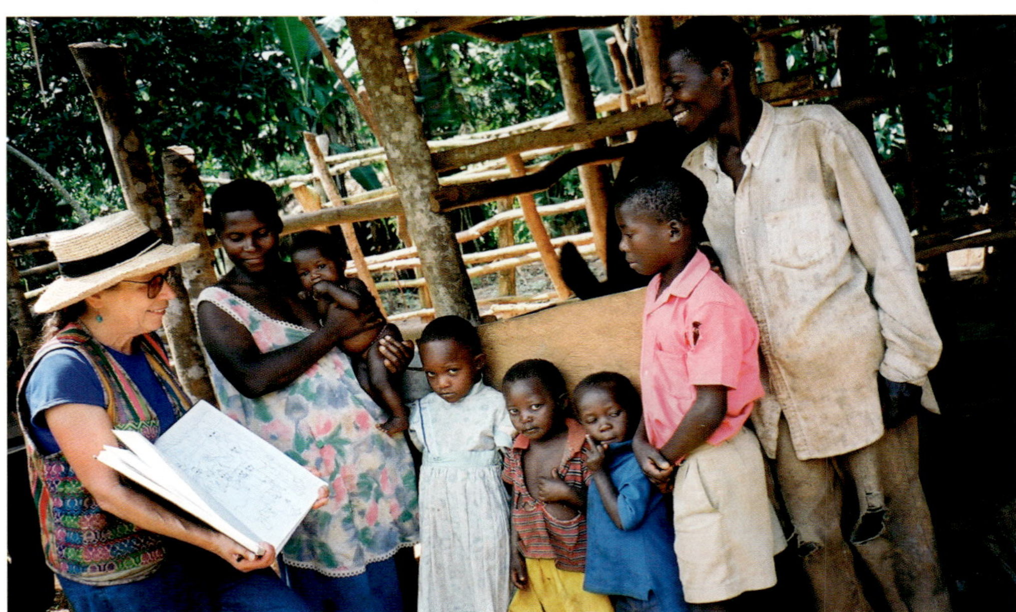

Betty with Sekatawa family, sharing drawings, 2003

Uganda: Dreaming Cows p. 55

This painting set the stage and gave Betty the title for her "Dreaming Cows" exhibit. "Throughout the tour," she says, "I watched people love—and even name—their cows." One might be introduced to Joy, Consolation, Cow of Love or Imaragahinda ("companion" in Rwandan).

To Betty, the value of Heifer's program "is that a single cow makes a big difference." It has for the Sediri family. After suffering the loss of four of their five children to AIDS, the grandparents assumed responsibility for the care of 21 grandchildren. The gift of a cow has been lifesaving.

The Sekatawa family in Mukono became the inspiration for her *Uganda: Dreaming Cows* painting. Fred and Stella Sekatawa joined a Heifer group a year before being chosen by the group to receive a cow. As with all Heifer groups, participating families had determined their own training needs and Heifer had hired local people to coach them. The training provided "how to" instruction about adequate care and shelter of Heifer animals and constructive use of by-products such as manure, urine and bio-gas. The family was selected on the basis of need as well as their ability to care for an animal. Now comfortably settled in, the cow is well-tended and loved—practically a member of the family. In turn, it provides milk, which is made into yogurt and sold for extra income, enabling the family to purchase what is needed to send the children to school.

Betty notes that "any time people stand patiently while I sketch them, they reveal what is important to them – because we have established an element of trust. Before the Heifer

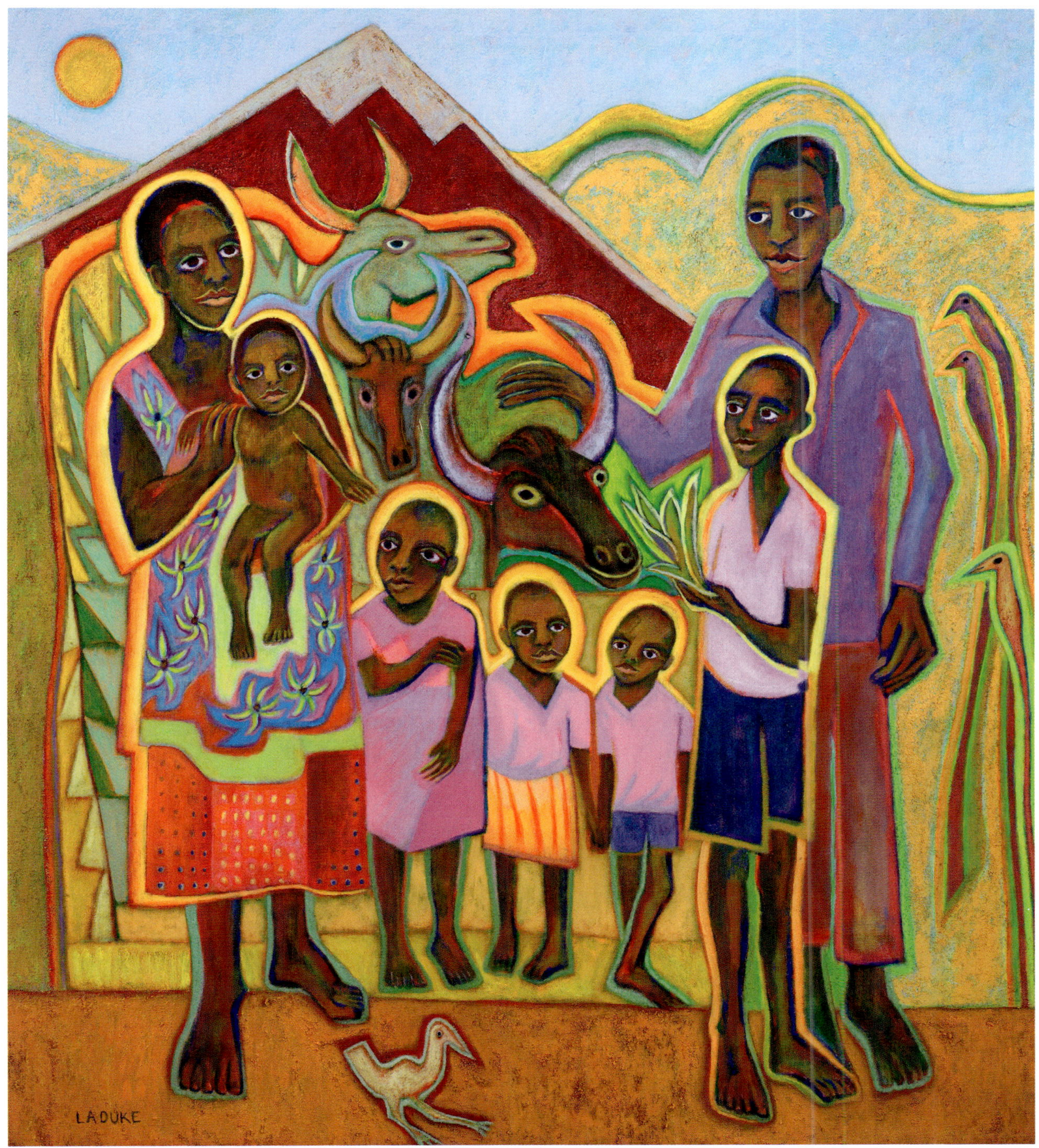

Uganda: Dreaming Cows • 60"x54" • 2003

cow, this family had little. Now they have hope. The family now has a way to be generous to others (such as sick children or families with new babies) in that they can give away surplus milk. If the cow has offspring, the community will benefit." In the painting, the father pats the cow's head affectionately while the oldest son feeds her. The cows represent the family's dreams—more cows mean more food security and money for clothes, healthcare and school supplies. The children can go to school rather than work in the fields.

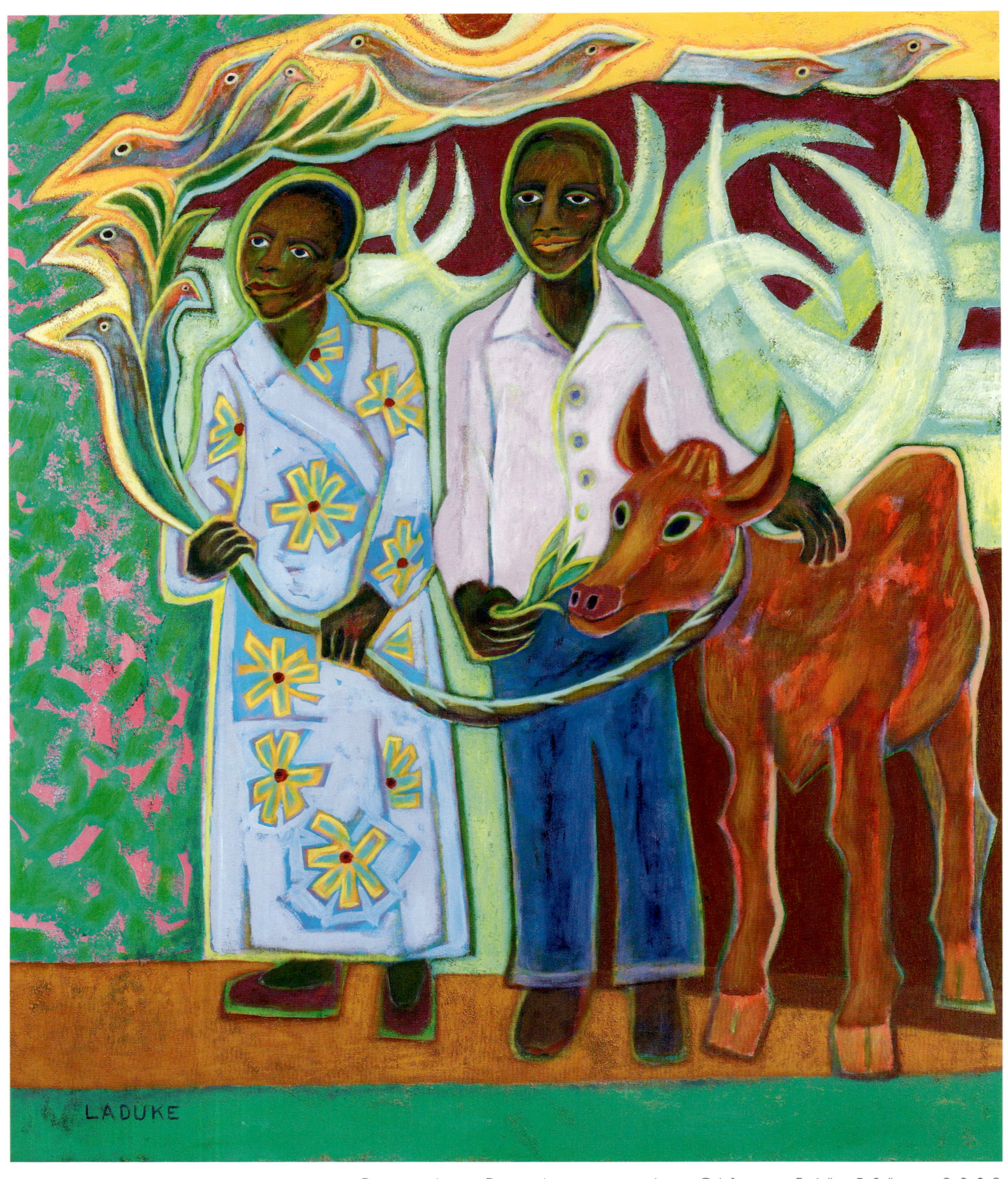

Rwanda: Passing on the Gift • 54"x50" • 2003

Rwanda: Passing on the Gift p. 56

Those on Heifer Educational Study Tours have the privilege of experiencing "Passing on the Gift" ceremonies in which families whose Heifer animals have given birth pass on the offspring to other families in need. These events, which reach broadly into the community, bring together many families in a celebration of sharing.

Families chosen to receive a Heifer animal have prepared long and hard for this day. During the training, they learn how to maintain healthy plots of land by using natural fertilizers and other practices that renew the soil. They are taught planting techniques that resist erosion. They are trained to contain and feed their livestock within enclosed shaded areas, which preserves the environment and minimizes the spread of disease. Families who have accumulated more animals also learn how to build bio-gas plants and use bio-gas units for cooking and lighting their homes to minimize the impact of deforestation.

Betty was drawn to the people she painted here because "there was something very humble about this husband and wife. They were in a daze about taking a calf home that would nourish their bodies and their dreams." The man extends a welcome to the cow by offering food. The rope that leads the cow flows upward to the sky as a symbol of the couples' hopes and plans for the future. The rope morphs into birds that represent timelessness and possibility. Behind them, the deep red reflects the horror of the past. Likewise, the sharp horns of the Ankole cows are in the background while the Heifer cow resides upfront with the family. The Heifer gift is a beacon of hope and light that is represented by the flames and the birds in the background.

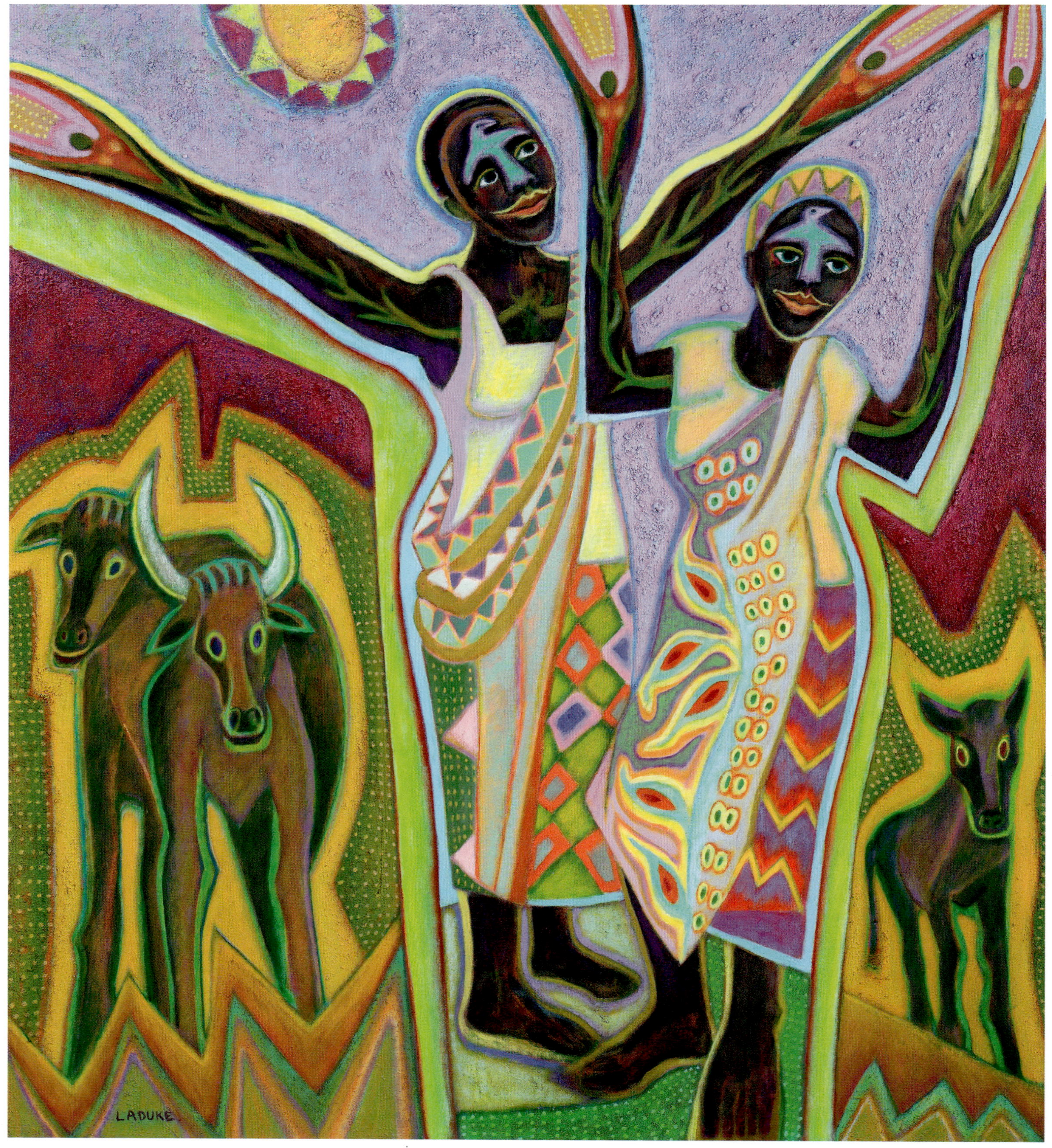

Rwanda: Celebrating the Gift of the Heifer 'Consolation' • 60"x54" • 2003

Rwanda: Celebrating the Gift of the Heifer 'Consolation' p. 58

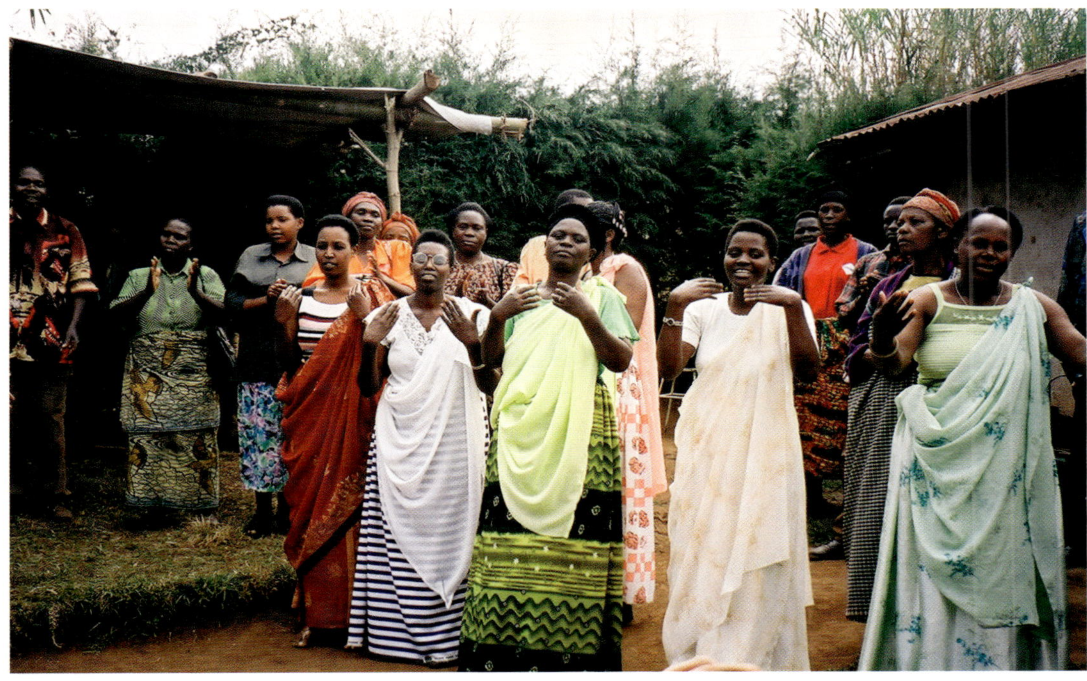

Left: Women in Ruhengeri at the Passing on the Gift ceremony, 2003; Below: Pass-on Ceremony, Heifer 'Consolation,' 2003

Two women joyously raise their arms to the skies as they dance to celebrate Heifer's gifts to the community, which surround them in the form of three cows. Smiles and birds permeate their faces, invoking "a sense of the spirit." Within their strong arms, growth enhances the female shapes that symbolize women's fertility. The painting honors the fertility of these women—who give birth and create food for their children, and who persevere.

Within the village of Ruhengeri (an older and more established Heifer community), the cow population has increased significantly. The women express their gratitude to the Heifer staff: "We want to thank you for this good act, what you have done for our community. Before we received heifers, we had no hope in life."

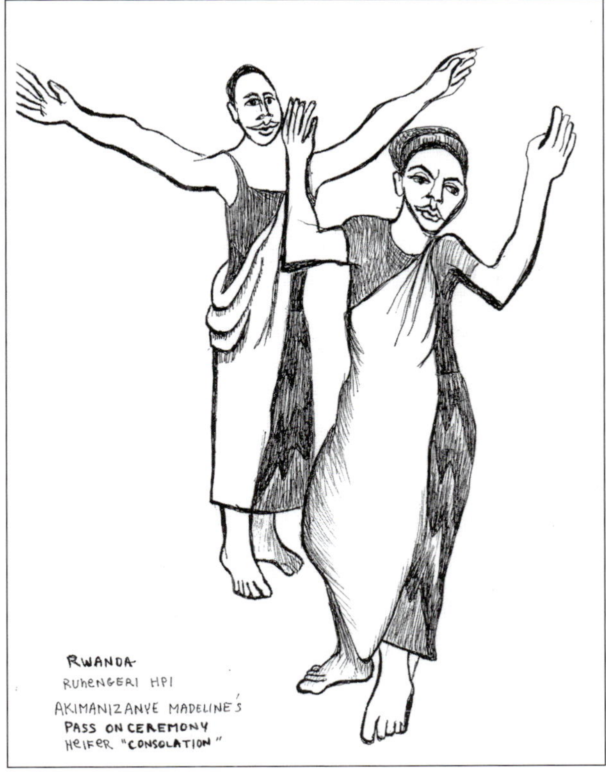

Uganda: Mrs. Nanfuka Teopista's Goats p. 61

When Nanfuka Teopista assumed responsibility for supporting two orphans, her limited income did not adequately sustain them until she was presented with a Heifer goat. She received training in goat management as well as in fodder[5] and tree planting before accepting this gift. Now the proud owner of three beloved goats, Nanfuka will not forget how that first goat changed their lives. The goat's milk reversed the youngest child's malnutrition and the goat's manure enriched the soil of her new vegetable garden. Additional income from selling surplus goat milk and breeding bucks has allowed her to buy the children's school supplies and uniforms. Since then, Nanfuka has passed on a female goat to the Nalukenge Rose family as well as her knowledge about how to care for the animal and the land.

---

[5] Fodder trees control soil erosion and provide firewood and food for livestock.

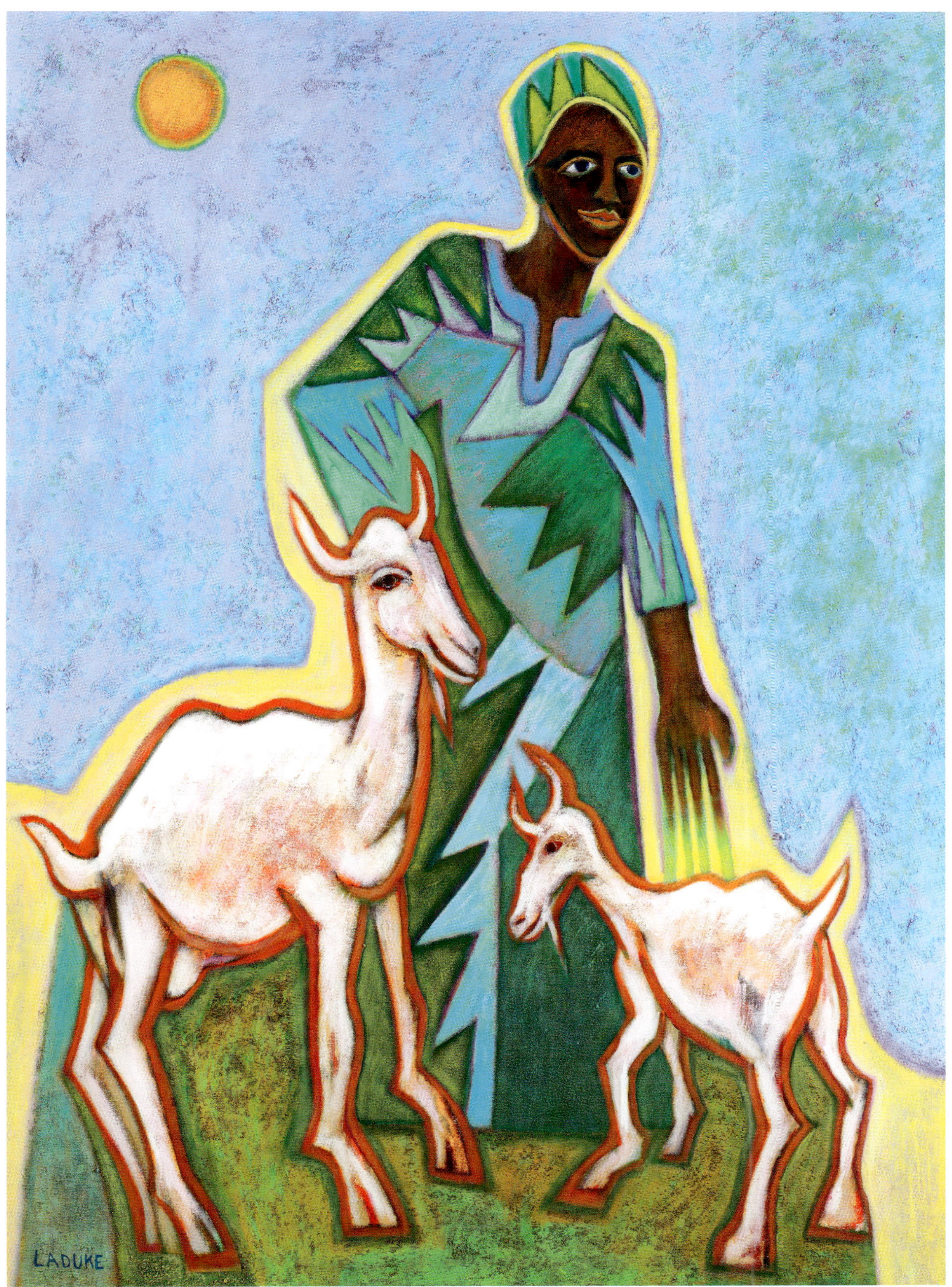

Uganda: Mrs. Nanfuka Teopista's Goats • 44"x32" • 2003

Tanzania: Masoud Joseph, Farmer

Masoud Joseph's farm represents a wonderful example of integrated farming. Every inch of his plot has been put to use. Although Betty captured the farmer alone in his garden, Joseph's wife, children and mother are nearby, supporting his efforts. In this man, Betty has found a "true role model for others in the community. By example, he teaches others to diversify beyond the care of one animal or crop."

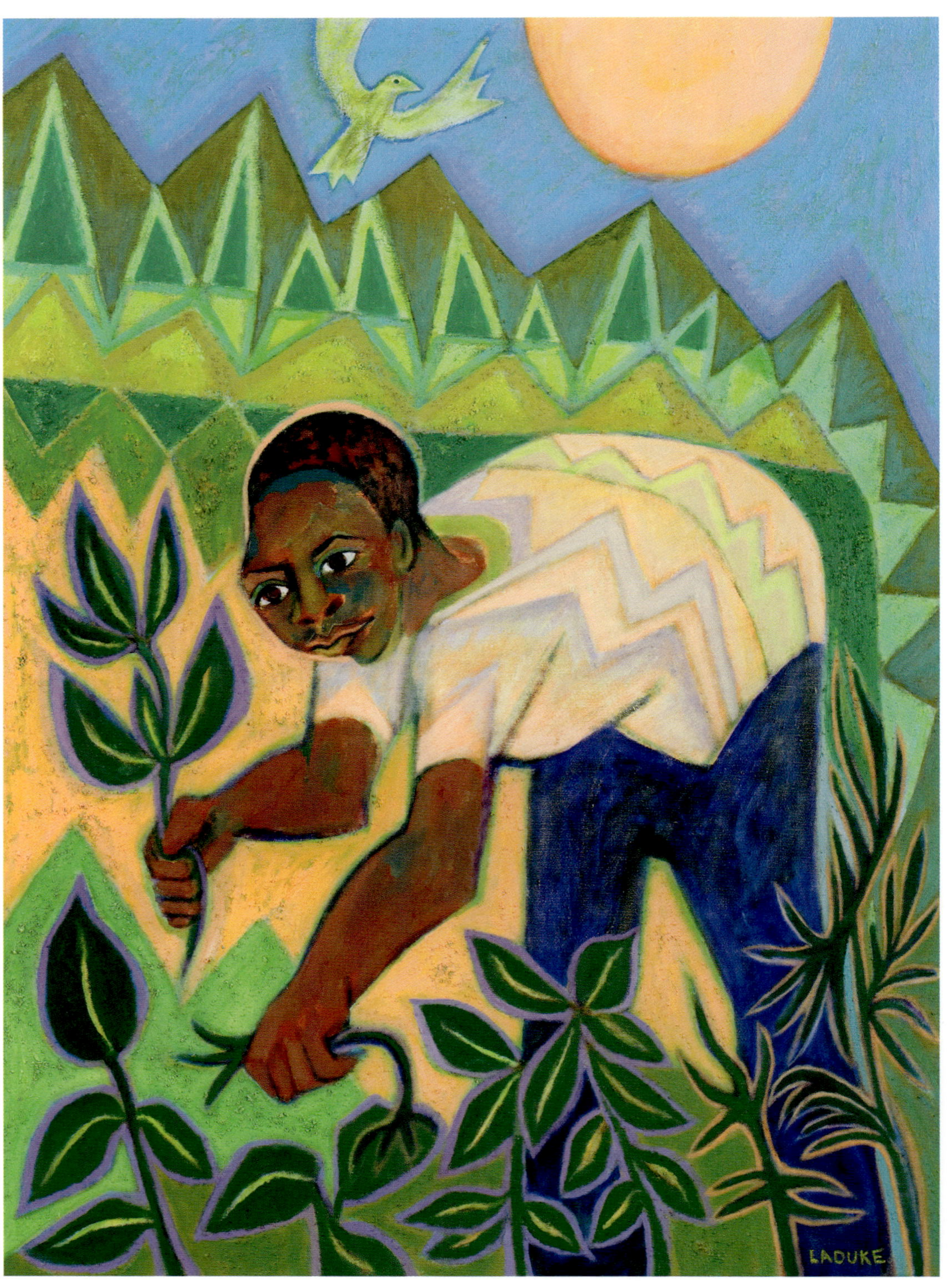

Tanzania: Masoud Joseph, Farmer • 44"x32" • 2006

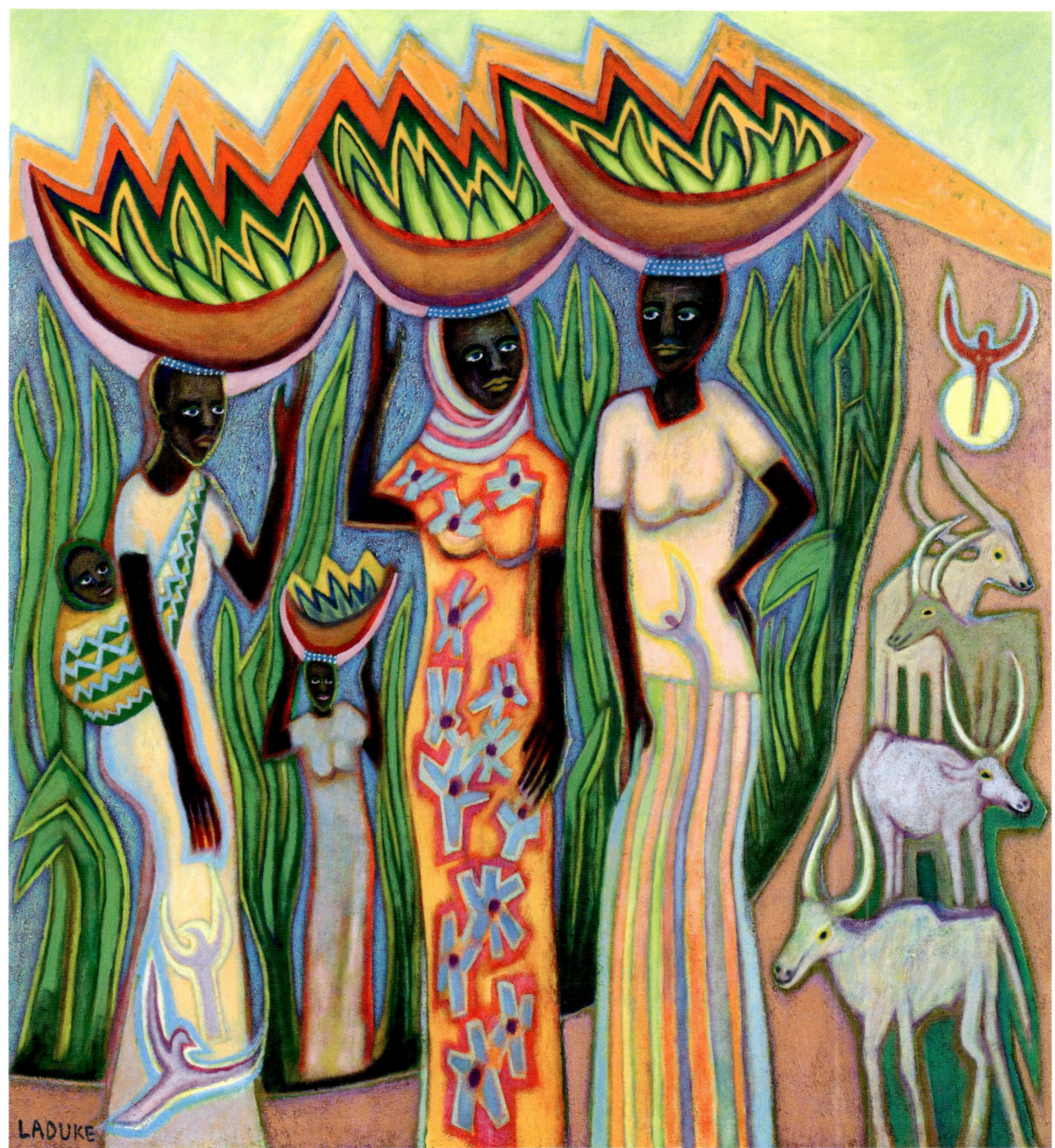

Green Bananas and Ankole Cows • 52"x44" • 2003

Green Bananas and Ankole Cows

The painting is filled with positive energy of women working and socializing together. This small group is on its way to market to sell the green bananas that they cultivate. In Rwanda and Uganda, everyone eats bananas. In contrast, the meat of the Ankole or long-horned traditional cow is primarily eaten by the wealthy. Heifer's high-yielding milk producing heifers offer a needed source of protein to poor families.

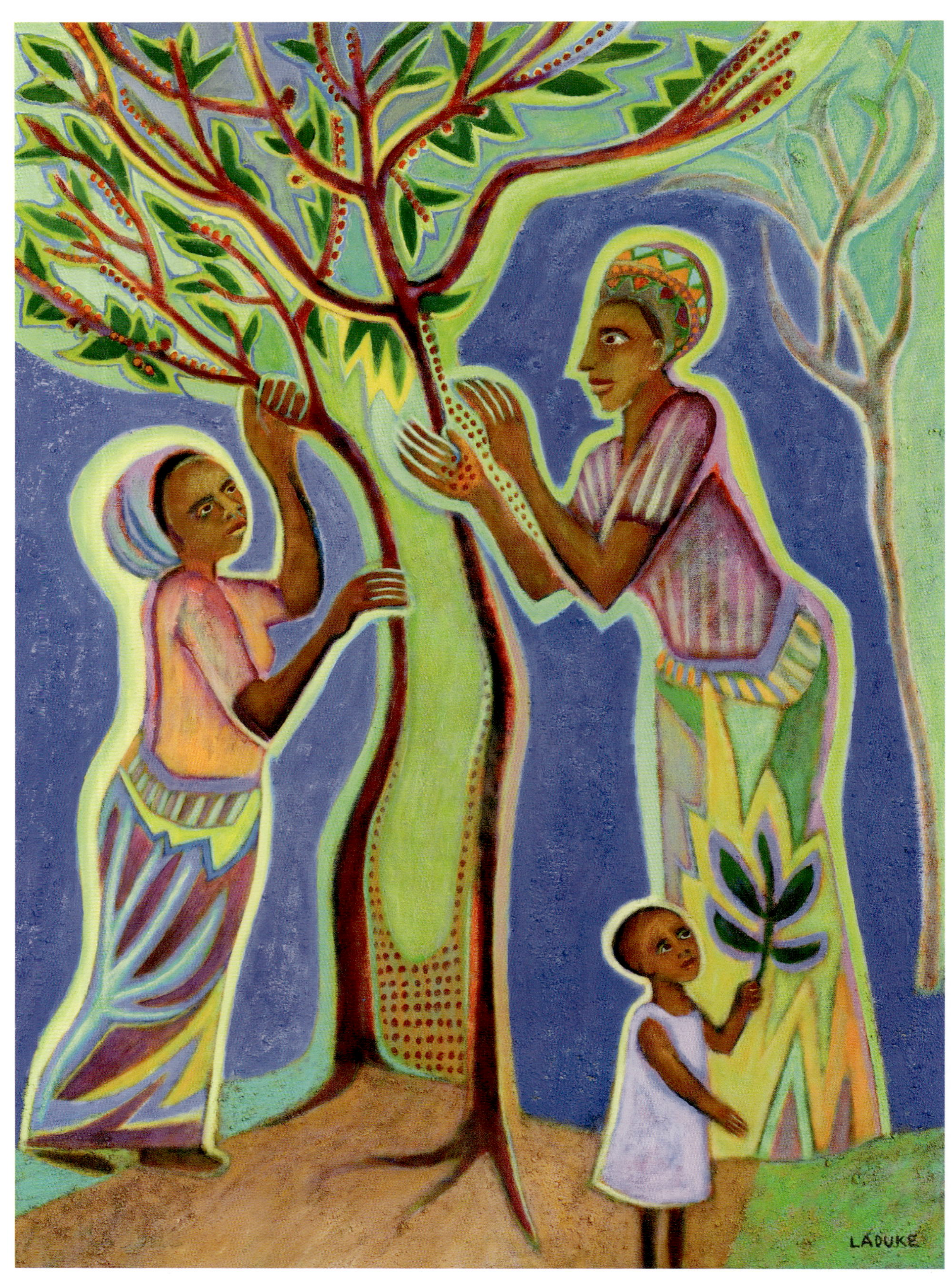

Rwanda: Coffee Harvest • 44"x32" • 2006

Rwanda: Coffee Harvest p. 64

Small coffee plantations along Rwanda's steep slopes provide some women with a seasonal opportunity to augment their family incomes. The women work together as the young children, who often accompany their mothers, play nearby. Soon enough, they will begin to care for their younger siblings, haul wood and gather firewood.

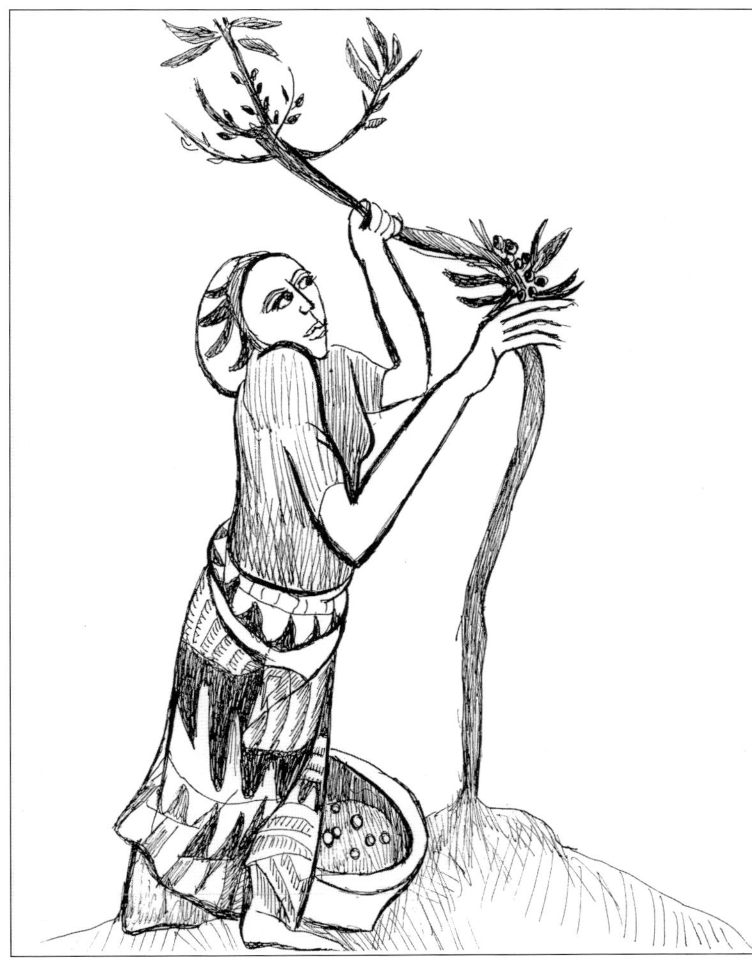

Rwanda Coffee Harvest, drawing, 2006

Rwanda: Reconciliation p. 67

This powerful panorama embodies many of Betty's experiences in Africa. Completed after her second trip to Rwanda in 2006, the collage of ideas represented in this painting has served as a catalyst for many of the Africa mural panels.

Betty's basic premise is that the people of Rwanda must find ways to connect to each other in order to heal. Heifer helps this to happen by enabling families to pass on animals to families they have wronged. The "Passing on the Gift" begins to restore harmony.

The painting illustrates a symbolic act of reconciliation between a Hutu and Tutsi family. On this trip, Betty found that village people were beginning to comprehend the need to talk about what had happened during the war in order to co-exist. By this time, the government and the people of Rwanda understood that the work of the International Criminal Tribunal for Rwanda (ICTR) was operating too slowly to have a direct impact on their lives. According to Rachel Rinaldo of the Global Policy Forum, it would take decades for conventional courts to try the suspects (which sources put at about 80,000 and upwards) due to a shortage of judges and lawyers. As a result, the government turned to a traditional system of justice known as "gacaca" (translated as "justice on the grass") to relieve the burden on prisons and courts. The gatherings are traditionally led by community elders or household heads who have been trained to serve as judges in the resolution of community disputes. The system is based on voluntary confessions and apologies by wrongdoers.[6] While these village assemblies (originally designed to settle village or familial disputes) are controversial because some believe that the "gacaca" system of justice poses a threat to survivors,[7] the intent is to promote healing and reconciliation.

Charles Kayumba, Heifer's Rwanda country director, notes that cows have become a symbol for healing in Rwanda: "People are put together as a group, and that exposes them to rub shoulders with each other and it opens up a dialogue for families. That is why some beneficiaries are calling it a 'Cow of Peace,' because when they share benefits and challenges and formulate solutions, it makes them come into contact with families that they may not have wanted to talk to previously."[8]

Rwanda: Reconciliation also portrays cows as a fundamental symbol of nourishment, sharing and healing. In this painting, a large cow is the landscape for the drama unfolding below. Within that context, the smaller cows represent sustenance. The animals, people and land flow into each other. In the left-hand corner, someone works the soil. The sun's compassionate expression warms the scene. The soft green of steep hillside garden plots in the background signifies growth and vegetation. The color green deepens as it works its

[6] Rinaldo, Rachel, "Can the Gacaca Courts Deliver Justice?" Inter Press Service; April 8, 2004; Global Policy Forum; gpf@globalpolicy.org.

[7] Corey, Allison & Joireman, Sandra, "Retributive Justice: The Gacaca Courts in Rwanda;" Oxford Journals 108:73-89, African Affairs; 2004.

[8] Bugbee, Geoff Oliver, "Cows, Miracles, and Peace;" World Ark, November/December 2007; Heifer International; p. 26.

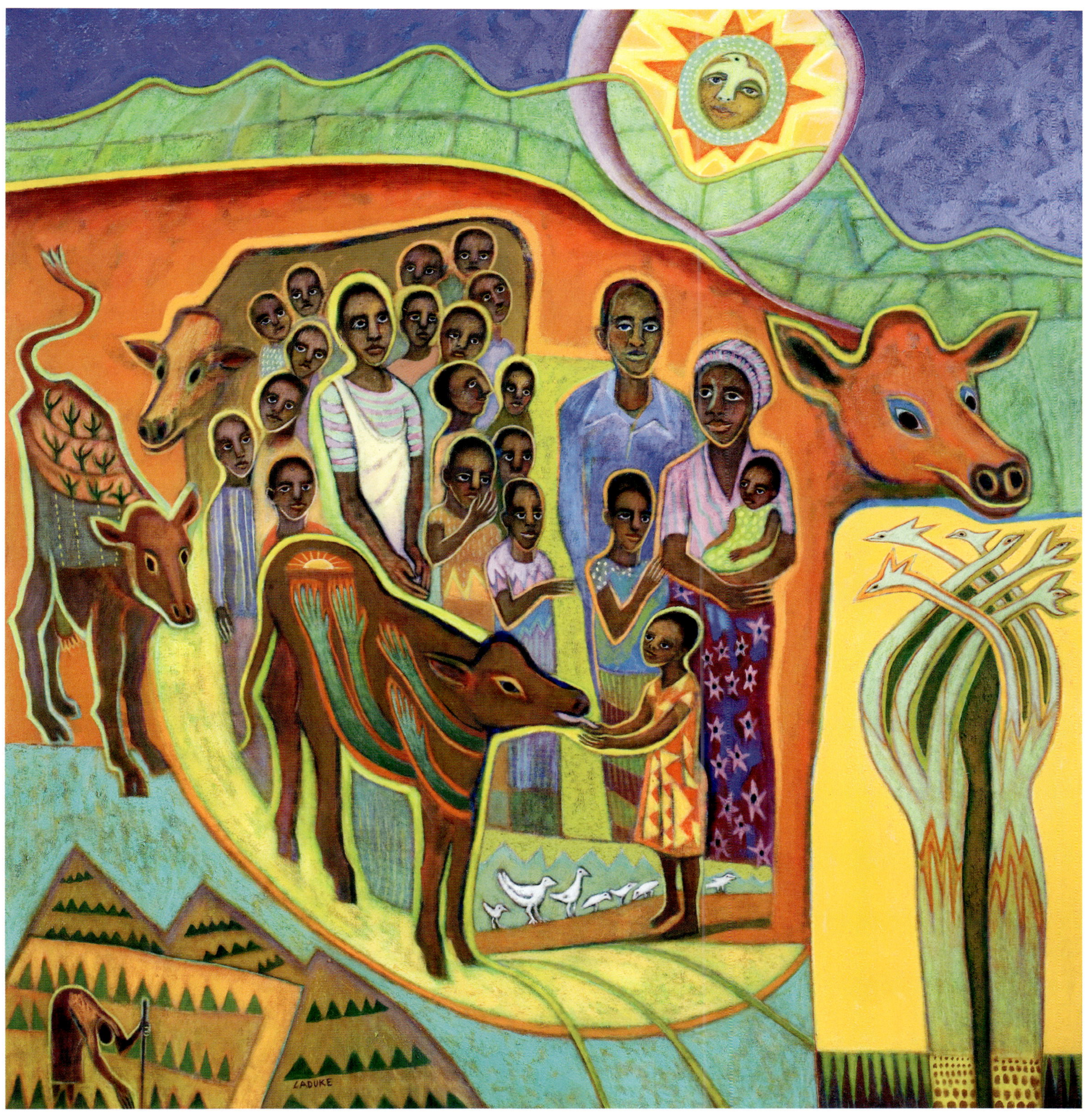

Rwanda: Reconciliation • 72"x68" • 2006

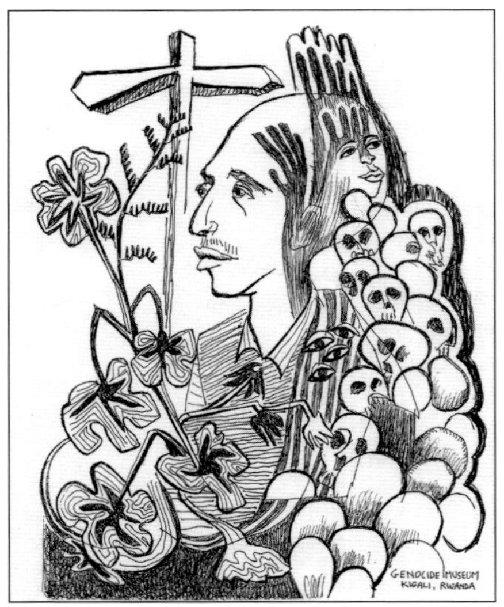

Genocide drawing, 2006

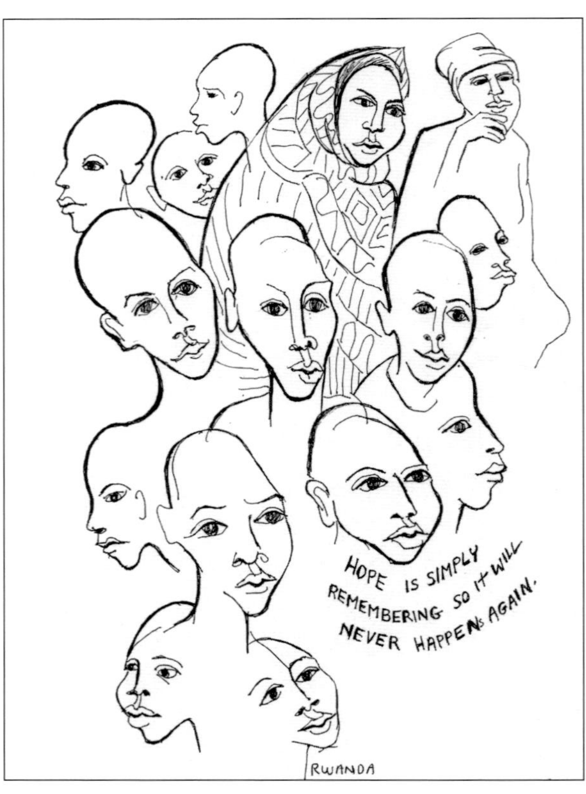

Hope is Simply Remembering , 2006

way from the land into one of the smaller cows. Nutritious grasses that Heifer has encouraged villagers to plant are represented by these deep green hands that reach toward the sun. Plants growing within another cow remind us that they fertilize the land. Nothing within this cycle of life goes to waste: extra manure can be sold and the cow's urine can be used as insecticide.

The energy between the hills and the cows flows in circular fashion: the cows need the land and the land needs the cows. Likewise, the people need their cows, goats and gardens just as the animals and plants need tending by the people. Working together produces positive outcomes for all.

In the right-hand corner of the painting, Betty has created a symbolic image of reconciliation in the form of two hands clasped in prayer that rise from parallel trees. The fingertips evolve into birds of possibility that look out on the broader community. Just as the tree changes into hands, so must people evolve in order to achieve reconciliation. This symbolic image is the starting point for one of the twenty-one murals panels exhibited at Heifer's national headquarters.

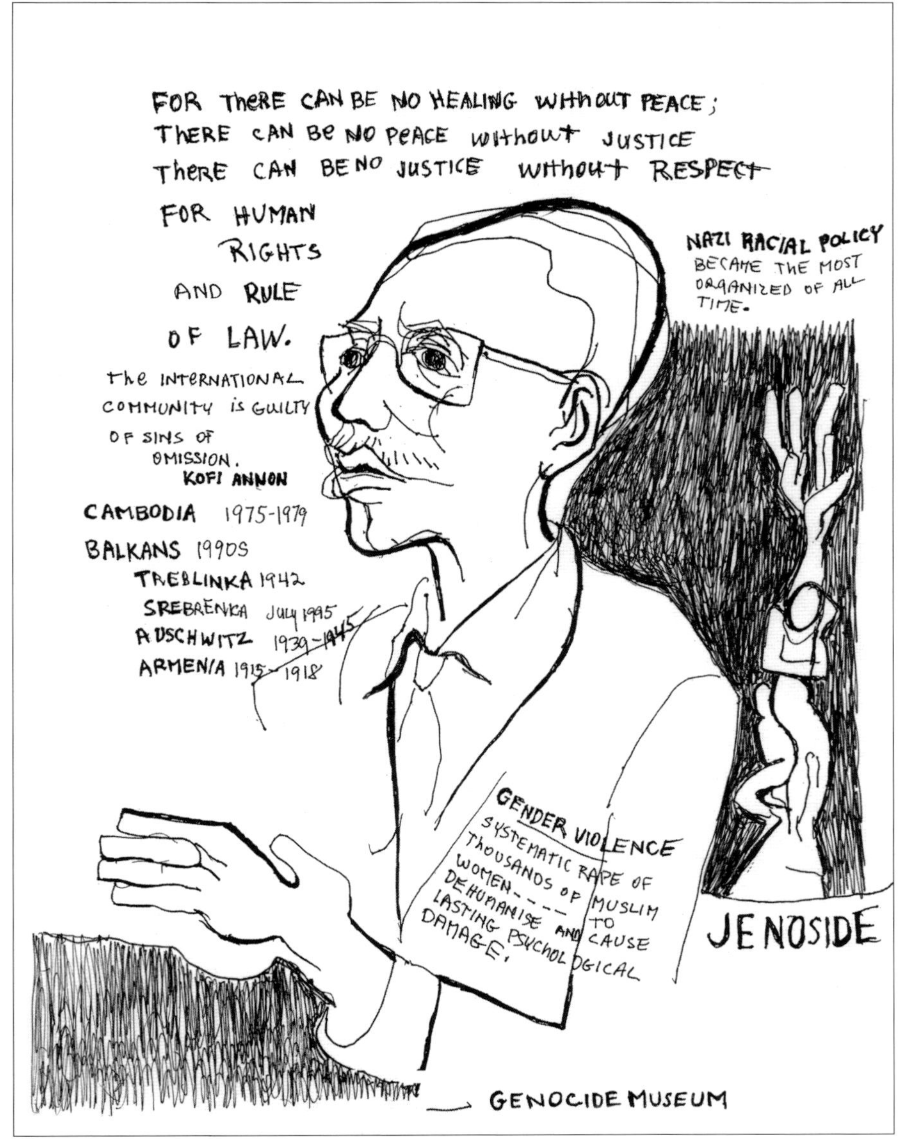

Genocide drawing *"No Healing Without Peace,"* 2006

"For there can be no healing without peace. There can be no peace without justice. There can be no justice without respect for human rights and rule of law."

—Kofi Annan

Africa: Reconciliation p. 71

In this mural panel, the concept of reconciliation is characterized by clasped hands rising from parallel trees. Two figures, one male and the other female, appear at the base of the trees. The man faces the woman who subtly looks his way, suggesting their need to talk about unresolved conflicts including issues of gender equality and economic disparity. People must face each other without weapons and talk!

An earlier version of *Africa: Reconciliation* can be seen in the painting *Rwanda: Reconciliation.*

All murals in "Dreaming Cows" series are acrylic on routed wood.

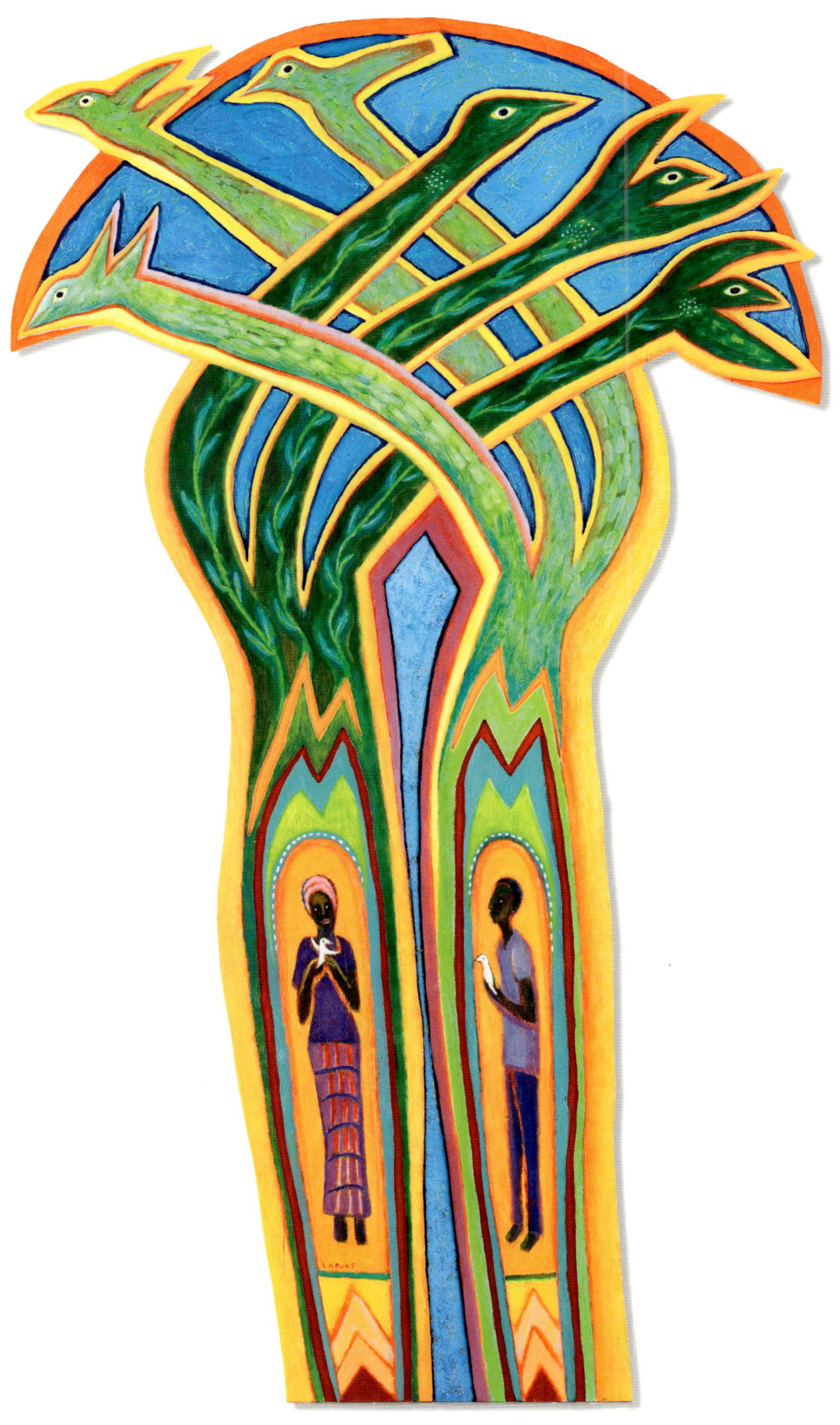

Africa: Reconciliation • 80"x48" • 2007

Africa: Dreaming Cows p. 73

In this mural panel, Betty uses key forms from *Dreaming Cows*, the painting that gave the exhibit its title. She emphasizes the closeness of this family. Five children and their parents are contained within a cow landscape that supports them with food and shelter. One child offers food to the cow while another's hand becomes the ever-present symbolic bird of possibility.

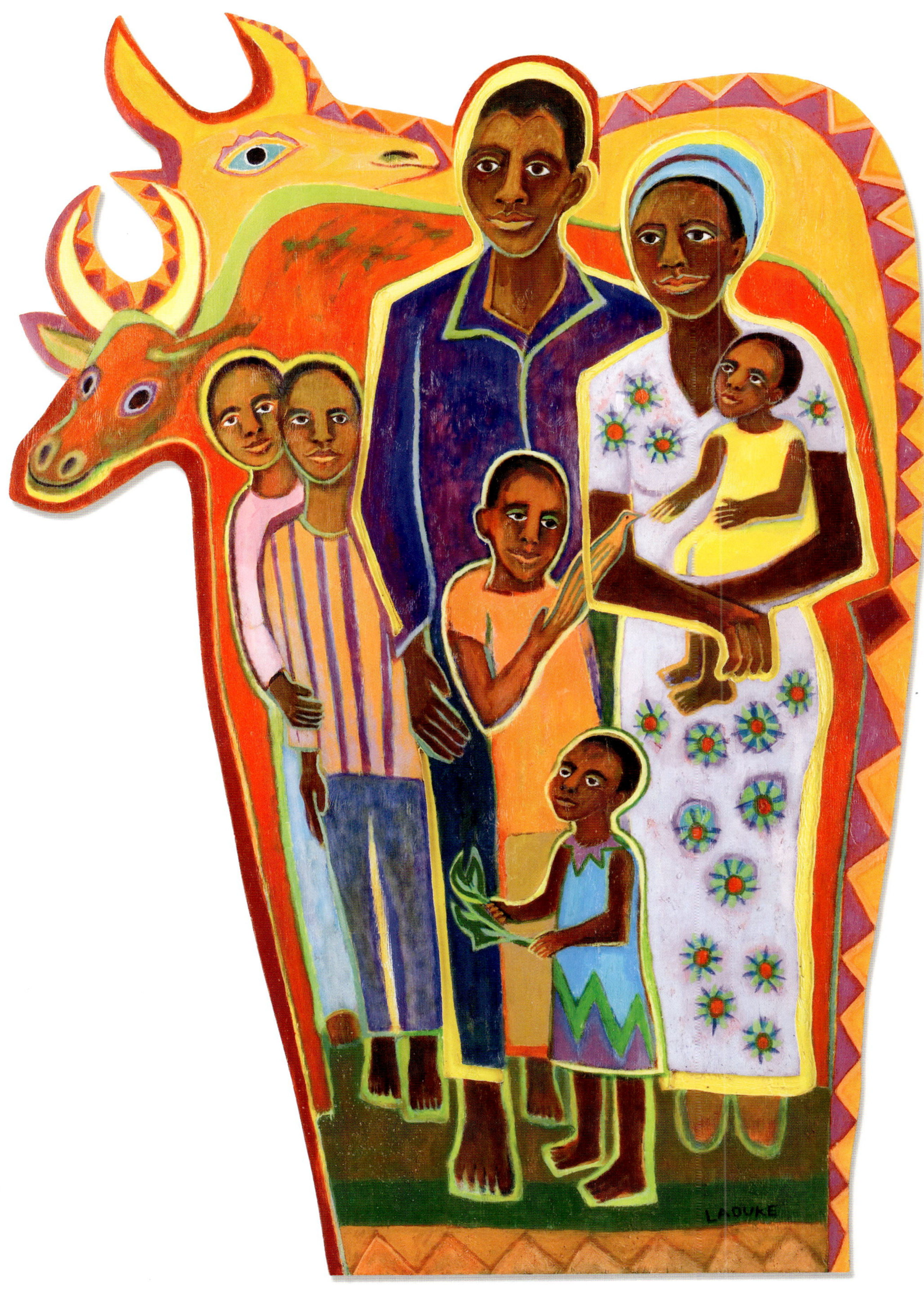

Africa: Dreaming Cows • 78"<48" • 2007

Africa: Planning for the Future p. 75

From the ashes of social upheaval, Heifer helps families to rebuild their lives and communities. A child feeds the calf that his family has received. As in the painting *Rwanda Reconciliation*, the calf's green hands symbolize growth and hope for the future as they reach toward the sun. A beneficent and much larger sun (with its ubiquitous spirit bird) radiates above the scene, surrounded by farmers who cultivate the land. This latter image becomes another piece of the Mural Project entitled *Africa: Beneath the Sun*.

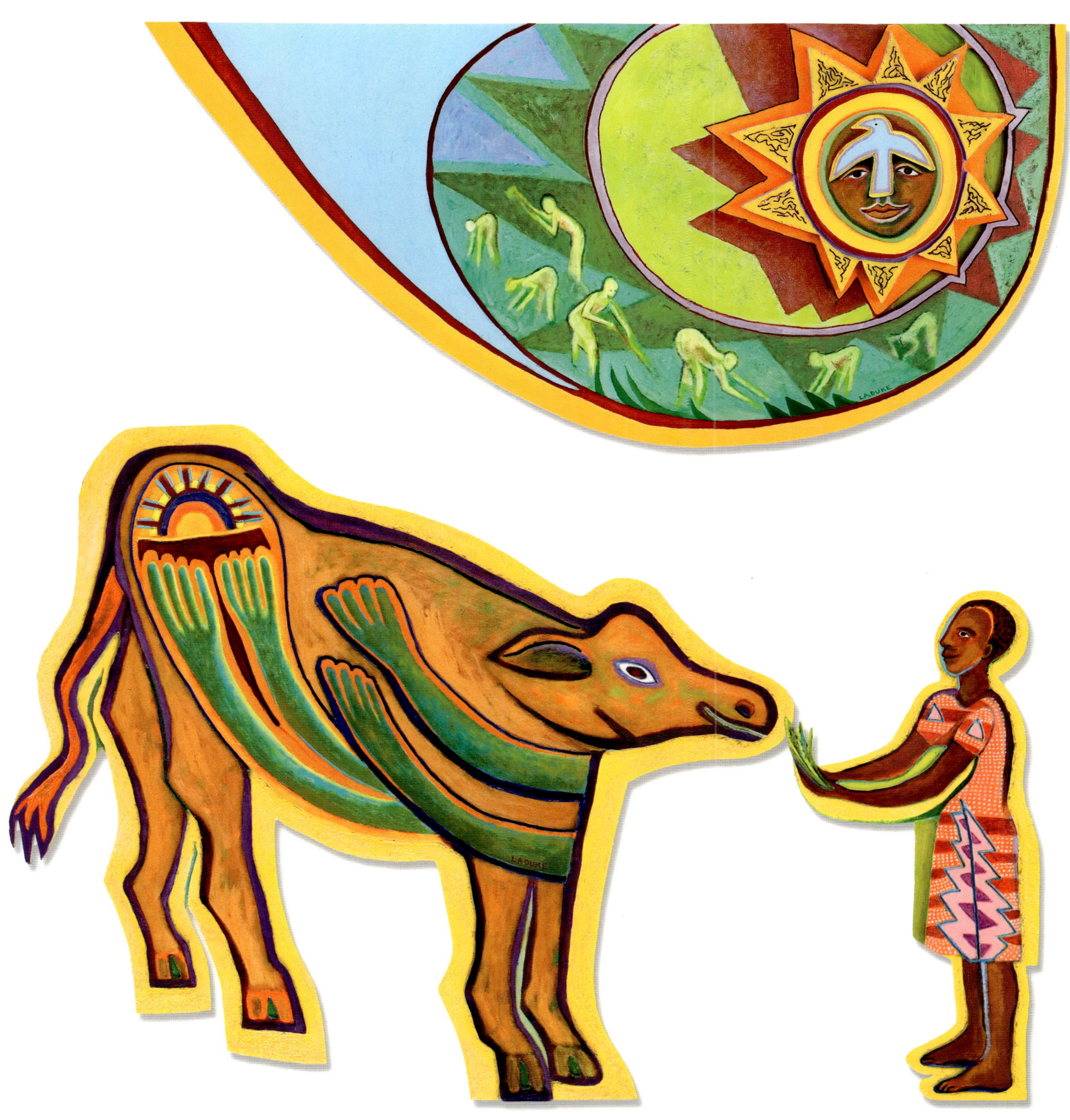

Africa: Planning for the Future • cow+girl 50"x48" • sun 62"x32" • 2007

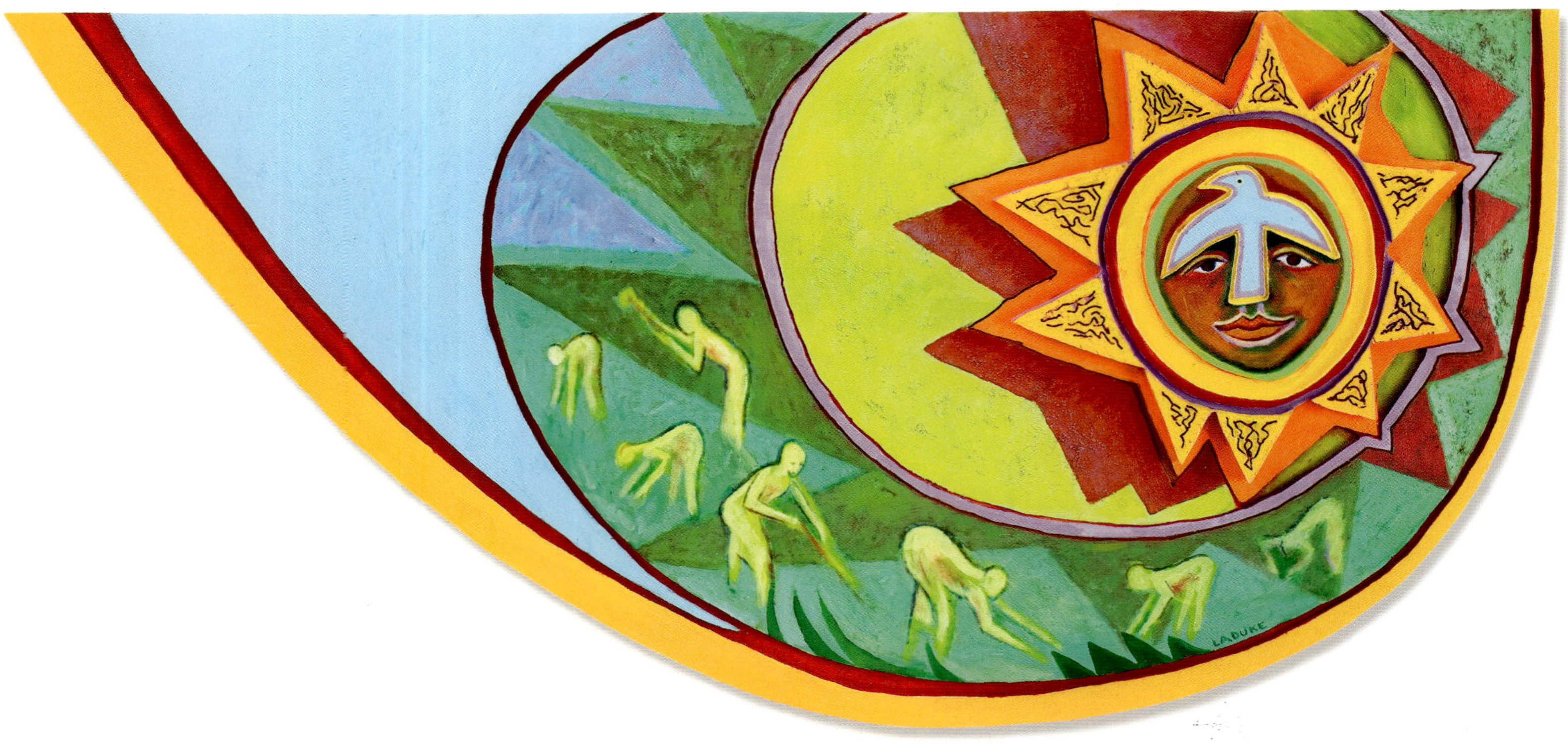

Africa: Beneath the Sun • 62"x32" • 2007

Africa: Beneath the Sun

The seasonal rhythms of plowing, planting, weeding and harvesting are guided by sun and rain. Silhouetted against the Earth, families work together to produce food that they can share. Then the process begins again. This is a larger image of a piece of the mural panel *Africa: Planning for the Future*. Both mural panels are more evolved versions of the sun in the painting *Africa: Reconciliation*.

Africa: Returning From School p. 77

This mural panel portrays a mother who envisions more options for her children in the future. The lucky ones in school uniforms meet up with those who have cared for younger siblings or worked on the farm during the day.

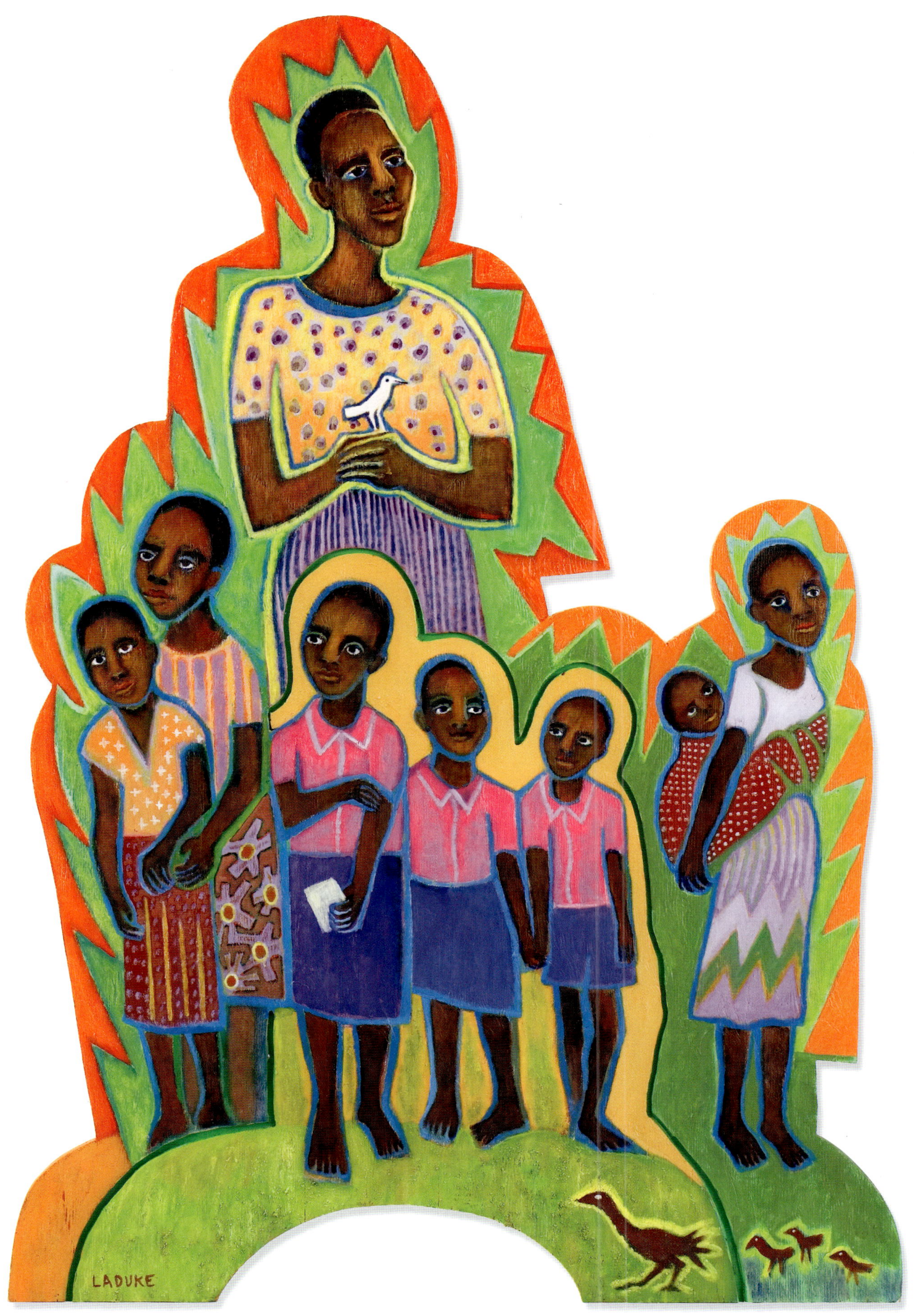

Africa: Returning From School • 72"x48" • 2007

Cow Landscape with Rain Birds p. 79

The cow and the landscape are integrated as one image. Cows contribute to the landscape by fertilizing the crops and the landscape contributes to the cow's nutrition. The arrival of rain birds predicts the weather and planting seasons.

The cow image in this mural panel was seen earlier in the painting *Rwanda: Reconciliation*.

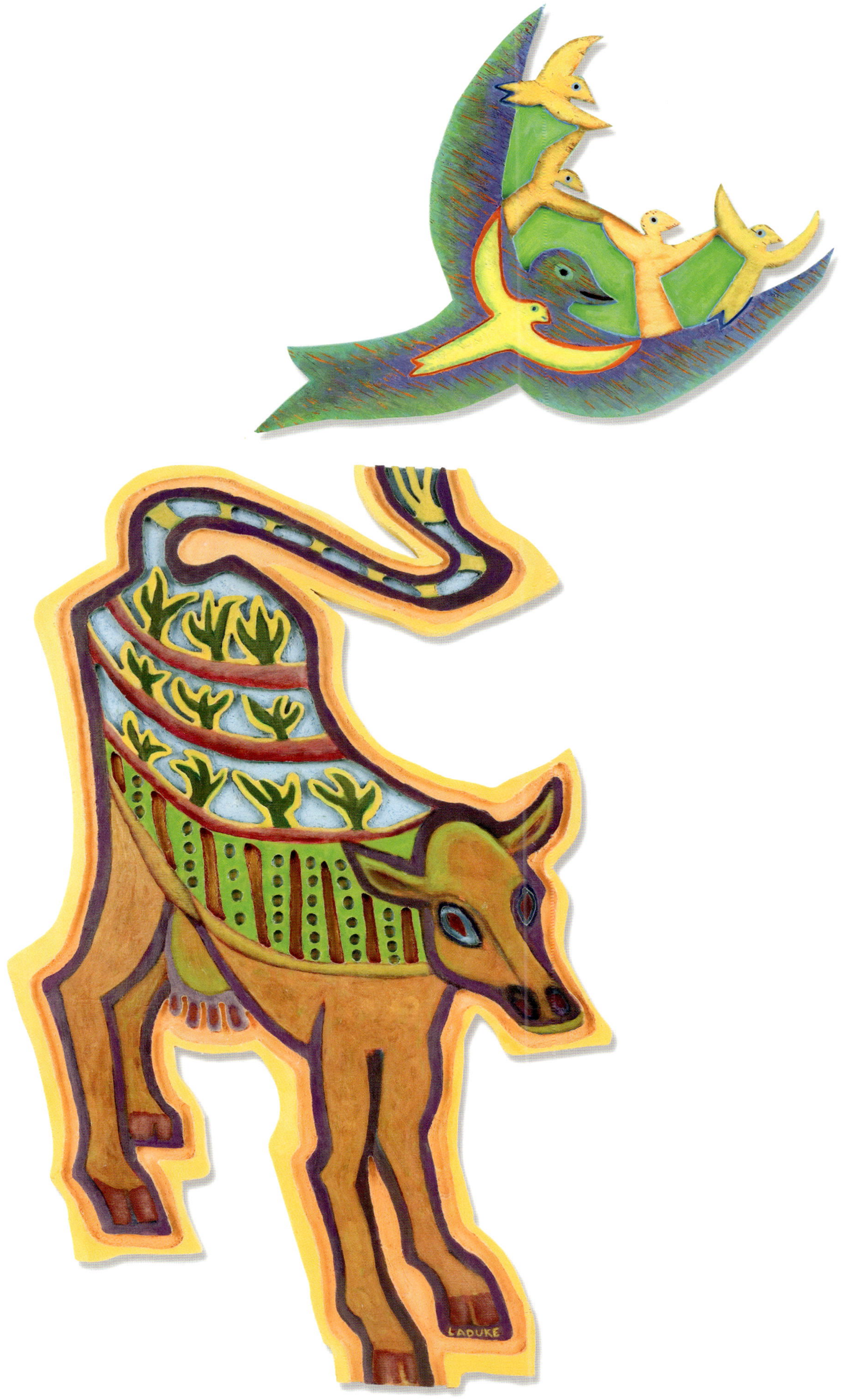

Africa: Cow Landscape with Rain Birds • cow 60"x39" • rainbird 20"x28" • 2007

Painting process of
Africa: Celebrating the Gift
Mural Sequence, 2007

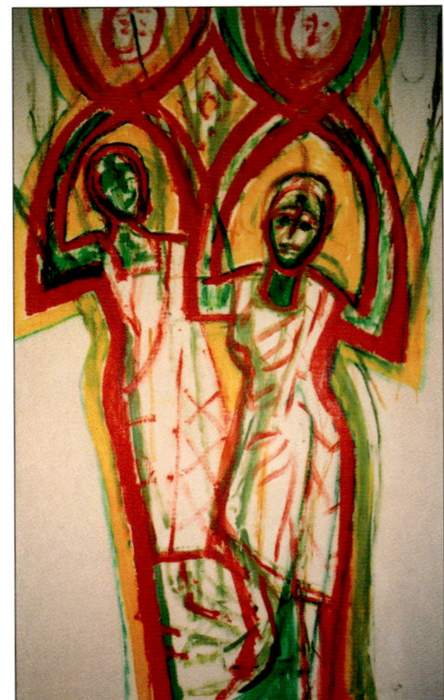

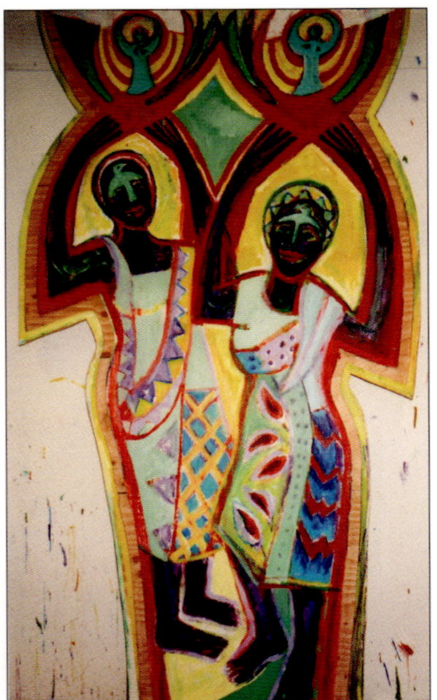

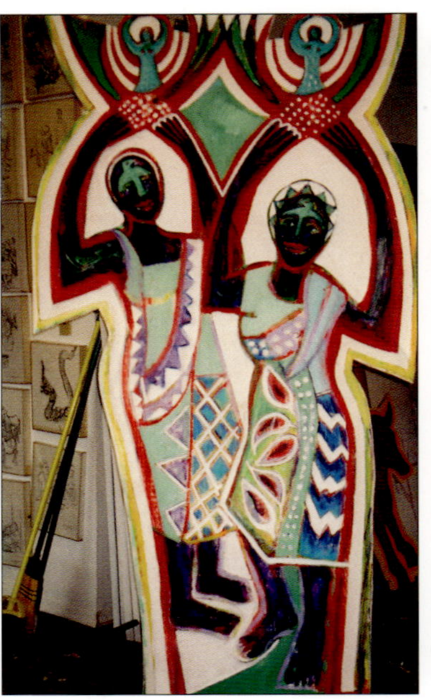

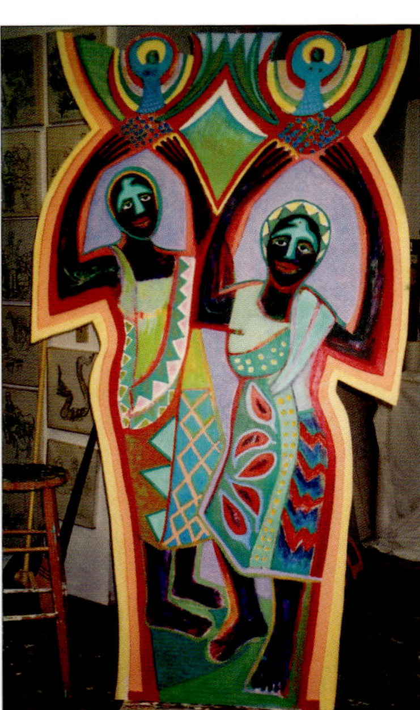

Africa: Celebrating the Gift p. 81

The two women are deeply grateful to Heifer for lifting the village up with the gift of animals, education and a focus on shared benefits.

This mural panel is reminiscent of the painting *Rwanda: Celebrating the Gift of the Heifer 'Consolation.'* When the mural panel was begun, the uplifting spirit of arms and hands were reaching toward angels. By the time it was complete, the angels had transformed into cows. What prevails is the energy of these women and the deep appreciation that they feel for what they have been given.

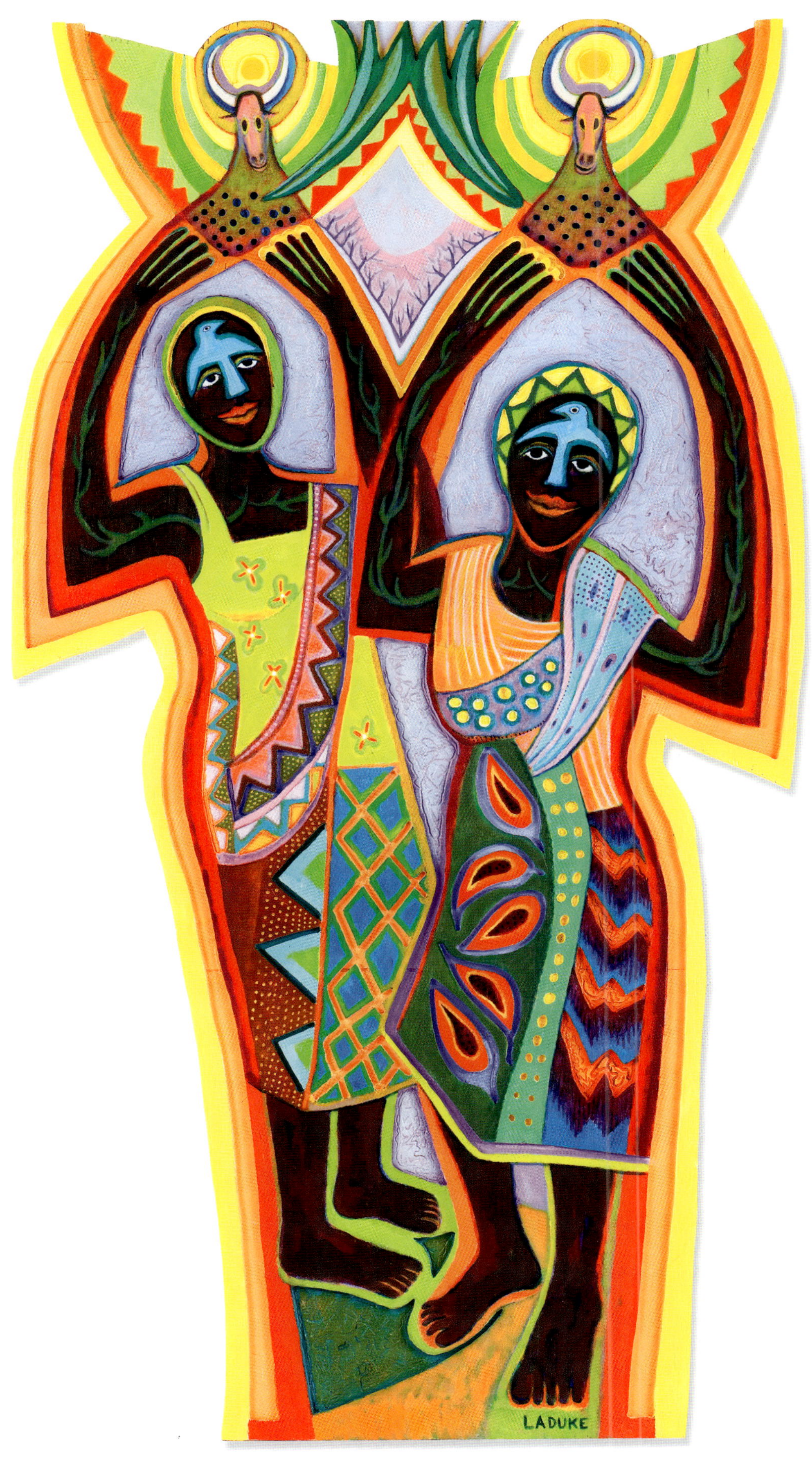

Africa: Celebrating the Gift • 84"x48" • 2007

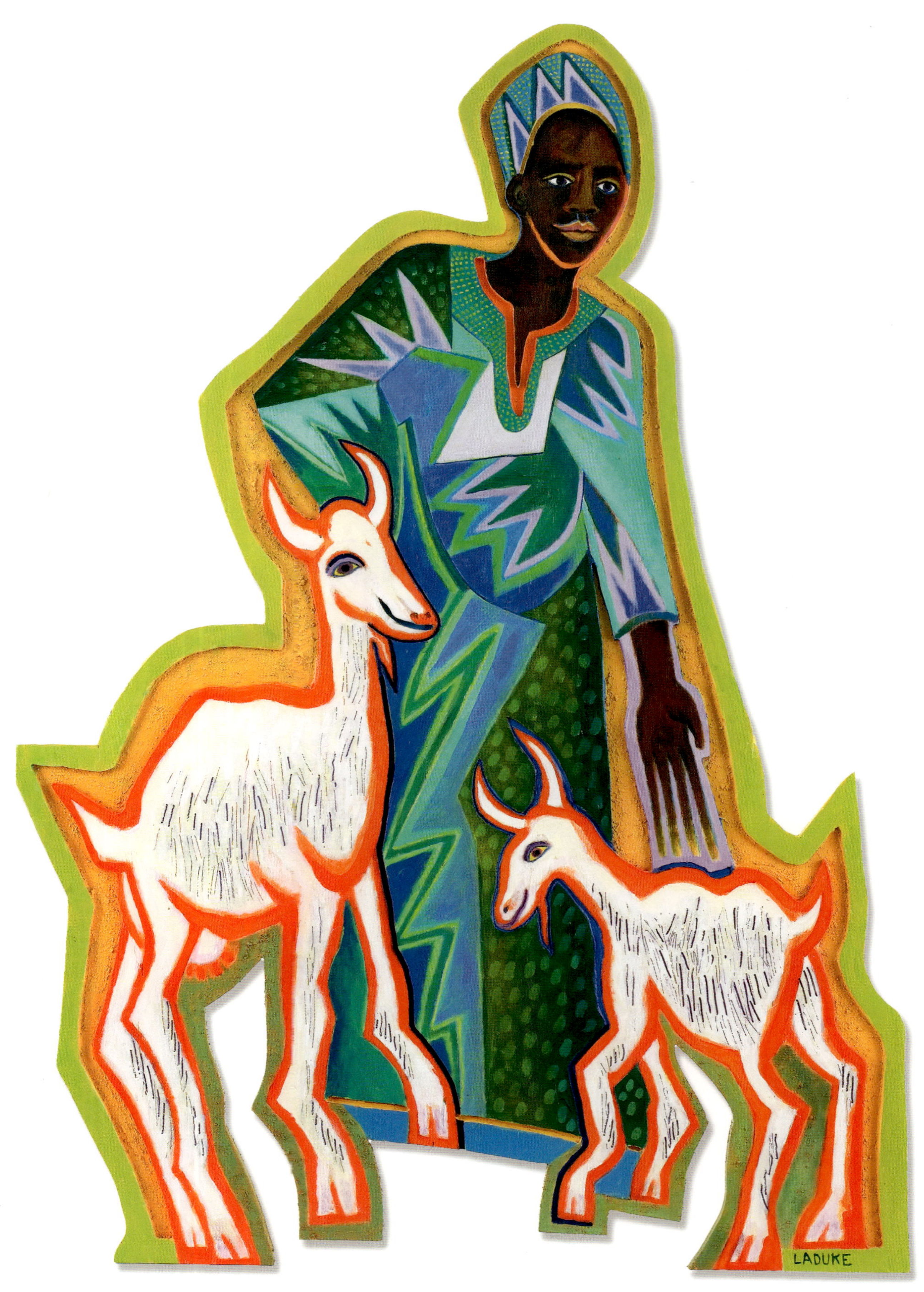

Africa: Goat Pride • 66"x44" • 2007

Africa: Goat Pride p. 82

Here, we revisit the dignified Nanfuka Teopista from Uganda, whose pride in the goats is evident as her hands reach toward them. While her silhouetted form is now engulfed in a bright yellow and green aura, she and her goats have previously been the subjects of a sketch and the painting *Uganda: Nanfuka Teopista's Goats*.

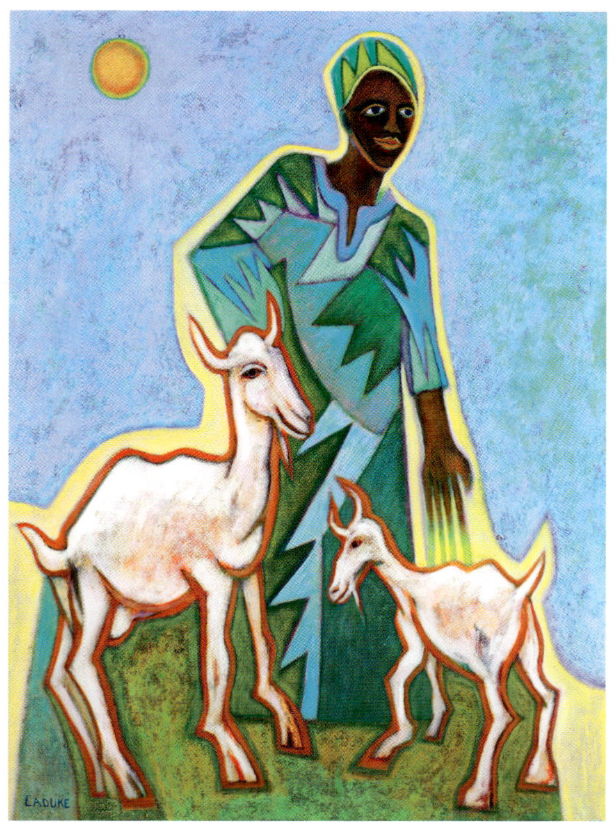

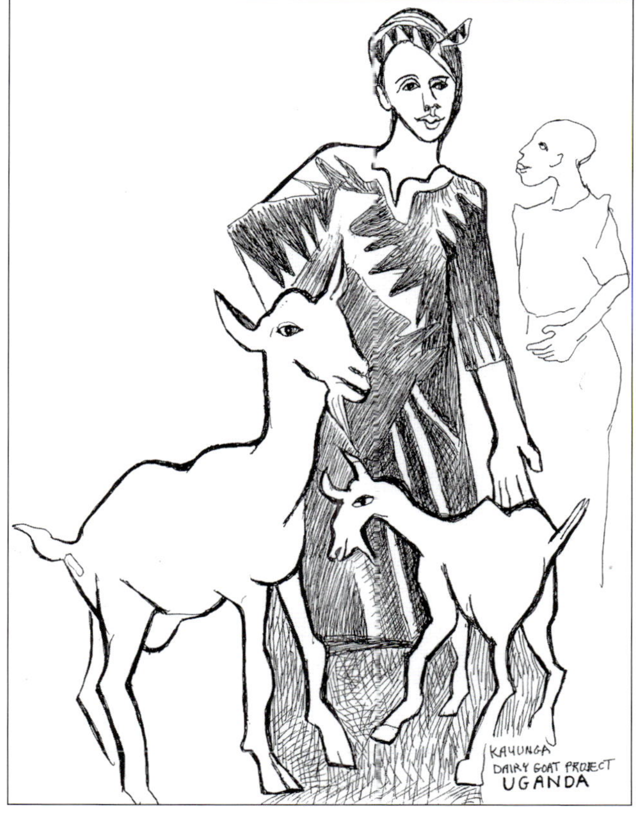

Uganda: Nanfuka Teopista's Goats, painting and pen and ink drawing, 2003

ASIA

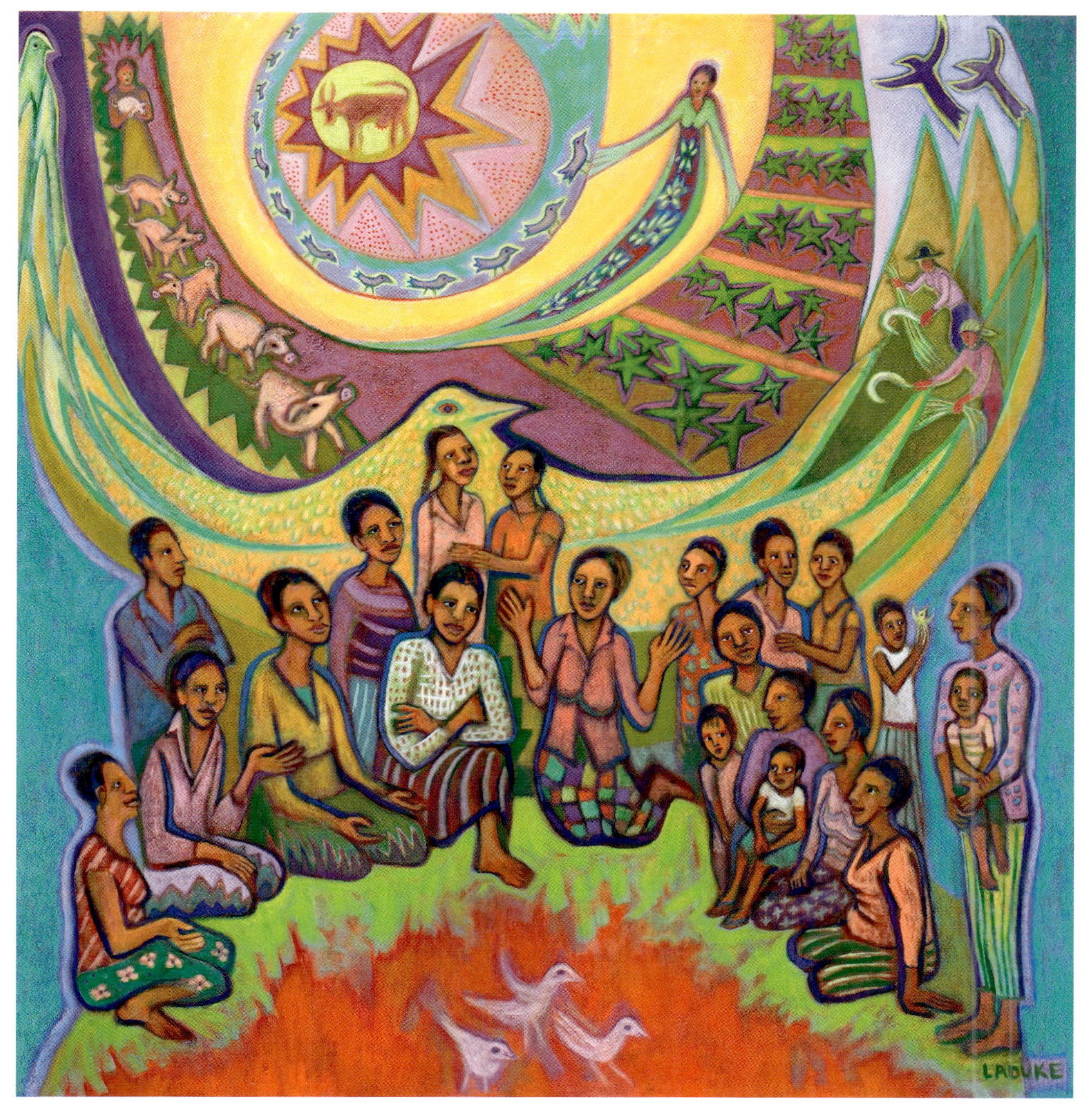

CAMBODIA

VIETNAM

THAILAND

MYANMAR

The Asia Murals

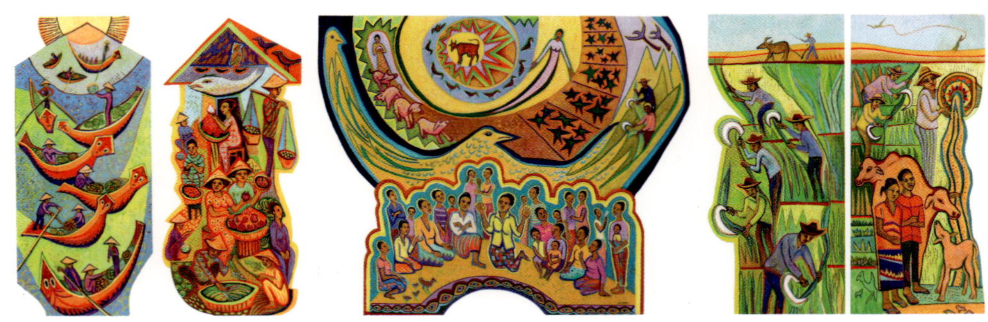

"Your pictures are so attractive with their deep bright color and the vivid paintings, which show the active daily life of people in community. We use these pictures widely to share with communities and teaching. We are proud of "Building Community Leaders" pictures, which become a mural for new [Heifer Village]. This encourages us to work harder and inspire us in involving in community development work for deeper impact."

—Senator Sovann, Country Director,
Heifer International Cambodia

Cambodia, Vietnam, Thailand and Myanmar

In 2005, Betty took a Heifer Study Tour to Cambodia and Vietnam and two years later, to Thailand and Myanmar. While the focus of these tours was on Heifer's efforts to improve the quality of life and the environment in rural Asia, participants also learned about the impact of significant events that have left their mark on rural and urban populations and economies: the Killing Fields of Cambodia; the Vietnam War; Vietnam's occupation of Cambodia and Laos until 1989; the military juntas; the ongoing house arrest of Aung San Suu Kyi and the imprisonment of other dissidents in Myanmar; the 2004 tsunami in Thailand; and the high incidence of HIV/AIDS and drug addiction throughout the region.

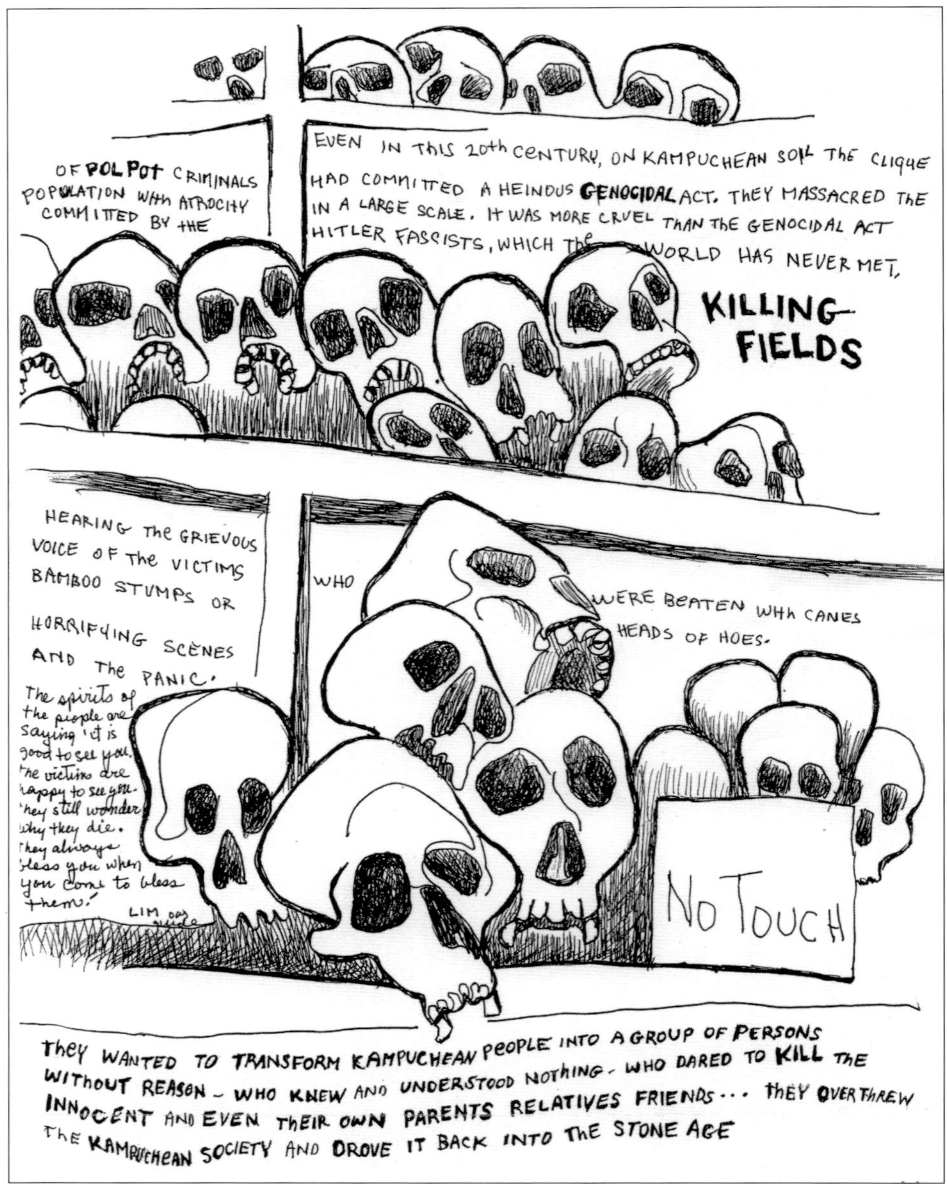

The Killing Fields, 2005

Betty's first Asia Study Tour introduced participants to sobering sights such as the Hoa Lo Prison in Hanoi, Vietnam, and the Tuol Sleng Genocide Museum in Cambodia's capital Phnom Penh. This former high school (used as a Security Prison known as "S21" by the Khmer Rouge regime from 1975–1979) is named after the hill on which it stands or "sleng tree," known to bear poisonous fruits. Its glass shrine holds thousands of human skulls and mass graves.[1]

Throughout rural Asia, rice farming is the primary occupation. Animal farming is a good source of supplementary income and nutrition for families, especially during times of drought. Betty was particularly moved by her visits in densely populated villages such as Pro Lit in Cambodia, where so many had been killed or displaced during the Pol Pot regime, only to return years later to rebuild their communities.

[1] Jul 2, 2008; Archive for the Tuol Sleng Category; Cambodian Genocide Program; Yale University, Center for Holocaust and Genocide Studies; genocidestudies.wordpress.com/category/museums/tuol-sleng-museums/.

Cambodia

As with many of Betty's paintings, the peaceful and bucolic scenes of people working in the fields, tending their animals and building community have been developed against a backdrop of genocide and destruction that cannot be ignored. To understand the Cambodia of today, one must know something of its past. In the September/October 2005 issue of Heifer's *World Ark*, Michael Haddigan wrote that "during its reign of terror, made chillingly real in the Hollywood film *The Killing Fields*, the Khmer Rouge ruled without mercy. The guerrillas outlawed private property and targeted suspected enemies for execution. They dragged people off into the night to be strangled, suffocated, shot, stabbed or beaten to death with hoes. It is a legacy of bitterness that would seem impossible to overcome." It is estimated that 1.7 million or 21% of the population lost their lives during this horrific reign of terror (1975–1979).[2]

And yet...former enemies now work side by side to create communities of peace. Heifer International's Peace Project is helping former soldiers develop small farms by providing cows, chickens and training.

Cambodia: Rice Harvest p. 90

The motion and rhythm of hand-held sickles used for rice harvest binds together the men and women who work in the fields. In the background, our eyes gravitate back toward a blood red road of genocide. But, the image's primary force lies with communal activity that focuses intently on the work at hand. Rice is the basic food in Cambodia. It takes many hands to plant, weed, harvest and process this precious commodity.

Such all-encompassing activity is offset by a mighty water buffalo in the background that helps the farmer to plow the land. The manure of this indigenous and majestic animal (provided by Heifer) fertilizes crops and fruit trees. The beauty of integrated farming is evident as water buffalo and ducks consume leftovers of the rice harvest.

This painting represents life in the Mekong Delta region, a primary rice exporting region that brings needed resources into the country. Heifer is encouraging Cambodian farmers to decrease dependency on one key product by diversifying, especially because many go hungry between rice production periods.

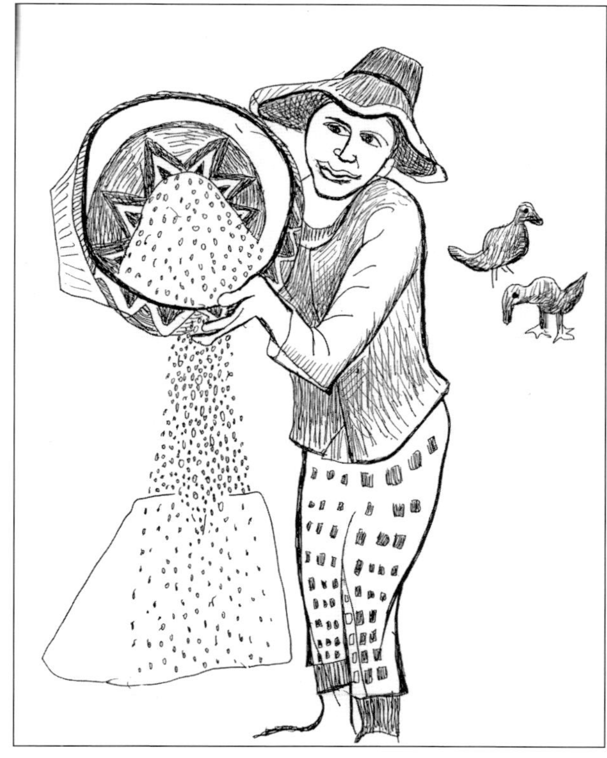

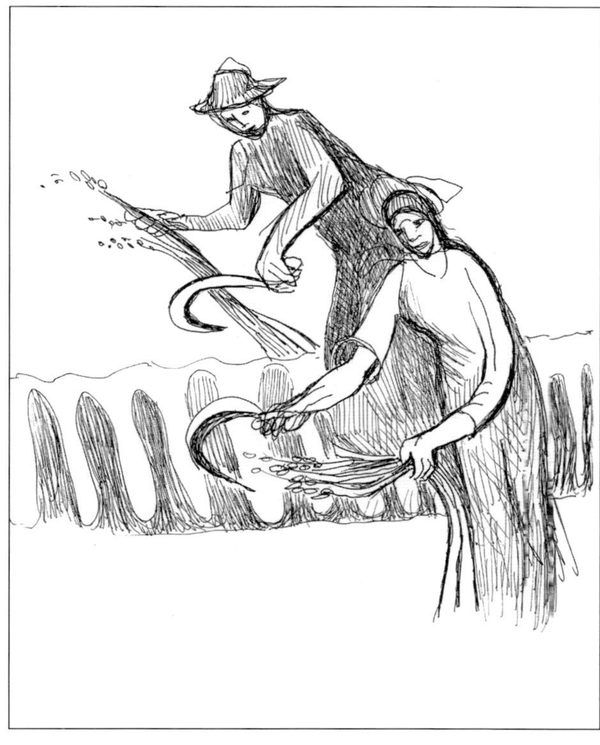

Above and below: *Cambodia Rice Harvesting*, 2005

[2] Yale University, Cambodian Genocide, www.yale.edu/cgp.

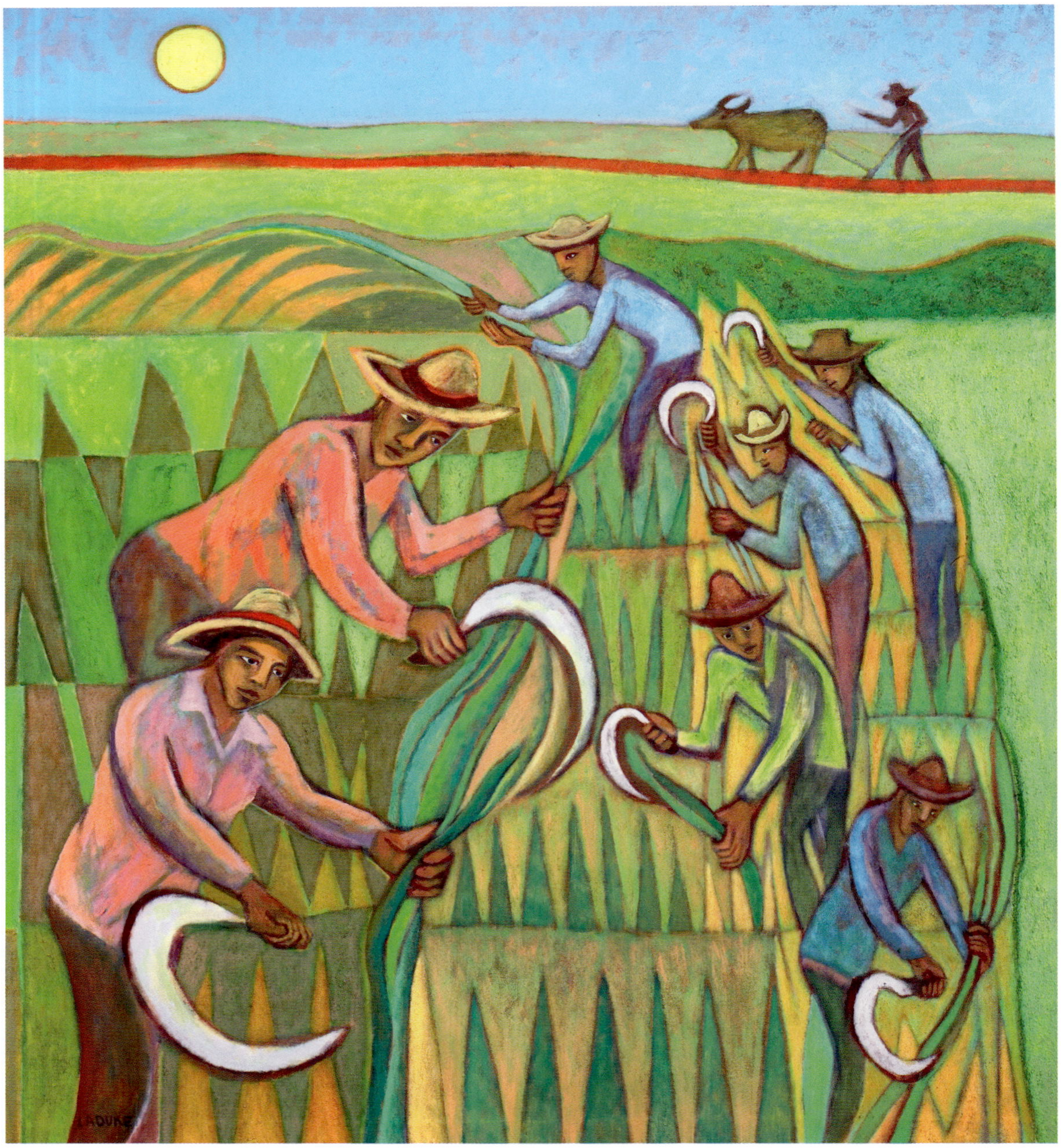

Cambodia: Rice Harvest • 60"x54" • 2006

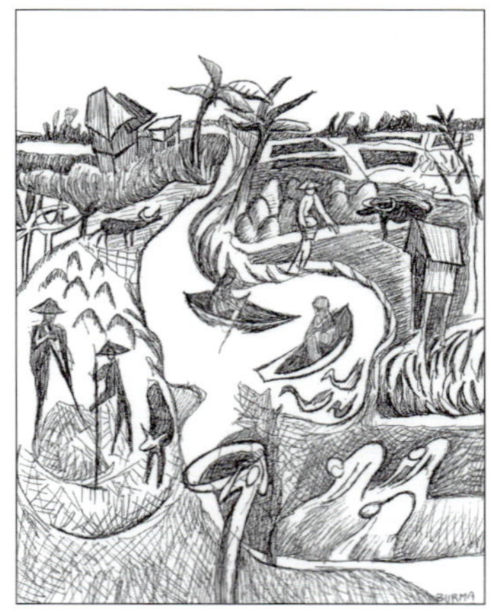
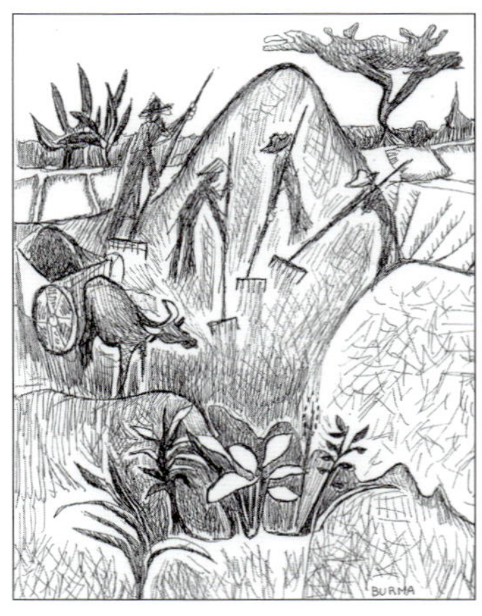
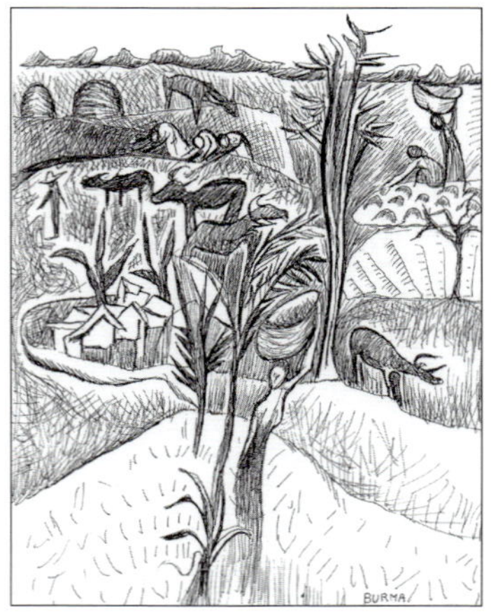

Myanmar Landscape, Rice Field, 2007

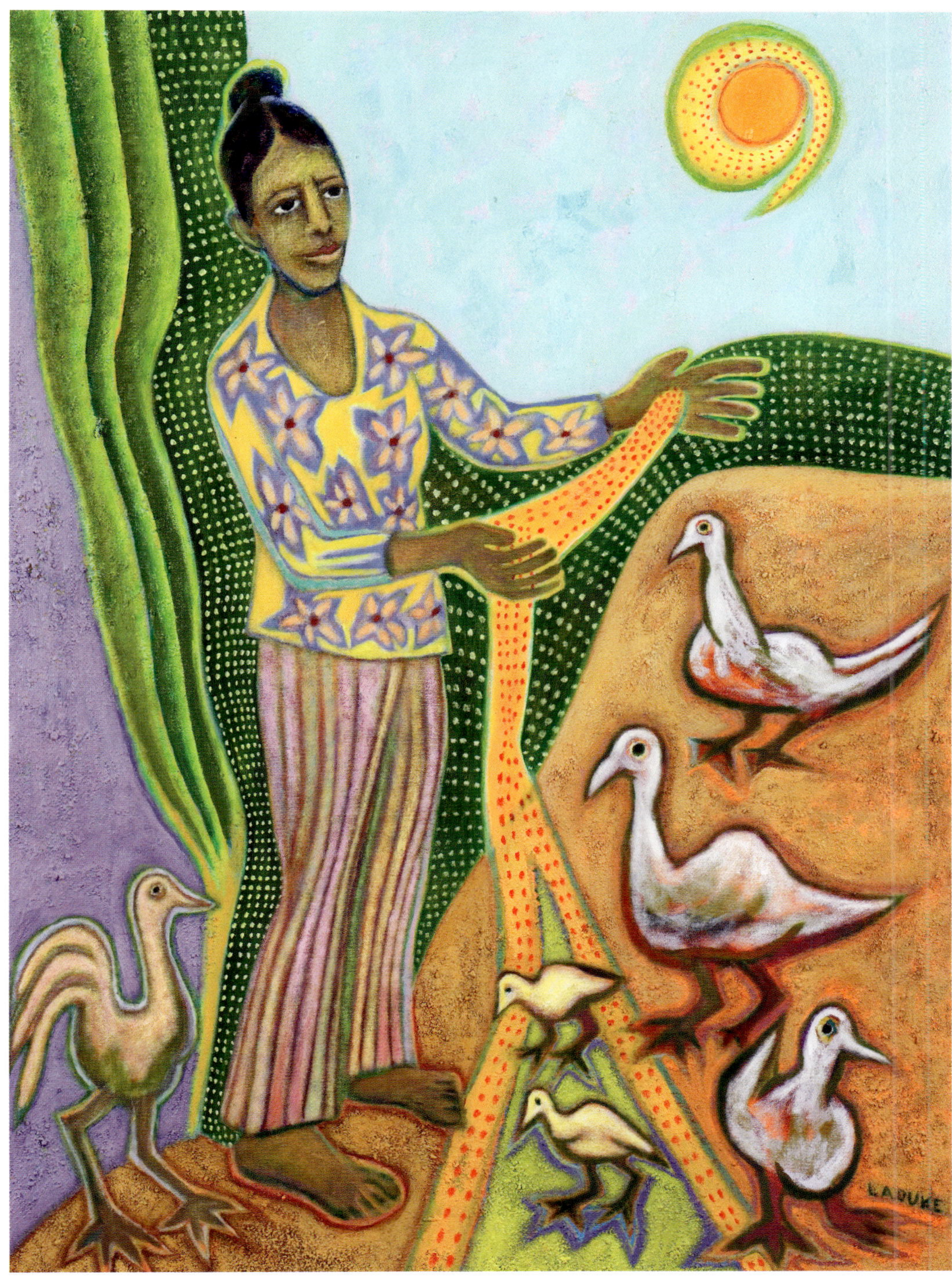

Cambodia: Mrs. Sim Roen's Ducks • 44"x32" • 2006

Cambodia: Mrs. Sim Roen's Ducks

In 2001, Mrs. Sim Roen was a 42-year old impoverished farmer in Trokeat Village in the Kampong Speu Province. This mother of five had the additional burden of caring for an abusive husband with chronic illness. She owned no animals or agricultural tools and could not afford to send her children to school. Then she was selected to be trained by Heifer as a village animal health worker (VAHW), at which, over time, she excelled. Since then, Mrs. Sim Roen has increased her family's food production with a home garden and has generated enough income to send her children to school. She is able to save food for lean periods. Her husband, who now receives medical treatment, helps care for the family's animals (three cows, one pig, thirty chickens, and five ducks). In addition, she has acquired tools and built a pond to raise fish and water the garden. Currently, her VAHW services and chicken sales provide the family with a steady income. This successful entrepreneur has moved beyond the boundaries of her own family to address issues of domestic violence, family health care and sustainability within her community. In 2004, Mrs. Sim Roen was the only Cambodian to be awarded Heifer's Golden Talent Award, which brought her to Little Rock, Arkansas, to celebrate Heifer International's 60th Anniversary.[3]

The painting portrays a proud woman who knows that she has done well. She has managed the ducks given to her by Heifer with such success that she has become a role model within the community. A ribbon of grain flows from Mrs. Sim Roen's hands to her ducks and chickens. The green ribbon behind her symbolizes a garden that has grown beyond the borders of the painting. The elements are strong components of this composition: one can almost feel the soft movements of a multi-hued blue sky; the darker currents of blue water; and the cyclical nature of the sun, the gardens and their connection to the nourishing grains that she feeds to her animals.

Cambodia: Building Community Leaders p. 93

While the site of this painting is Prolet Village in Siem Reap Province, the message of its striking image symbolically represents what is happening in many villages that Betty has visited. Here, the villagers tell her, "The heritage we want to pass on is not only cows, but good education. We want to build community leaders." The group of women gathered under the magnificent mythical bird or "garuda" (a large avian creature that appears in Hindu and Buddhist mythology) are proud to have assumed some control over their lives. They have built a school for their children. They are passing on heifers to others in need. They welcome the Heifer Study Tour with open arms and appreciation. A big feast is prepared for all to share, but the visitors must eat first.

In the painting, the past—represented by the bright red at the base of the painting—still holds much horror, especially for the older generation. Yet, a new future is being built upon the horrors of the past. The women convene on a bed of beautiful green that signifies new growth. Birds that exemplify freedom and possibility fly about. A woman in the sun reaches out to her beloved ducks while nearby, a woman holds tight to a piglet as she follows a family of pigs. The harvest scenes indicate more prosperous times to come.

[3] Information derived from Heifer's Golden Talent Award Description.

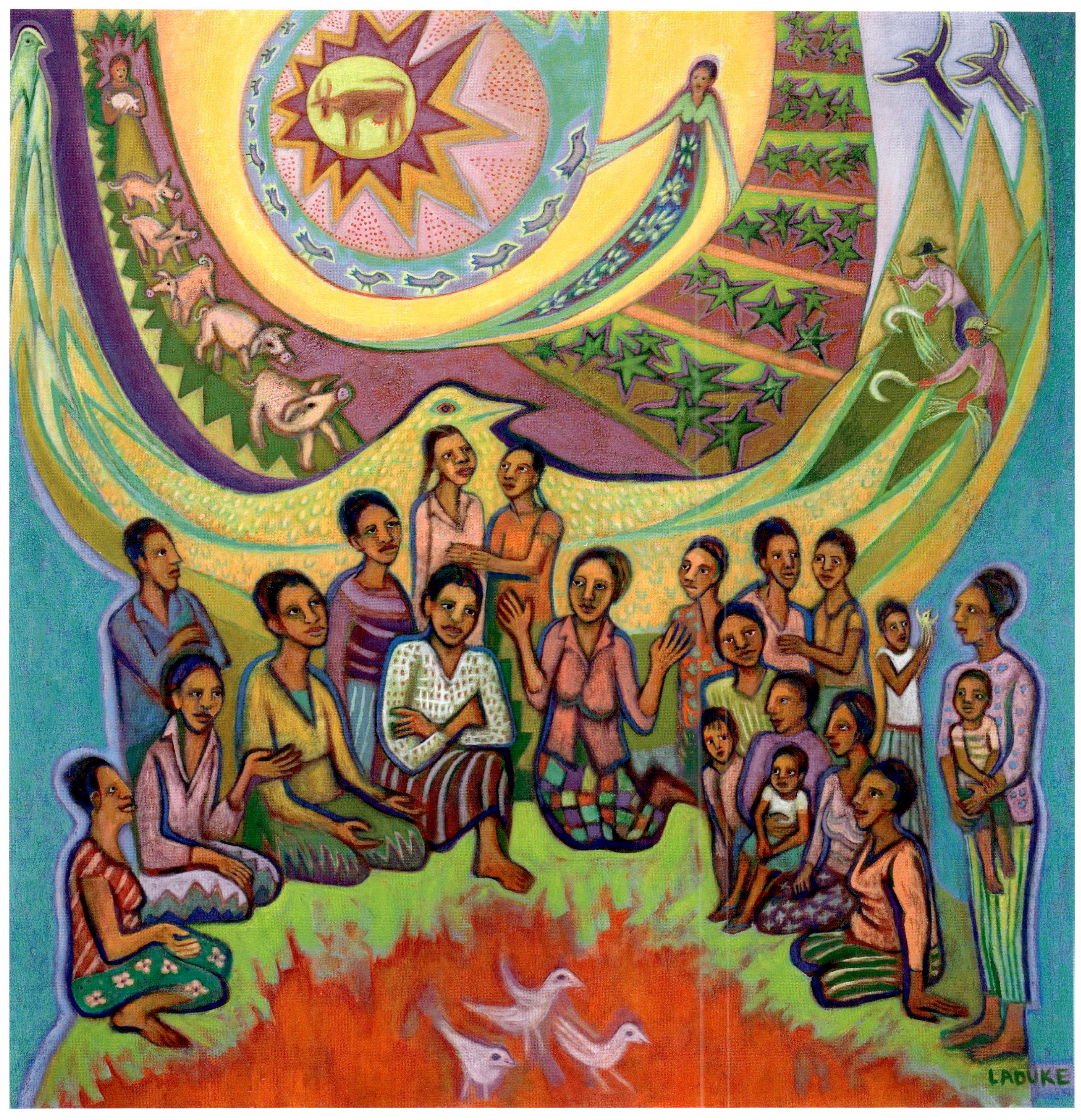

Cambodia: Building Community Leaders • 72"x68" • 2006

"The beauty of Heifer," says Betty, "is their support of the wholeness of a community. Education is a cornerstone—teaching, learning, sharing—it is about much more than animals."

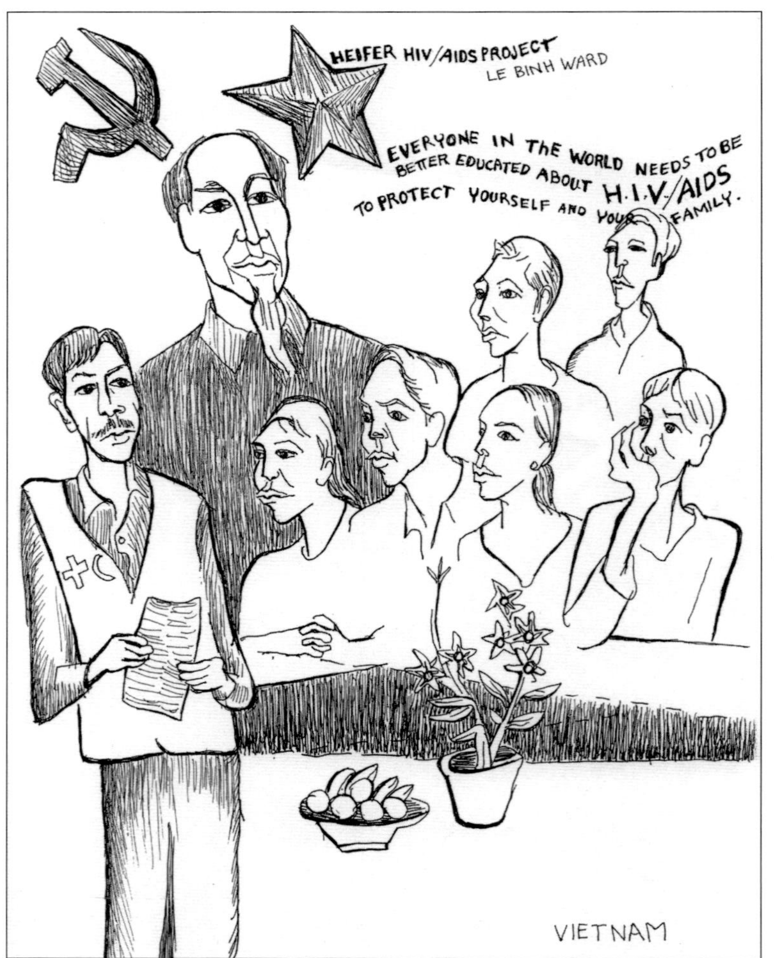

Heifer HIV/AIDS Project,
Le Binh Warc, 2005

Vietnam

Following the Vietnam War, the country experienced little economic growth until 1986, when a policy of "doi moi" or economic reform often referred to as "market socialism" was implemented by the Communist Party.[4] These structural reforms began to modernize the economy and open the country to foreign trade. "Doi moi" has generally been beneficial to farmers in rural Vietnam. People living in rural areas (comprising 73.12 percent of the population, 57.1 % of whom make a living from agriculture, forestry, and aquaculture)[5] work for themselves rather than for the state. They can choose what crops to grow. However, they must also grapple with higher taxes (especially on rice) and a higher cost of getting their products to market (processing and transportation). As such, many continue to function at a subsistence level.[6]

Heifer Vietnam began in 1987 with the intention of improving teaching, research and extension activities at the Animal Husbandry and Veterinary Medicine Division of Can Tho University in the Mekong Delta. Its programs have grown to include 16 provinces and more than 8,000 families, with a focus on integrated farming as well as on raising cattle that have been cross bred to best adapt to local climate and conditions. The Heifer program also works with youth at risk, handicapped children and people with HIV.

The focus is as much on empowering families as it is on helping families to improve their annual income and the environment. Because there are few local non-governmental organizations (NGOs) in Vietnam, Heifer primarily partners with the country's Province's Department of Agriculture and Rural Development, Department of Cooperatives, and Department of Labor, War Invalids and Social Affairs.

Vietnam: Dragon Fruit Dreams p. 96

The exuberance with which Betty describes her introduction to the dragon fruit is contagious: "At the market, the melon-like dragon was a new experience that I particularly enjoyed for taste as well as color. It is red on the outside and pure white with the tiniest black speckles on the inside. I had never seen this before and I was delighted!"

Betty's love of market places throughout the world is a recurrent theme. At market day in the Mekong Delta, she revels in the cone-shaped traditional hats that the women wear and the colorful patterns of their clothes.

Baskets are prominently featured: this renewable resource is often used in conjunction with bamboo poles to carry a multitude of wares and produce, as seen in the background.

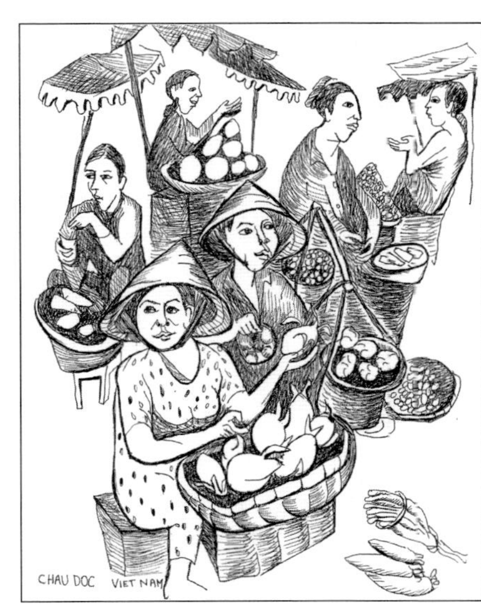

Chau Doc Market: Dragon fruit Dreams
drawing, 2005

[4] San José State University Dept. of Economics; www.sjsu.edu/faculty/watkins/vietnam/htm#DOIMOI.

[5] People living in rural areas (comprising 73.12 percent of the population, 57.1 % of whom make a living from agriculture, forestry, and aquaculture) According to the General Statistics Office of Vietnam; 2005; http://www.gso.gov.vn.

[6] California State University: www.csuchico.edu/~cheinz/syllabi/asst001/fall98/thompson/doimoi.htm.

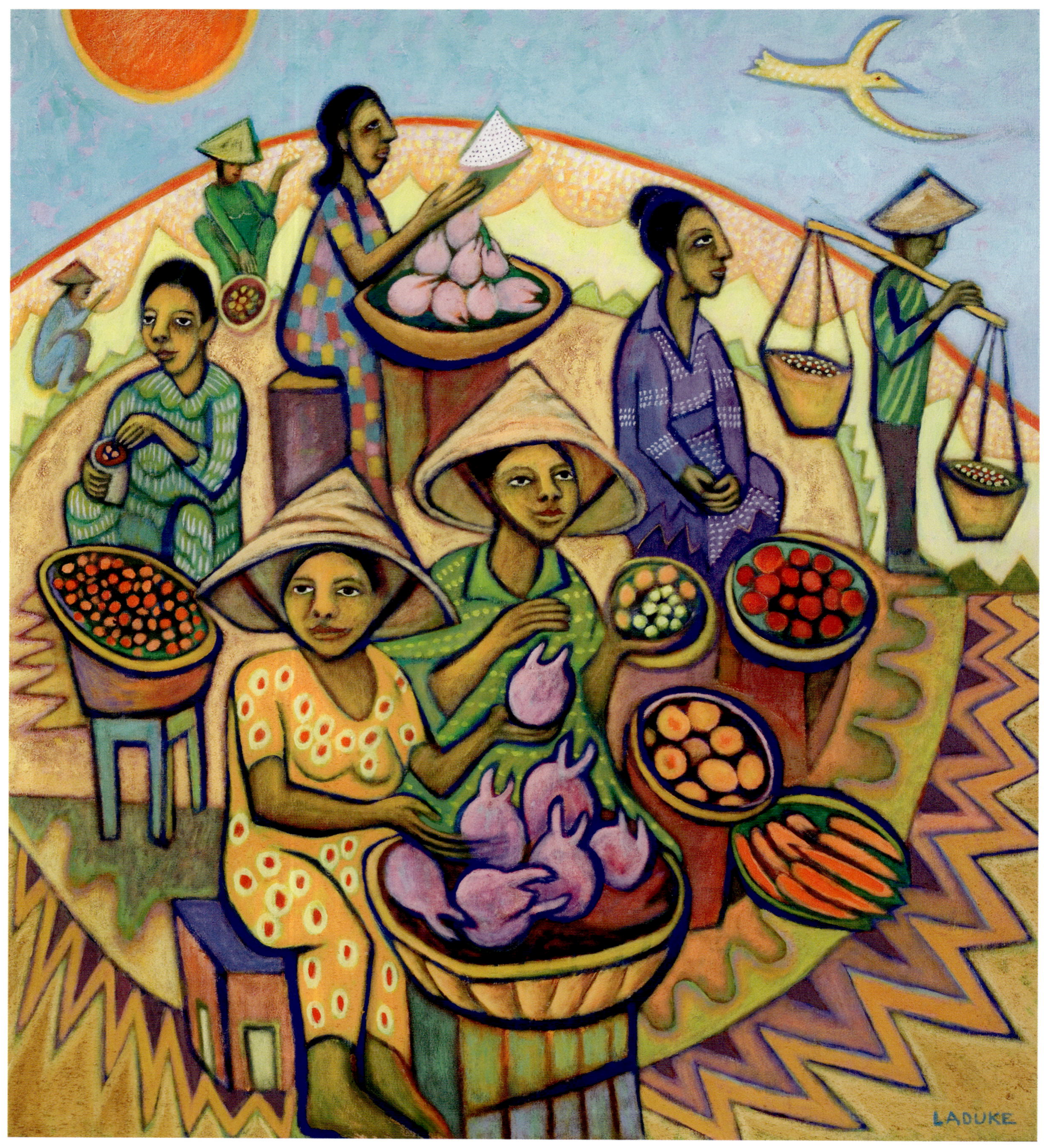

Vietnam: Dragon Fruit Dreams • 54"x50" • 2006

Vietnam: Mekong River Market

Women wearing traditional Vietnamese hats earn extra income by selling surplus produce at the lively River Market. The river is heavily trafficked with boats carrying all kinds of fruits, vegetables and flowers. The boats that carry them have expressive dragon faces that are vigilant and spirited.

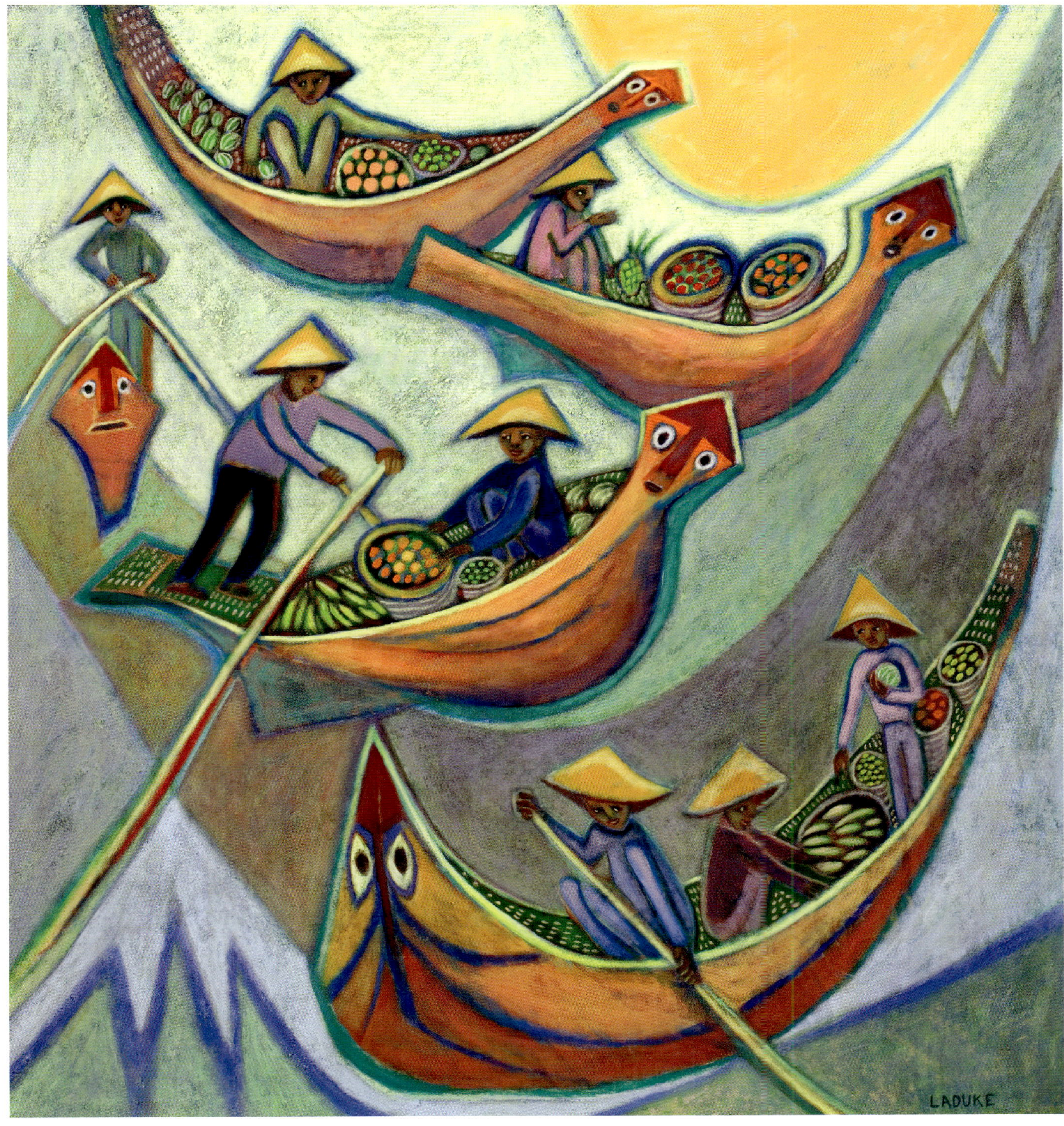

Vietnam: Mekong River Market • 54"x50" • 2006

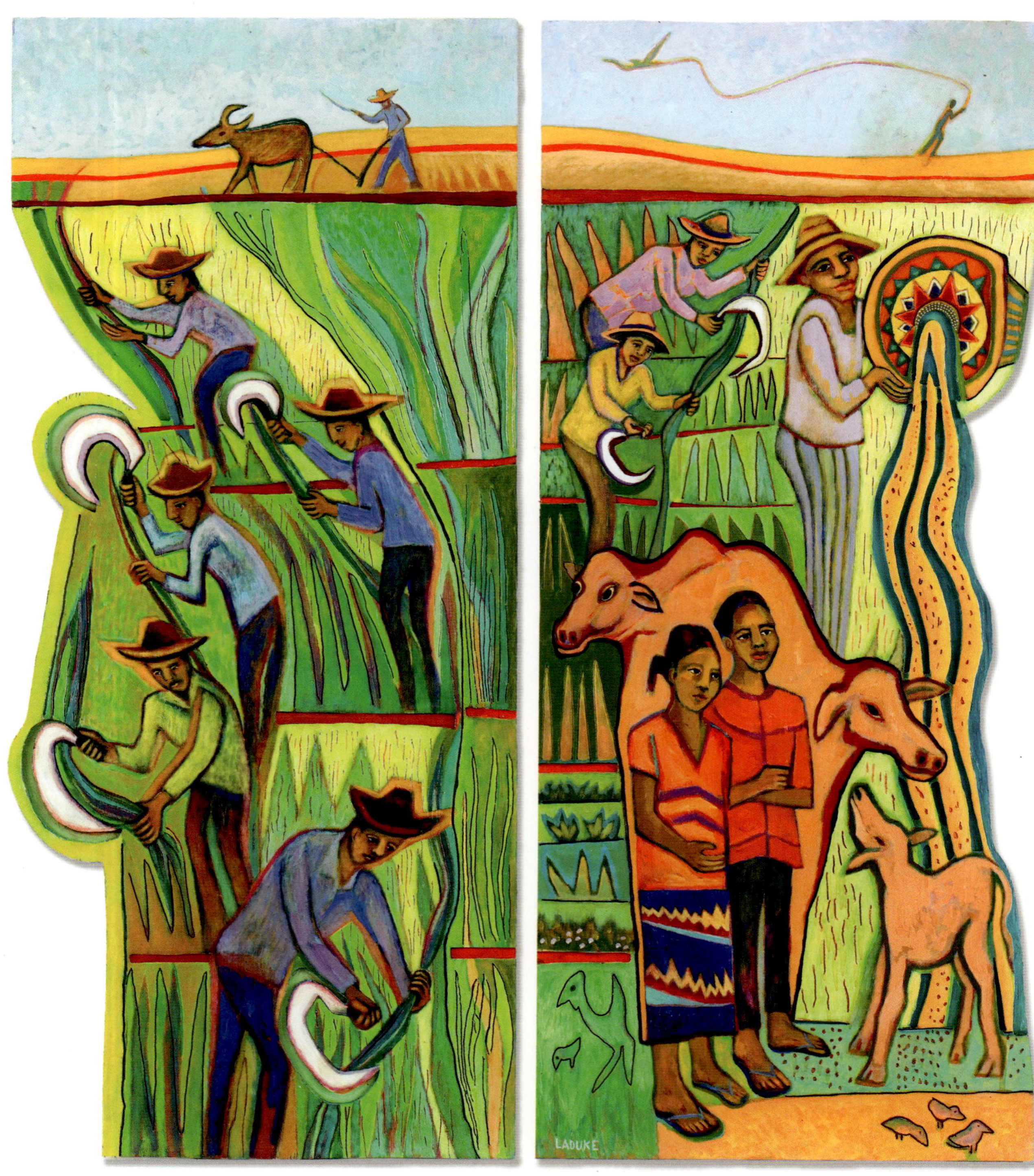

Asia: Rice Harvest • 84"x96" • 2007

Asia: Rice Harvest

Water buffalo help to plow the land while many hands contribute to the process of planting, growing and harvesting the rice. Heifer International provides water buffalo, heifers, goats, pigs, fish, seedlings and training to farmers who primarily grow rice, Asia's most basic food.

Asia: Building Community Leaders

With encouragement from Heifer community developers, villagers gather to talk about their hopes for the future. "The heritage we want to pass on is not only cows but good education. We want to build community leaders."

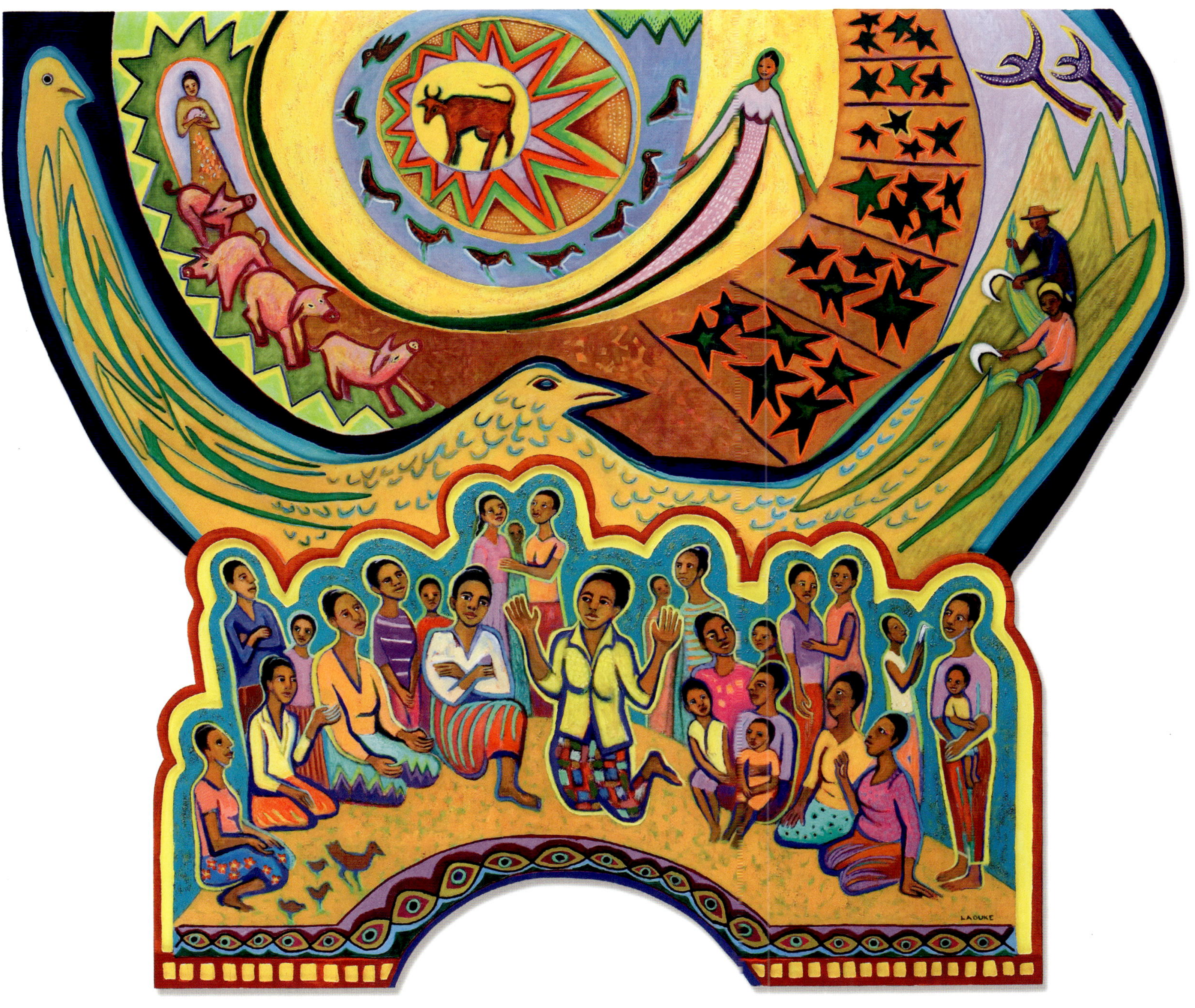

Asia: Building Community Leaders • 84"x96" • 2007

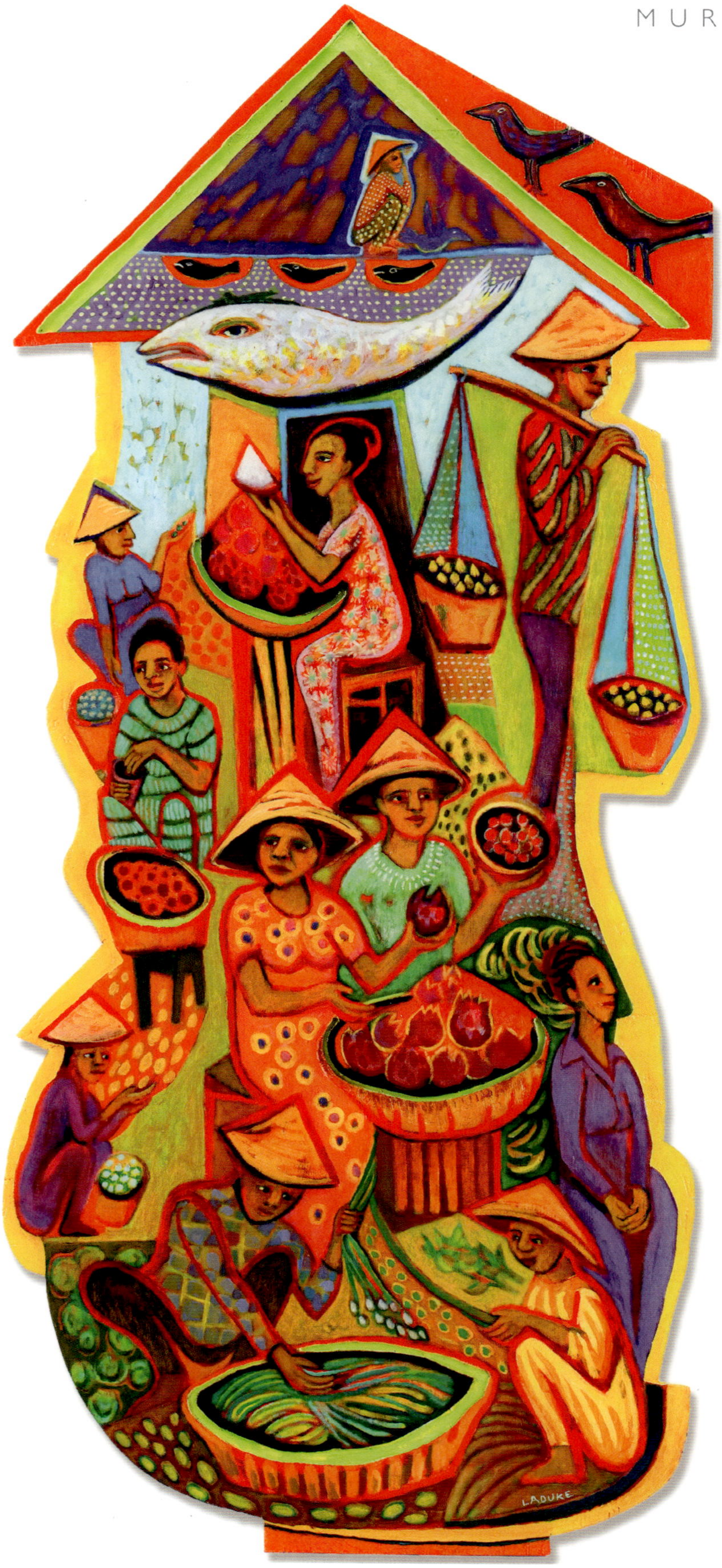

Asia: Village Market • 84"x48" • 2007

Villagers bring extra produce from their vegetable gardens and fruit trees to sell at the market.

Asia: Village Market

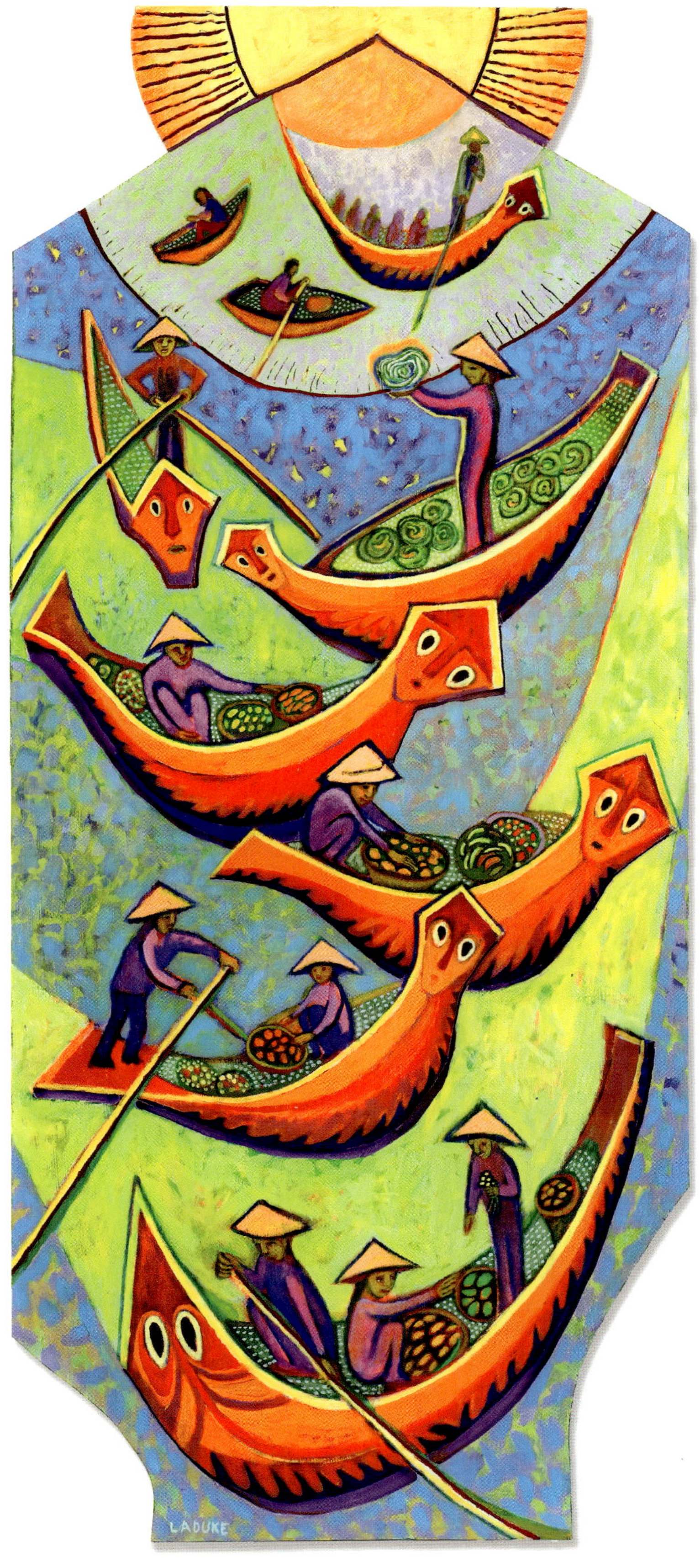

Asia: Mekong River Market • 84"x48" • 2007

Asia: Mekong River Market

As in the Mekong River Market painting, women selling colorful produce enrich the landscape. The whimsical dragon faces of the boats add a playful element to the scene

EASTERN EUROPE

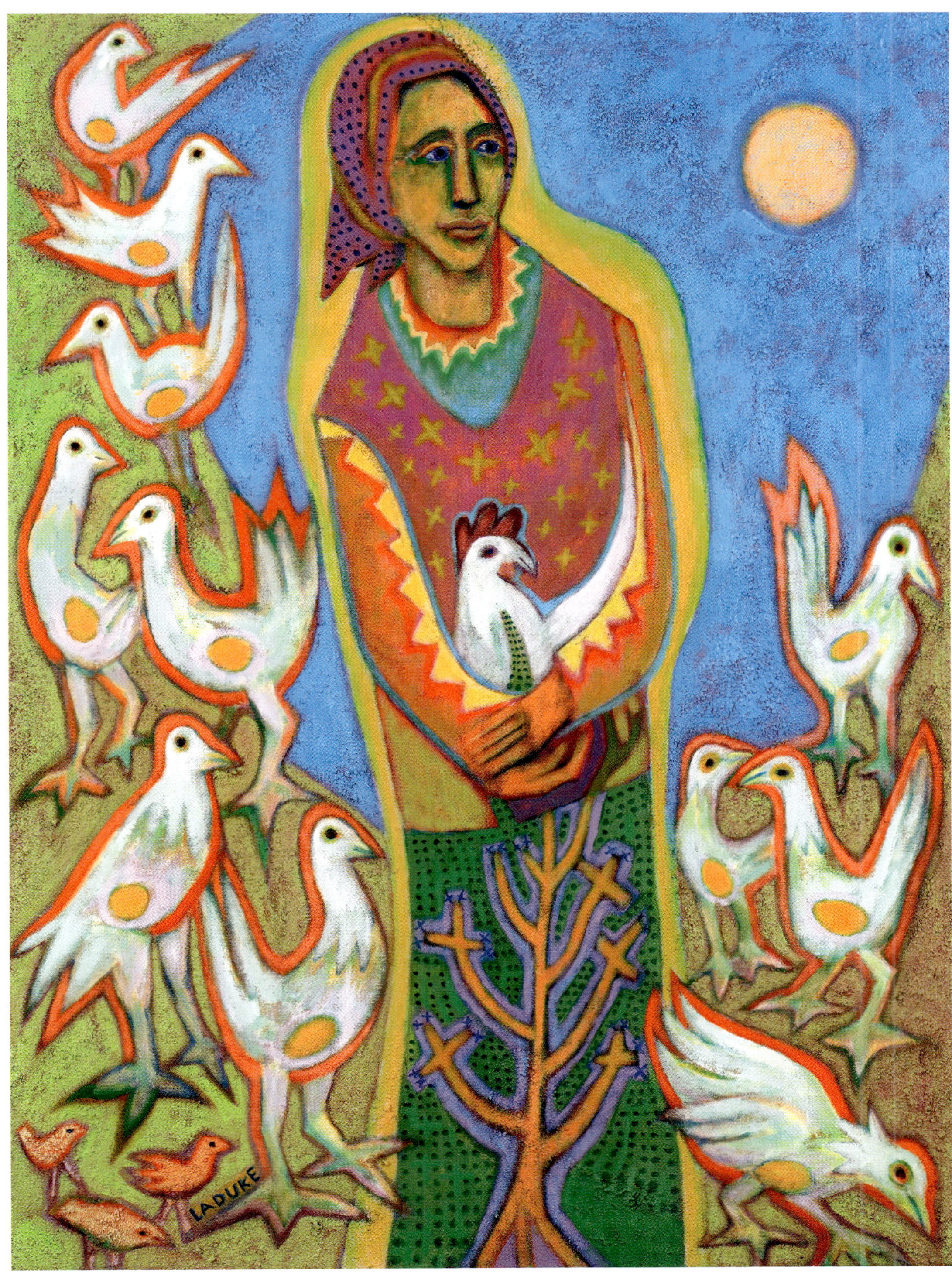

POLAND

KOSOVO

ALBANIA

The Eastern Europe Murals

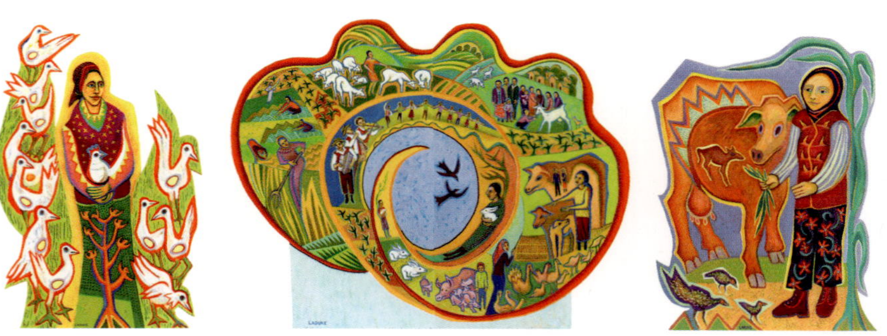

"For me, there is a lot of personal history and meaning. You can't be with people in this country (Poland) without feeling how the history is still alive and raw."

—Betty LaDuke

Poland, Kosovo and Albania

Introduction

Betty visited Poland in 2005 and Albania and Kosovo in 2006, where she was struck by a different face of poverty. Whereas she saw waif-thin people throughout Asia and Africa, here she observed many who were overweight from a heavy but insufficiently nutritious diet. Unemployment rates as high as 50% or more,[1] depressed economies and harsh weather conditions translated into high levels of depression and alcoholism throughout the region. Nevertheless, Betty found a deep sense of cultural pride and resilience among the people she met.

After decades of Soviet dominance, Eastern Europe has begun to slowly recover from economic collapse. Tightly controlled state farms under Communist rule have given way to individually-owned small farms. However, the success of these farms has been compromised by a severe lack of resources and equipment.

---

[1] *International Herald Tribune*, Jan. 29, 2008, "Kosovo's Independence Won't End Its Struggle;" United Nations Economic Commission for Europe: www.unece.org/stats/trends2005/employment.htm.

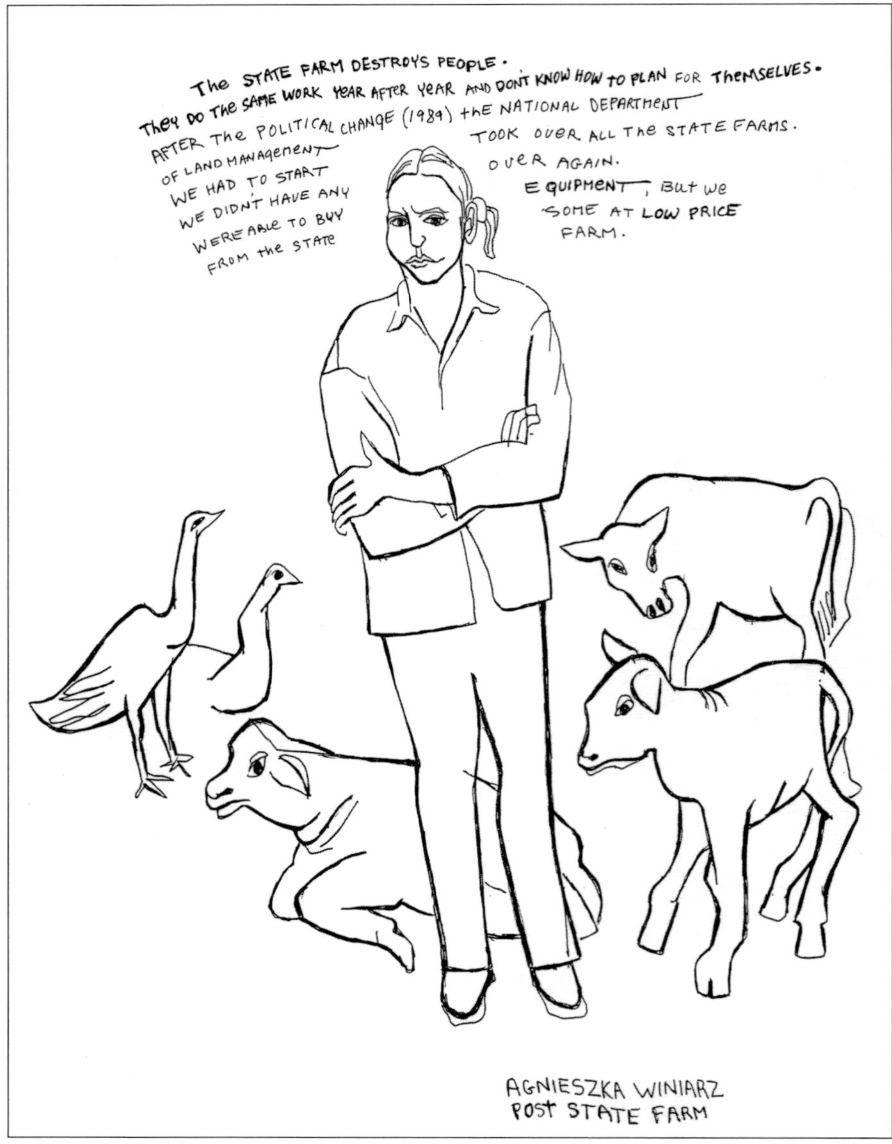

Agnieszka Winiarz, post-State Farm, 2005

Although countries such as Poland and Albania have moved toward a free market economy, they remain some of the poorest nations in Europe.

Since its first parliamentary elections in 1989, the republic of Poland has been recognized as one of the healthier economies of post-Communist countries. However, many challenges remain, particularly in rural Poland: low profitability for farmers as a result of the shift to a free market economy; lack of educational and job opportunities; and insufficient resources and farm equipment to allow small farmers to adequately support their families.[2]

Albania, Europe's only Muslim-dominated country, saw the end of Communist rule after forty years in 1999. That same year, war in neighboring Kosovo brought nearly half a million ethnic Albanian refugees into the country, straining already limited resources of this largely agricultural economy.[3]

Kosovo became a nation after declaring independence from Serbia on February 17, 2008. However, the atrocities of the war that took place a decade earlier left their mark, with many thousands of Kosovo Albanians killed and more than 1.5 million left homeless.[4]

Poor economic policies, international sanctions and limited access to trade and finance also contributed to what remains a severely damaged economy. Like its neighbors, Kosovo has also been identified as one of Europe's poorest countries.[5]

As with many of the Heifer sites, extreme poverty and lack of resource development in Poland, Albania and Kosovo are connected to long periods of economic and political instability. These rural economies consist of hardworking multigenerational families whose older generations remain far more connected to the land than their more Westernized offspring.

[2] HI Poland Study Tour booklet 5/28–6/10, 2005.

[3] National Geographic website: Eastern Europe facts: travel.nationalgeographic.com/places/countries/country_Albania.html: Text source: *National Geographic Atlas of the World*, Eighth Edition, 2004.

[4] www.state.gov/www/global/human_rights/kosovoii/homepage.html.

[5] National Geographic website: Eastern Europe facts: travel.nationalgeographic.com/places/countries/country_Kosovo.html.

Poland

Betty's mother was born in a poor farming village in Poland so the trip to the country of her ancestors was especially meaningful. On this, her second visit to Poland, Betty had an emotional response to time spent in the Warsaw Ghetto, the Lublin concentration camp (Majdanek) and the Warsaw Uprising Museum (dedicated to the Warsaw uprising of 1944 since opening in 2004): "For me, there is a lot of personal history and meaning. You can't be with people in this country without feeling how the history is still very alive and raw."

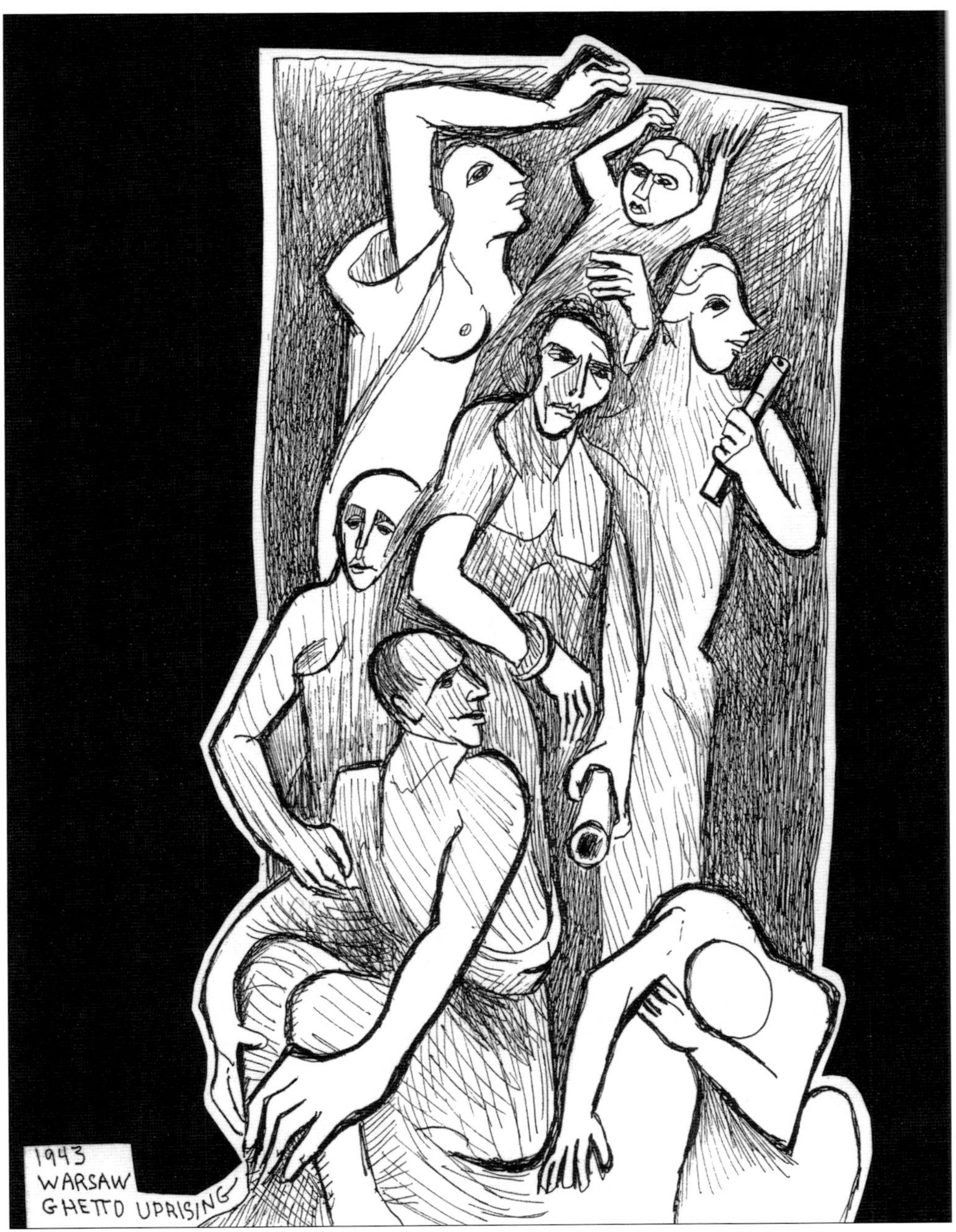

1943 Warsaw Ghetto Uprising, 2005

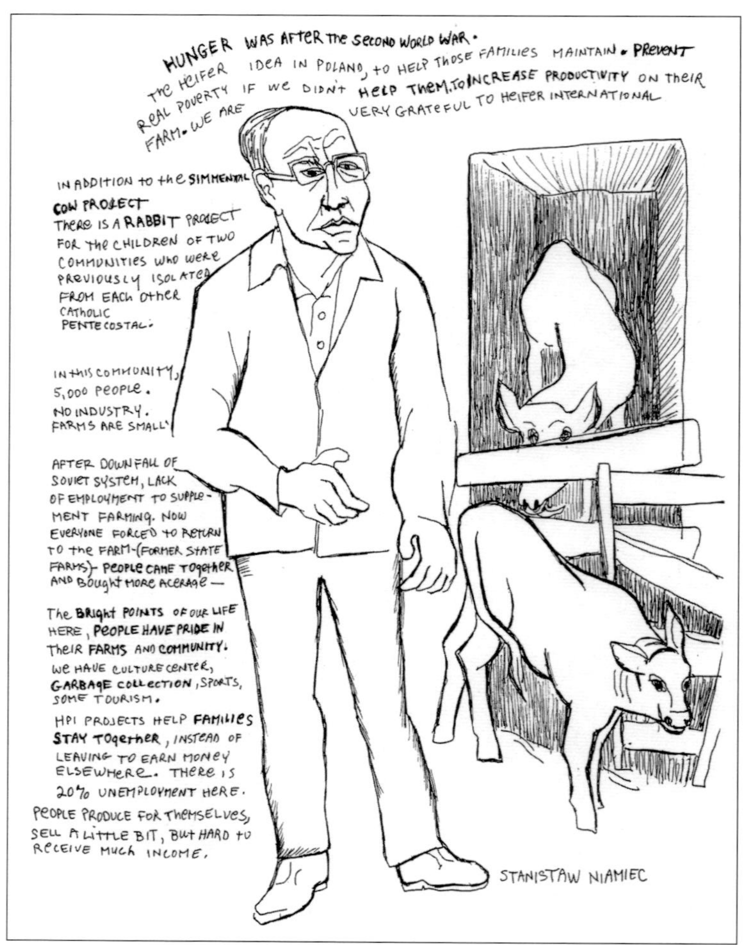

Hunger was after the Second World War,
Stanistaw Niamiec, 2005

Since 1992, Heifer has put energy and resources into helping small-scale farmers in Central and Eastern Europe develop a more integrated approach while encouraging sustainable development and biodiversity in agriculture. Although Heifer has had a presence in Poland since World War II, its first office opened in Warsaw in 1998. In this largely rural country, work is being done to improve the genetic and breeding value of animals such as cows, sheep and horses; increase milk production; develop an organic farming center that supports homeless people; revitalize livestock of families devastated by the great flood of 1997 and other natural disasters; provide an orphanage with sows and goats to improve the children's nutrition; restore sheep farms; develop rabbit and chicken farms; and deepen environmental awareness.[6]

Poland: Barka Project, Organic Farmer, Cherry Tree and Rabbits p. 109

The Barka Project (translated from Polish to mean "ark") was developed in the Poznan Region by Tomasz and Barbara Sadowski in 1989 to help homeless people rebuild their lives. Barka is an NGO that provides shelter, food, education, work and other supports to homeless people battling depression and other mental health and substance abuse problems.

[6] HI Poland brochure, 2005.

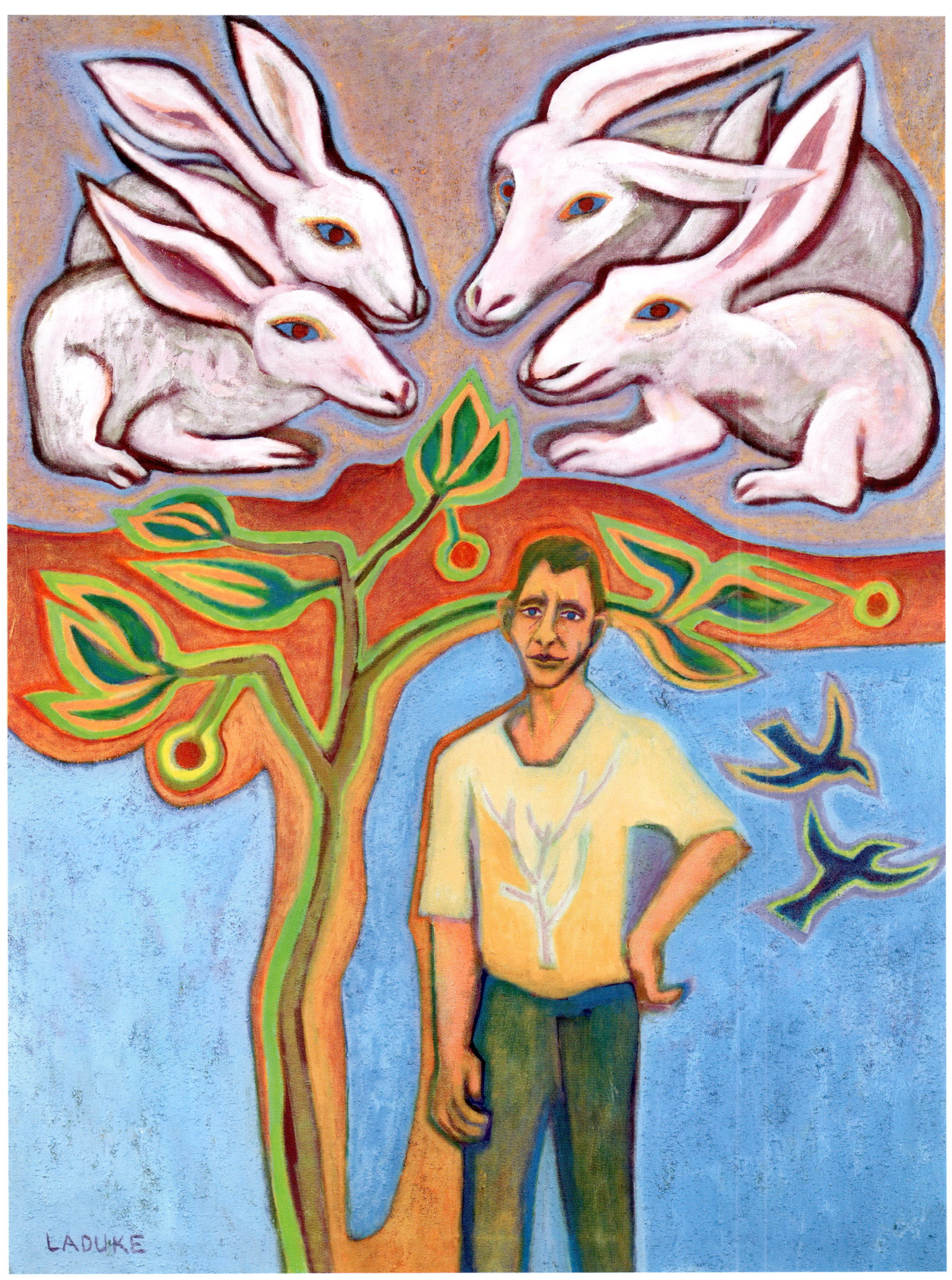

Poland: Barka Project, Organic Farmer, Cherry Tree and Rabbits • 44"x32" • 2005

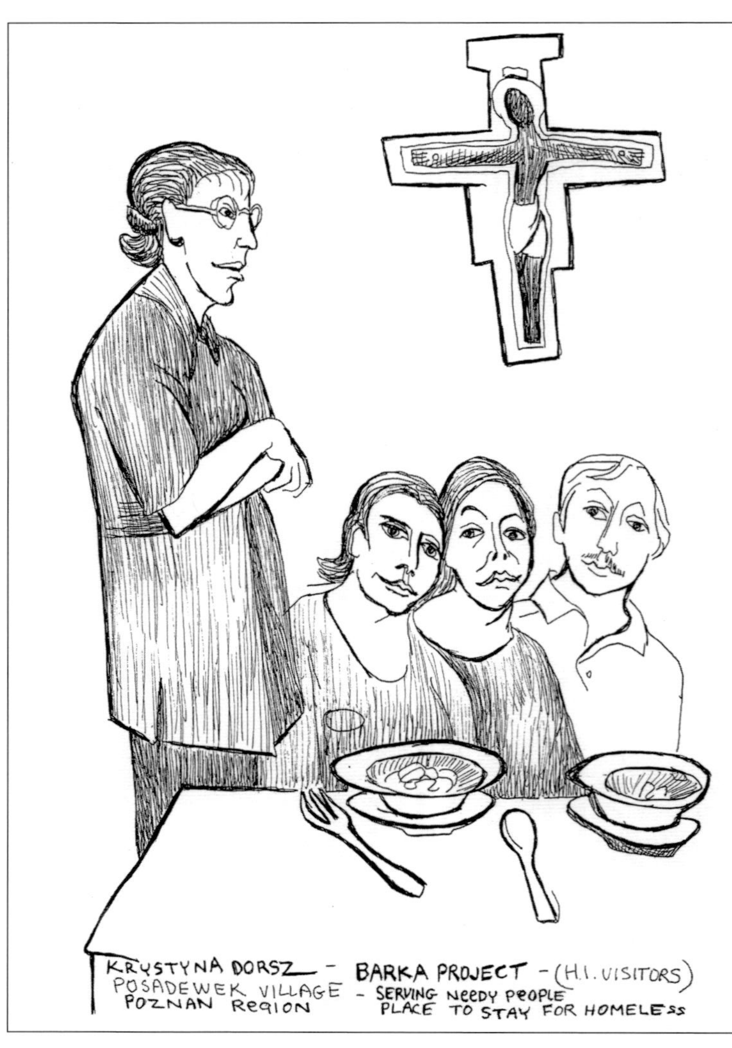

Krystyna Dorsz: Barka Project, Posadewek Village, 2005

Initially, low-cost state farms were purchased and renovated by the program's residents. Each farm has become a cooperative whose members oversee its management and growth. Within this structure, people share decision-making as well as the daily chores of cooking, household and work responsibilities.

Heifer became involved with Barka's Posadowko farm in 1999. Residents adapted farm buildings and secured fodder before receiving pigs and hens. In 2001, a second Heifer-supported project was created in Chudopczyce, where a conventional farm was converted into an organic farm. With an official organic farming certificate, the farm now sells produce at higher prices. Both farms contribute to the food supply of Barka's shelters and generate additional income for the organization.

The farmer in the Barka Project painting had been a down-and-out alcoholic before becoming a member of the community. Now, he participates in a state-of-the-art small-scale organic farm that is a community model as a farm and as a place of healing. He and his cohorts pass on sows to other farmers in the region. The man stands under a cherry tree full of rabbits who watch over him. There is new growth from within him as illustrated by the tree that spreads across his chest. The message of renewed hope is carried by the birds that cavort happily to his left. His name is Andrzei Wiater and his dream is to "build a better community and to help surrounding villages, step by step."[7]

Poland: Brzezowka Village Hen Project p. 111

In April 2004, the Association of Development and Transformation was established to support economic and social development and to protect the natural and cultural heritage of the Less Poland Voivodeship region. Heifer supports these efforts.[8] In the village of Brzezówka (located within a park protected by law to limit agricultural activity), thirty families each received 20 hens. Small-size poultry breeding preserves the environment as it helps farmers generate income from eggs and meat.

The portrait on the following page captures a grandmother who lives with her daughter and grandchildren. In this symbolic painting, she wears traditional decorative clothing that includes a head scarf and a skirt with a Tree of Life pattern. A repetitive pattern of the cross on her shirt conveys the importance of religion in this predominantly Catholic culture. The old woman is surrounded by hens, all of whom carry within them precious eggs that nourish and support the family and provide income for the grandchildren's education.

---

[7] quote from Betty LaDuke.

[8] HI Poland Study Tour booklet 5/28-6/10, 2005.

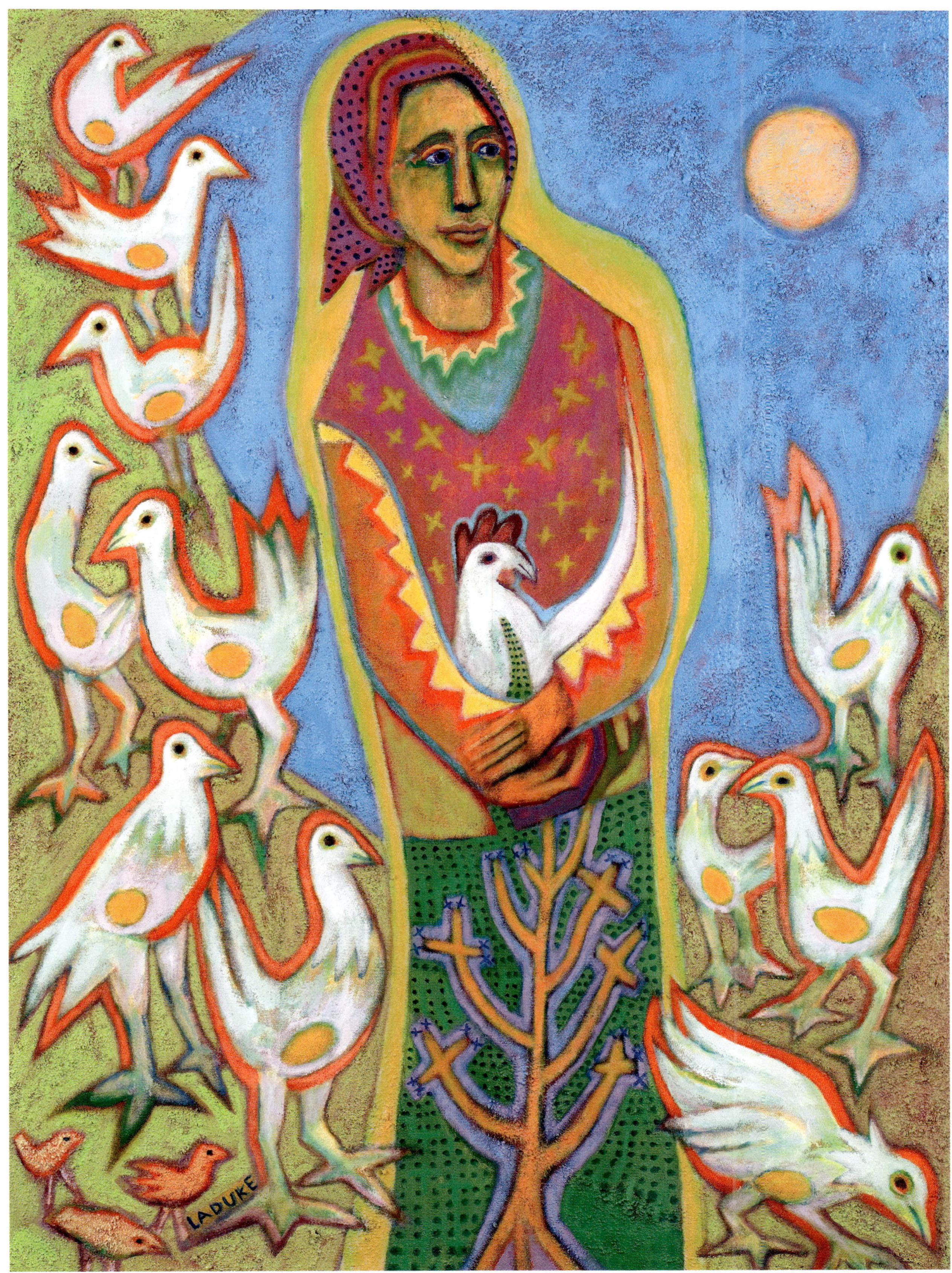

Poland: Brzezowka Village Hen Project • 44"x32" • 2005

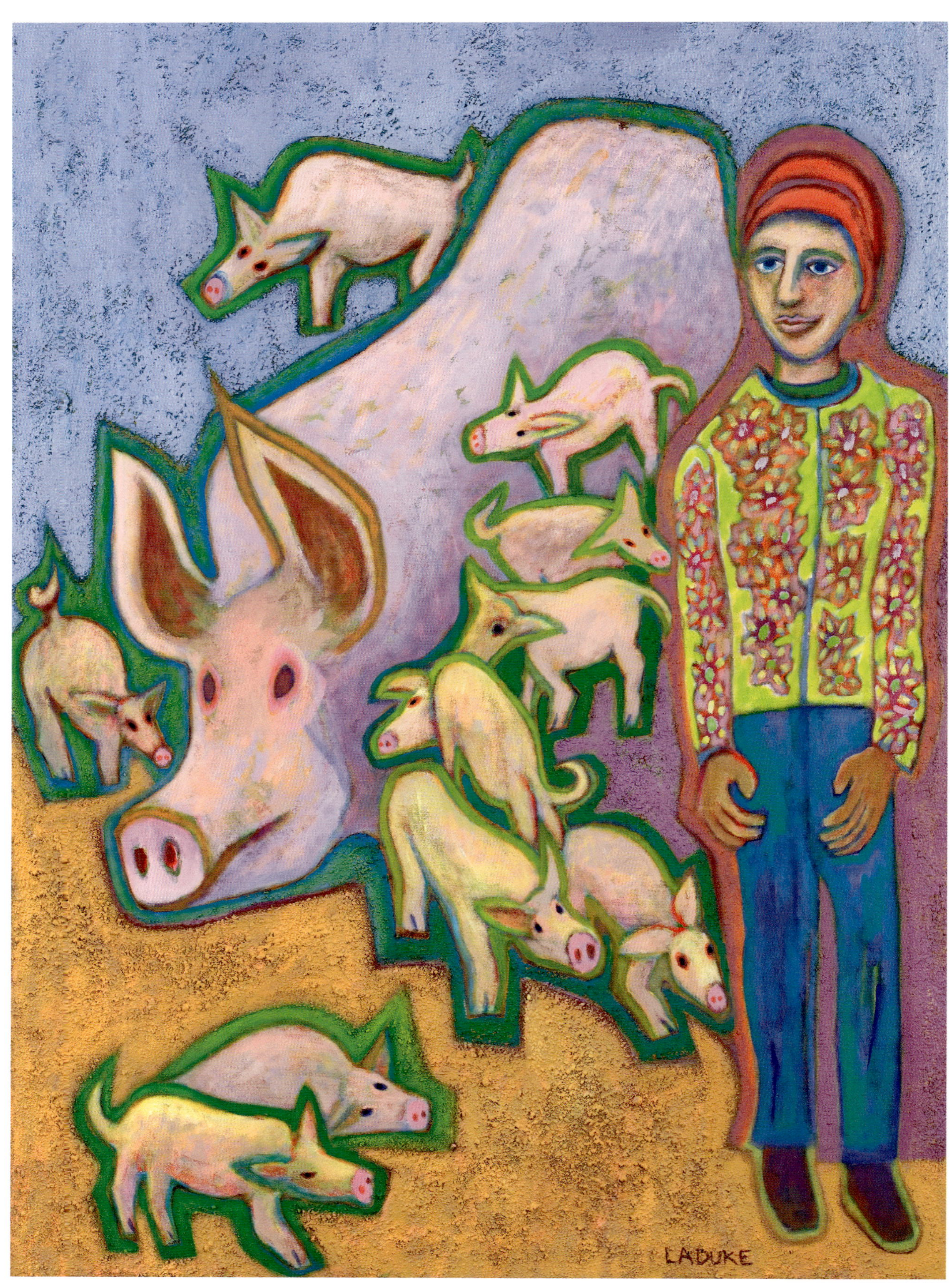

Poland: Wola Galezowska Orphanage Pig Production Project • 44"x32" • 2005

Poland: Wola Galezowska Orphanage Pig Production Project p. 112

Located in a small village in the Lublin area of Eastern Poland, the Wola Galezowska Orphanage was opened in 1946. The orphanage maintains a residence for almost fifty children from ages three to eighteen years and a small farm. The farm provides a loving environment for orphans and even children of parents who struggle with alcoholism and other disabilities. The children are busy with school work and responsibilities on the farm.

The farm had been involved in pig production until financial troubles shut down the operation. The purchase of two goats and two rabbits by two hardworking boys at the orphanage served as a catalyst for a small group of children who were interested in raising animals. In 2001, they asked Heifer to help them reestablish the farm's animal production capacity and so it began again. Heifer has since provided sows, goats, rabbits, cows and education to the children. These young people benefit from what they learn about responsibility, caring for others and productivity as well as from enhanced nutrition. The children pass on two piglets to orphanage graduates for every sow that they receive from Heifer.[9]

It is typical for a sow to have ten piglets, which Betty has captured in this painting. A girl with a wool cap and a colorful jacket watches the mother sow and her babies enjoy the green gardens that surround them. The animals and the children flourish from the loving care that they receive on the farm.

[9] HI Poland Study Tour booklet 5/28-6/10, 2005.

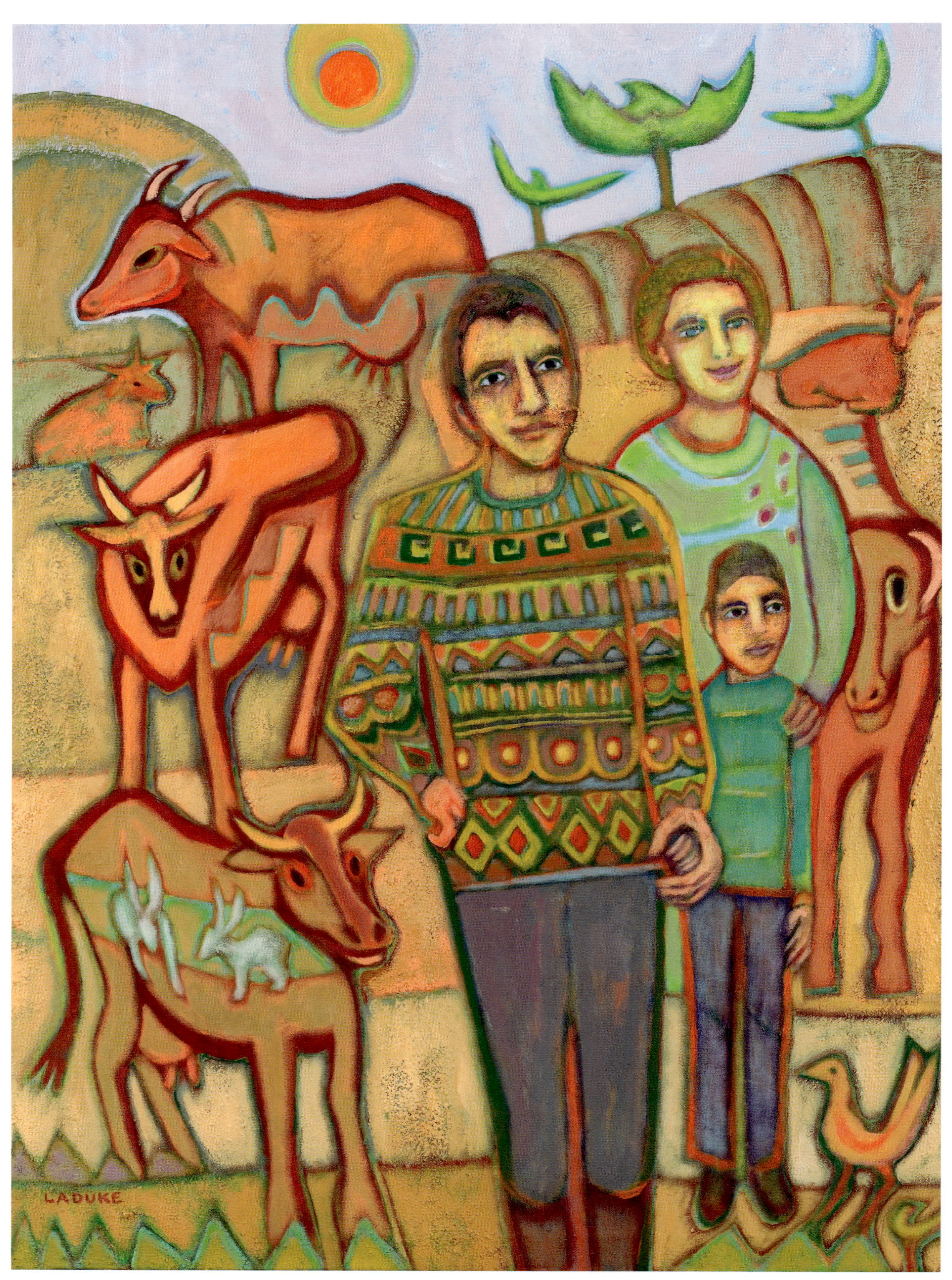

Poland: Red Cow Family • 44"x32" • 2005

Poland: Red Cow Family p. 114

Heifer has four projects that work to revitalize the Polish Red cow. According to Dr. Terry Wollen (Heifer's Director of Animal Well-Being and Staff Veterinarian), Red cows are "Poland's last breed and are in danger of extinction." These hardy, fertile cows are ideal for local farmers because they live long lives and have relatively high milk production. They survive comfortably on mountainous terrain with low fodder requirements and maintenance costs.[10]

Betty visited a Red cow project supported by Heifer in Mochnaczkaa (Southeastern Poland), close to the Slovak border. The harsh climate of this hilly region exacerbates already difficult conditions for farmers who continue to struggle with the impact of market reform. Unemployment in the region is among the highest in Poland. Since 2003, when a group of farmers asked Heifer to help replace mixed-race cattle with Polish Red cattle, Heifer has provided Red cows and education about integrated farming to the community. In turn, the farmers have created an emergency fund with money collected from those receiving Heifer cows in order to help people whose animals die. They understand that helping their neighbors helps the community as a whole to survive.

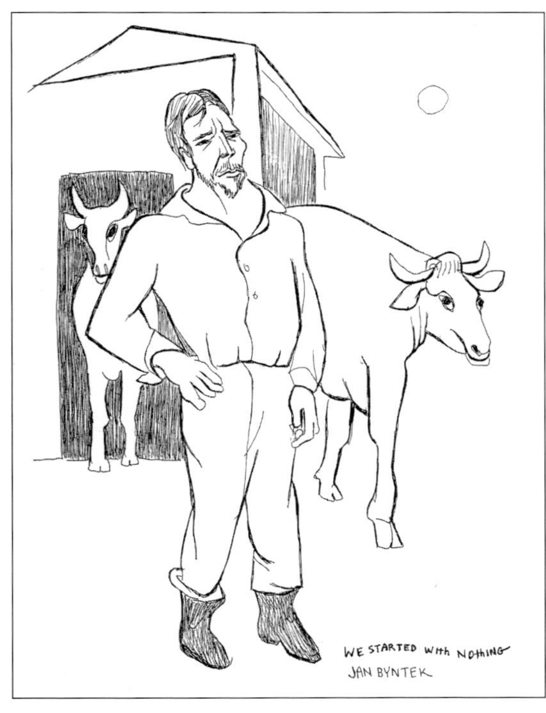

We started with nothing, Jan Byntek, 2005

The Red Cow Project is instrumental in keeping families together because fewer leave to seek work far from home. The painting portrays a smiling mother with her son and husband. A herd of Red cows basks in the sun. Birdlike trees in the background spread their wings and sing to the sun. Rabbits growing inside of a cow in the forefront represent the essence of integrated farming. The animals eat off the land and, in turn, produce manure that enriches the soil. The idea is to use every possible resource to develop a sustainable way of living while reducing waste and minimizing costs.

[10] "Sometimes, Alpacas Do It Better: The Difference Indigenous Livestock Can Make;" World Ark, March/April 2005, p.26.

Poland: Tree of Life p. 117

The past and the present are captured in this large and complex painting, which highlights the Madonna at the center of a Tree of Life. Worship of the Madonna is central to Polish culture, which is deeply influenced by the Catholic religion. Betty's Madonna has two faces: that which holds the sadness of Poland's history faces us directly. The other face, which conveys the present, signifies a more hopeful future. The Madonna embodies Mother Earth and the mother of all people, no matter what race or religion. She embraces cultural diversity and acceptance as she carries a message of peace. The green olive branch in her hand lying within a female form extends the reach of her love. The baby that she holds is fashioned after the Christ child, whose essence is associated with nurturing that all children need in order to thrive.

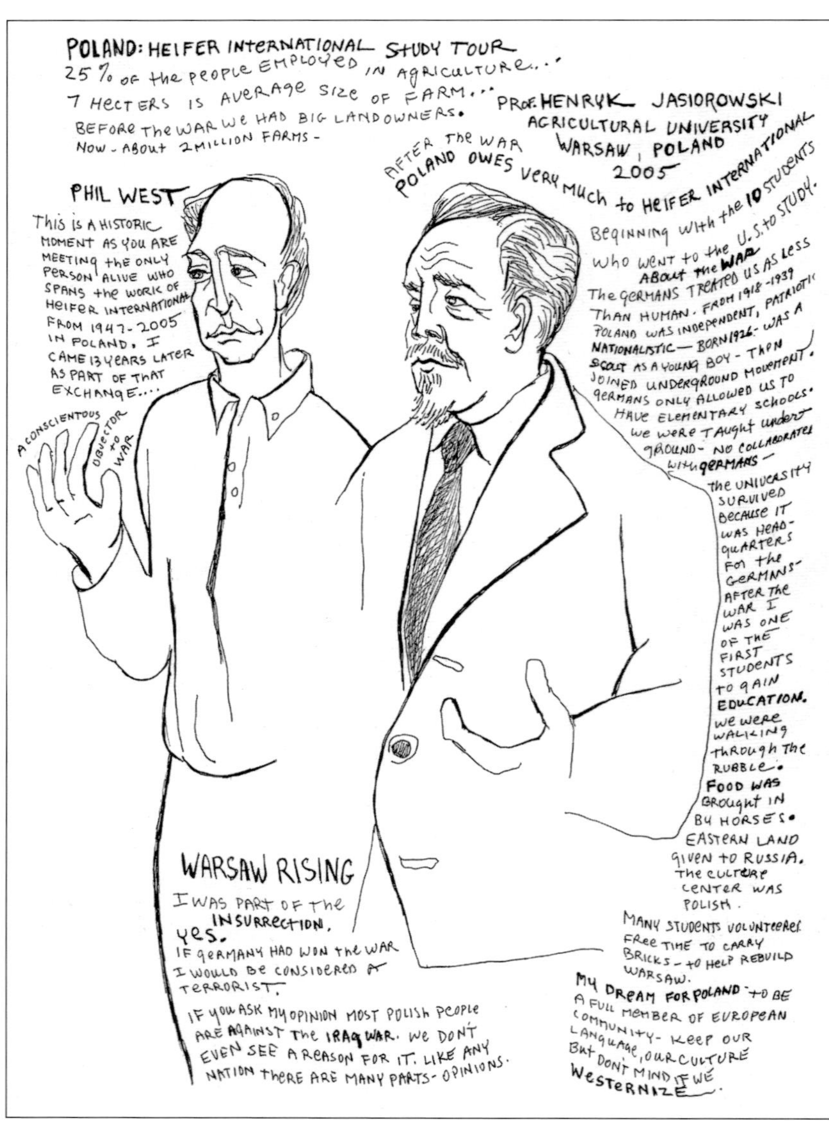

Phil West and Professor Henryk Jasiorowski portrayed, with accompanying text, 2005

The bottom of the painting depicts the horrifying and tragic history of Poland during World War II. A concentration camp has been recreated. Jews are symbolically portrayed as birds with Star-of-David badges (that they were forced to wear in German-occupied territories during the war). Imprisoned behind blood red and purple jail bars, they desperately want out, especially as the red crosses at their feet signify death. The green figures near them are flattened, crushed and surrounded by blood.

Above, tree branches carrying pleasant memories of Betty's experiences in rural Poland provide relief. Animals she encountered are omnipresent: the piglets in the Madonna's dress signify fertility; the sheep and cows remind her of various Heifer project visits; and the blue rabbits that face each other hark back to a project that helped villagers from neighboring Catholic and Pentecostal villages break through a longstanding animosity when their children learned to raise rabbits together. Betty notes that "Heifer bridges gaps between people who have historical animosity."

The people of Poland are very family-oriented. In the top left-hand corner, a family of six is portrayed within Poland's national symbol, the double eagle. On the bird's head is the ever-present Catholic cross. Below them, people are harvesting and weeding in the fields; the work

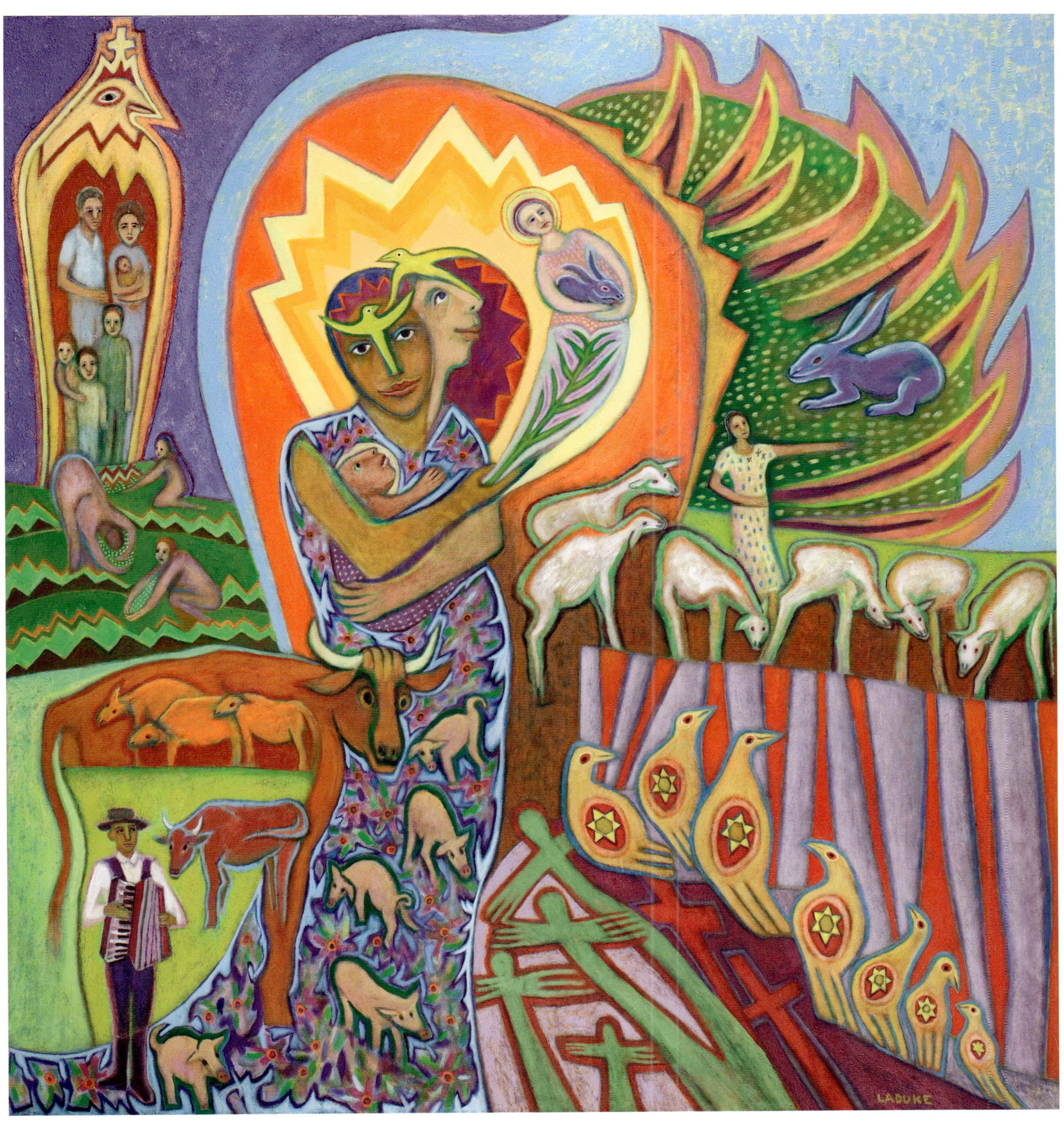

Poland: Tree of Life • 72"x68" • 2005

is sometimes backbreaking but necessary. In the lower left-hand corner, a man plays his accordion—a sweet reminder of how important it is for Polish people to maintain their cultural traditions, folk music and Polkas.

The future is also represented by new seeds embedded in green in the upper right-hand corner. Flames of the past become more flower-like as the past and present are reconciled.

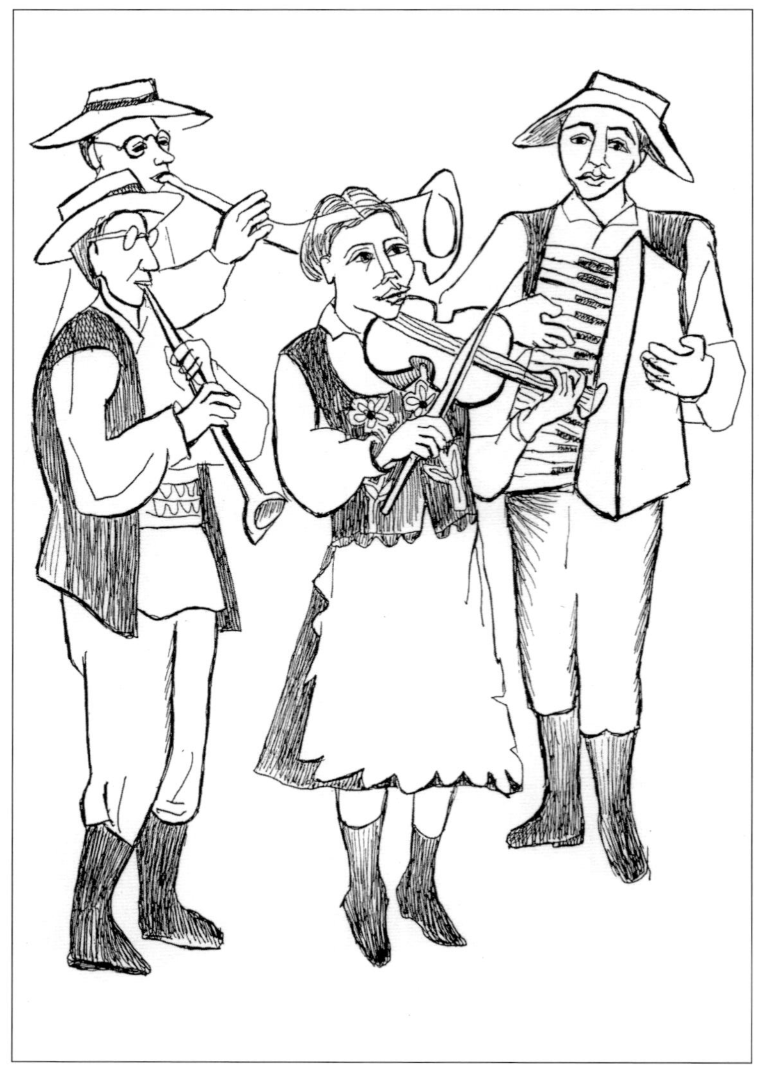

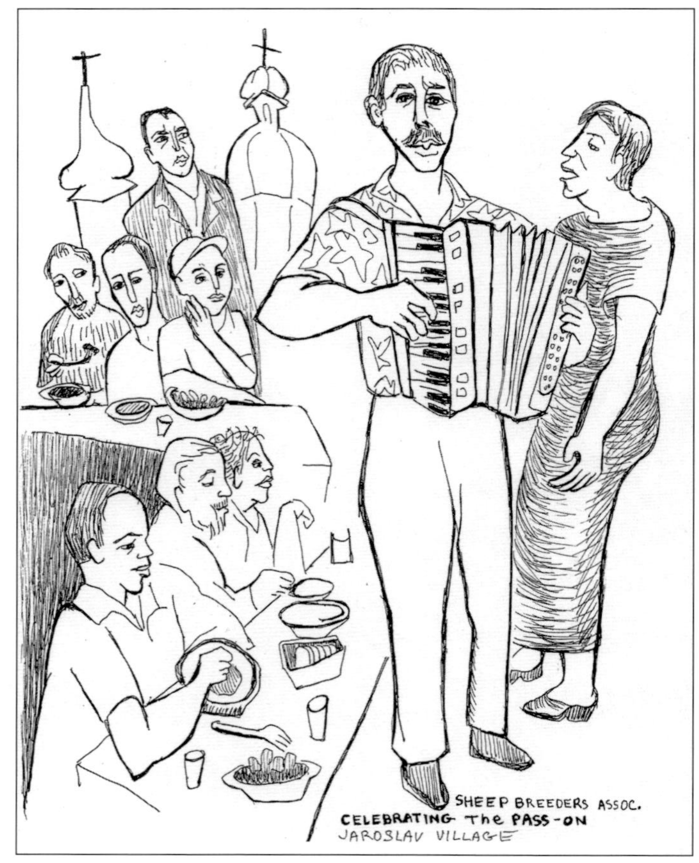

Left: Playing accordion, violin and wind instruments; Right: Jaroslav Village, Sheep Breeders Association Celebrating the Pass-On, 2005

Albania and Kosovo

During the Heifer Study Tour to Albania, Betty spent the night at a small farm with a family in the village of Dukat in the Orikum District. She was especially drawn to the grandmother, who reminded her of Bertolt Brecht's *Mother Courage*. As Betty sketched her, the old woman's jealous husband repeatedly asked, "When will you draw me?" "I will draw you at 7:00 a.m. tomorrow morning," she replied. At 6:45 a.m., grandfather unceremoniously walked into Betty's bedroom. She shooed him out and soon followed with her sketchbook:

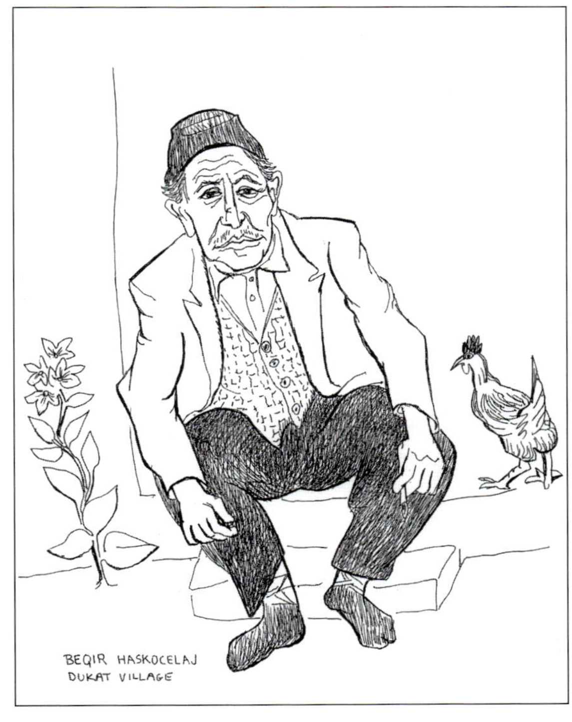

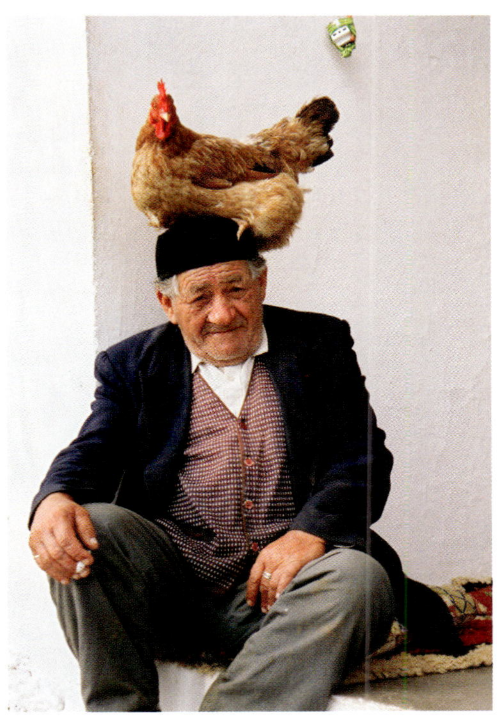

"The grandfather sat down, took off his shoes, and smoked a cigarette while I sketched. The chicken just stayed on grandfather's head. When they finally took the chicken off his head, it wandered into my bedroom where it proceeded to lay an egg on my bed! That's my story."

—Betty LaDuke

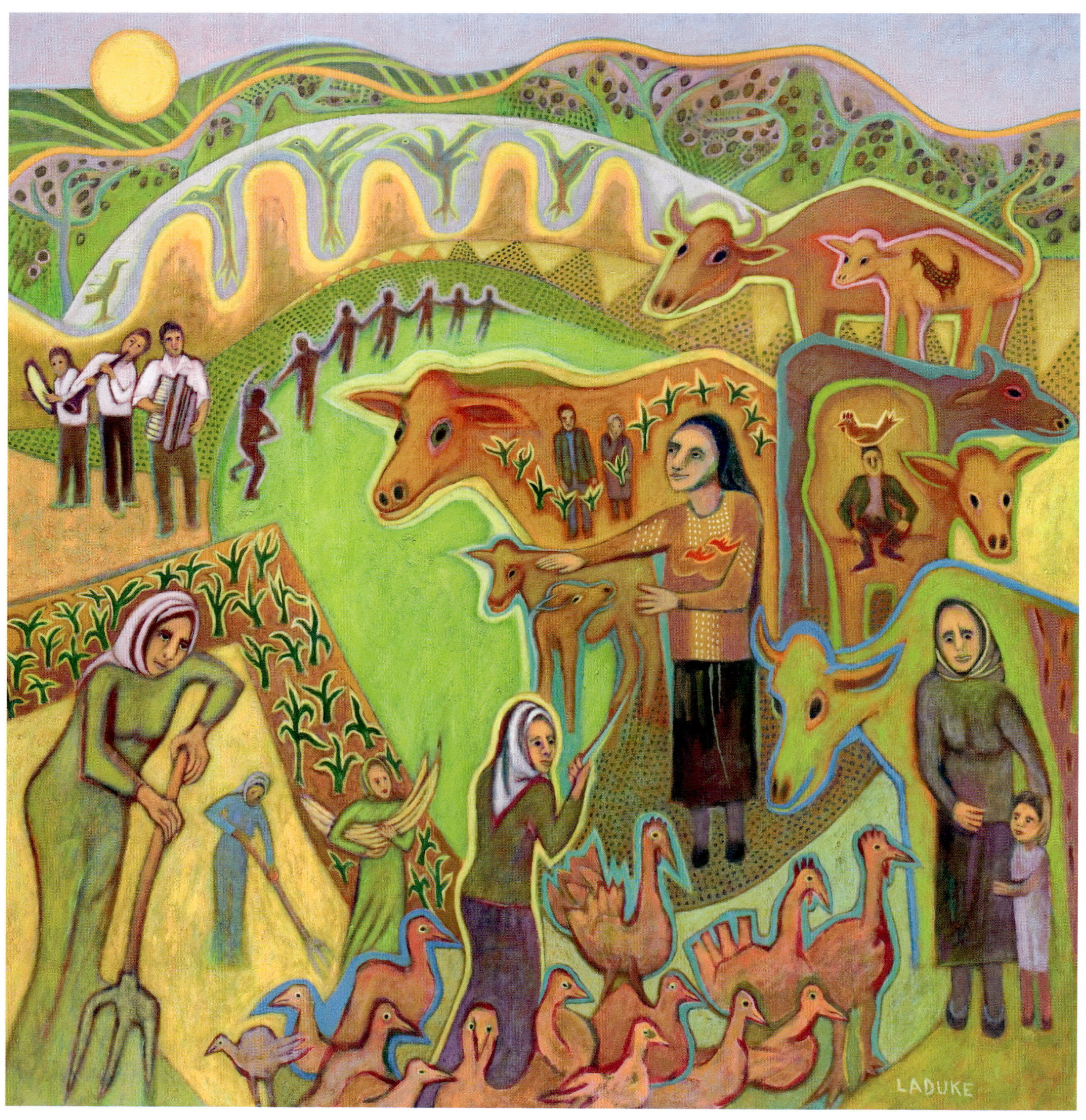

Albania: We may be Poor but our Culture is Rich • 72"x68" • 2006

Albania: We may be Poor but our Culture is Rich p. 120

Betty's Albanian experience is encapsulated within this multifaceted painting. What villagers at the Belshi Community Center shared has left a deep impression: "We may be poor but our culture is great and our hearts are open to everyone! No one from our state institutions has ever come to visit us. We thank you for coming from so far away to be with us. We thank you for the cows, the training and the hope that we now have for the future." Villagers thanked their Heifer visitors by providing a memorable lunch and afternoon of singing and dancing.

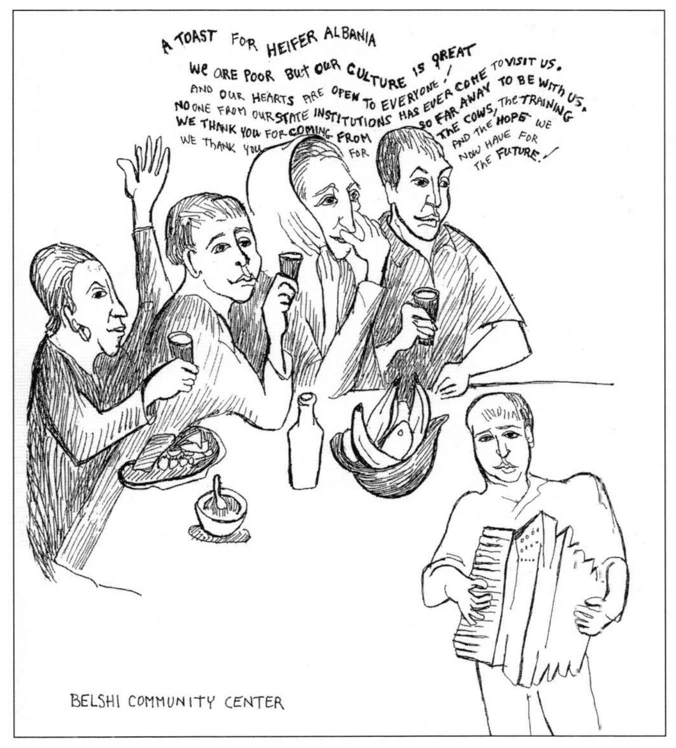

Belshi Community Center, 2006

So much is happening in this painting. Within a cow sits grandfather with the chicken on his head. Not far away, the ageless grandmother pets her cows. She gently reaches out to pet the animals; she is so appreciative of their ability to provide her family with milk, butter and cheese. In the foreground, the young woman holding a stick herds turkeys toward recently harvested fields to feed on leftover grain. To the left, women harvest hay with pitchforks that eventually form huge haystacks like the five yellow mounds in the background. These mounds are interspersed with birds that have tree-like characteristics. Above them, vineyards filled with grapes dot the horizon.

The sun bears down on all the activity of an industrious farm community at work and at play. A mother hugs her child and another carries a bundle of hay to feed the animals. Local musicians play the accordion, flute and tambourine as people celebrate a Heifer visit and dance in the green field. Roosters, families and new growth rise up from within the cows. Gardens and trees complete the landscape.

Betty explains, "I like the diversity of small farms—people churn their own butter and have their own root cellars. They work very hard to preserve everything they can during the summer months to carry them through the winter."

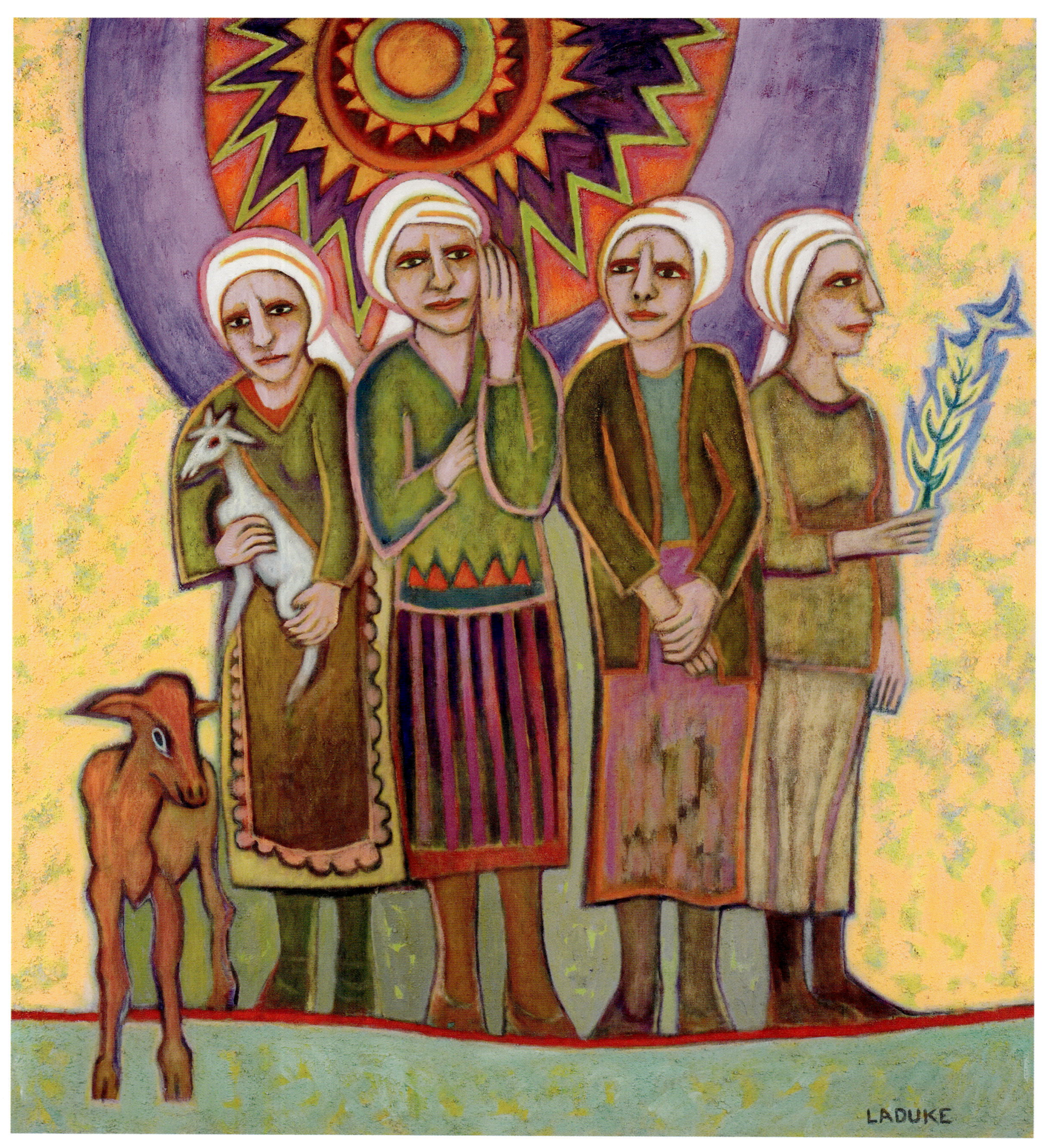

Kosovo: War Widows Project • 52"x44" • 2006

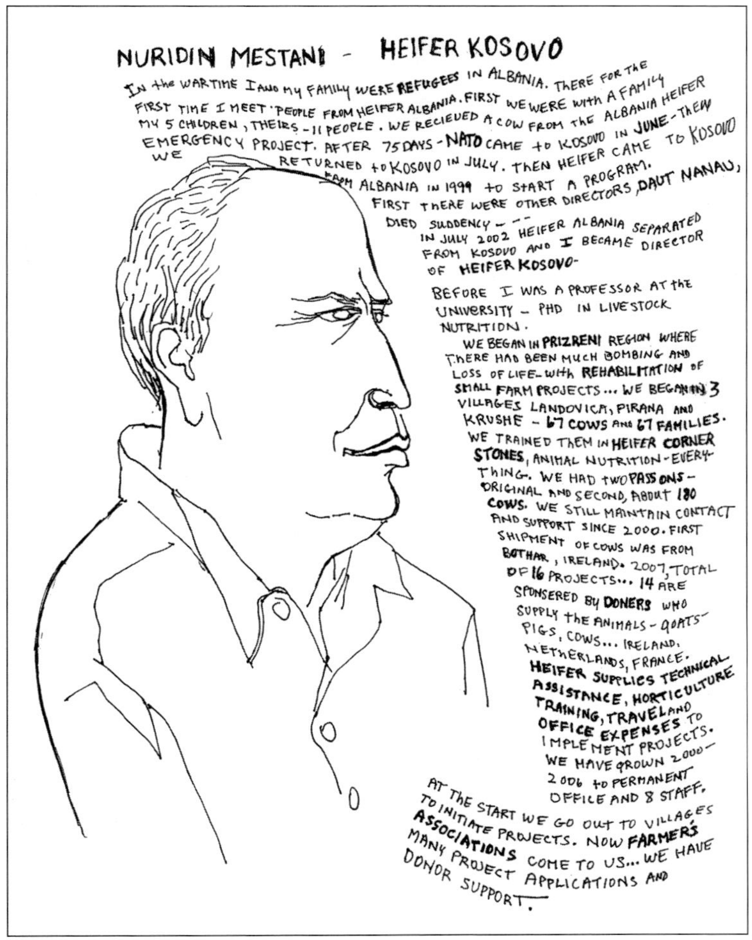

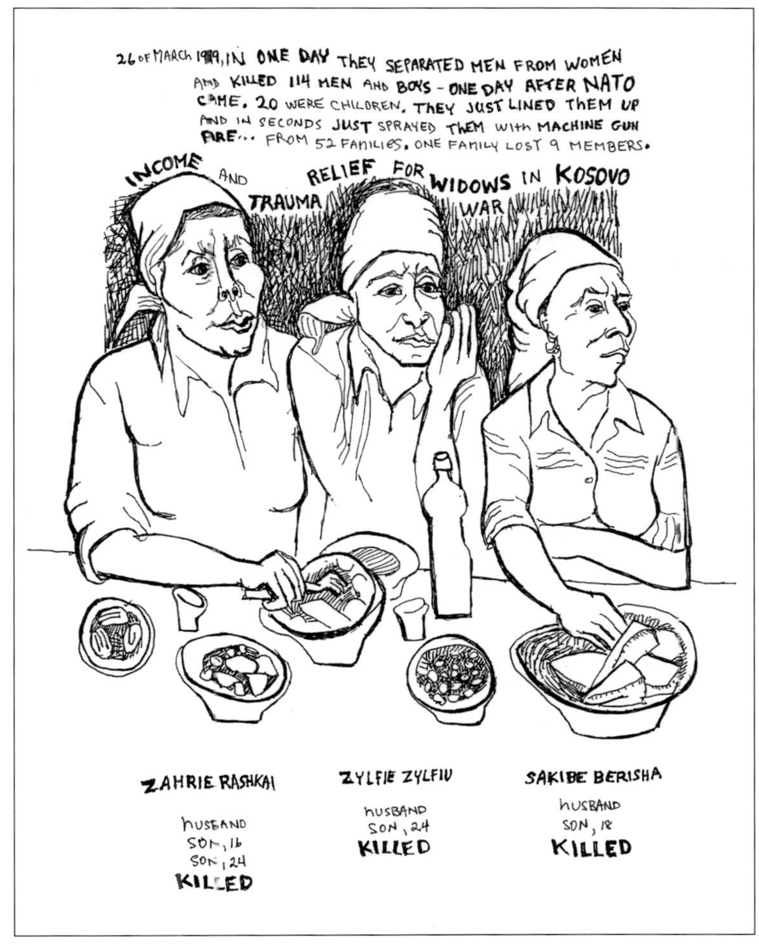

Left: Nuridin Mestani, 2006; Right: 26 of March, 2006

Kosovo

Betty's sketch entitled "Nuridin Mestani—Heifer Kosovo" conveys much about the hardship faced by the people of Kosovo during and following the 1998-1999 war. It also describes Heifer's part in helping the country to heal, one animal and family at a time.

Kosovo: War Widows Project p. 122

Betty's sketch and story about war widows serves as the backdrop to this painting. In the village of Krusha e Vogël in the Prizreni region, all Heifer beneficiaries lost their husbands (and in many cases, other family members) and most of their livestock during the 1998–1999 war. In 2004, Heifer Kosovo partnered with the Dutch Foundation De Brug International and Dorcas International to develop a program that would alleviate the extreme poverty and distress of these war victims. War trauma relief trainings were offered to widows and their children. Initially, thirty families were slated to receive a pregnant heifer. Beforehand, stables were rebuilt and widows were given technical assistance, supplies, milking equipment and medicine. As the women began to work cooperatively (e.g., a milk collection site was established and a bee project was developed), they became less isolated. In 2002, the Krusha e Vogël Farmer's Association was established.[11]

In the painting, four women dressed in traditional clothing and head scarves convey the sadness in their lives. And yet, their shoulders touch and they derive strength from each other as they work together to optimize their gifts from Heifer and its partners.

Kosovo: The Cow's Name is Nora p. 125

Nora, the cow, is the family's only source of income. Pregnant when she was given to the family, Nora gave birth to twins. One calf was very weak and its owner was told that she would die. The woman told Betty, "But I had already lost too much, so I fed her with bottle milk and covered her with a blanket. She survived and did well, and now I have passed her on. I still have Nora."

[11] Heifer Kosova brochure entitled "Income and Trauma Relief for War Widows in Kosova."

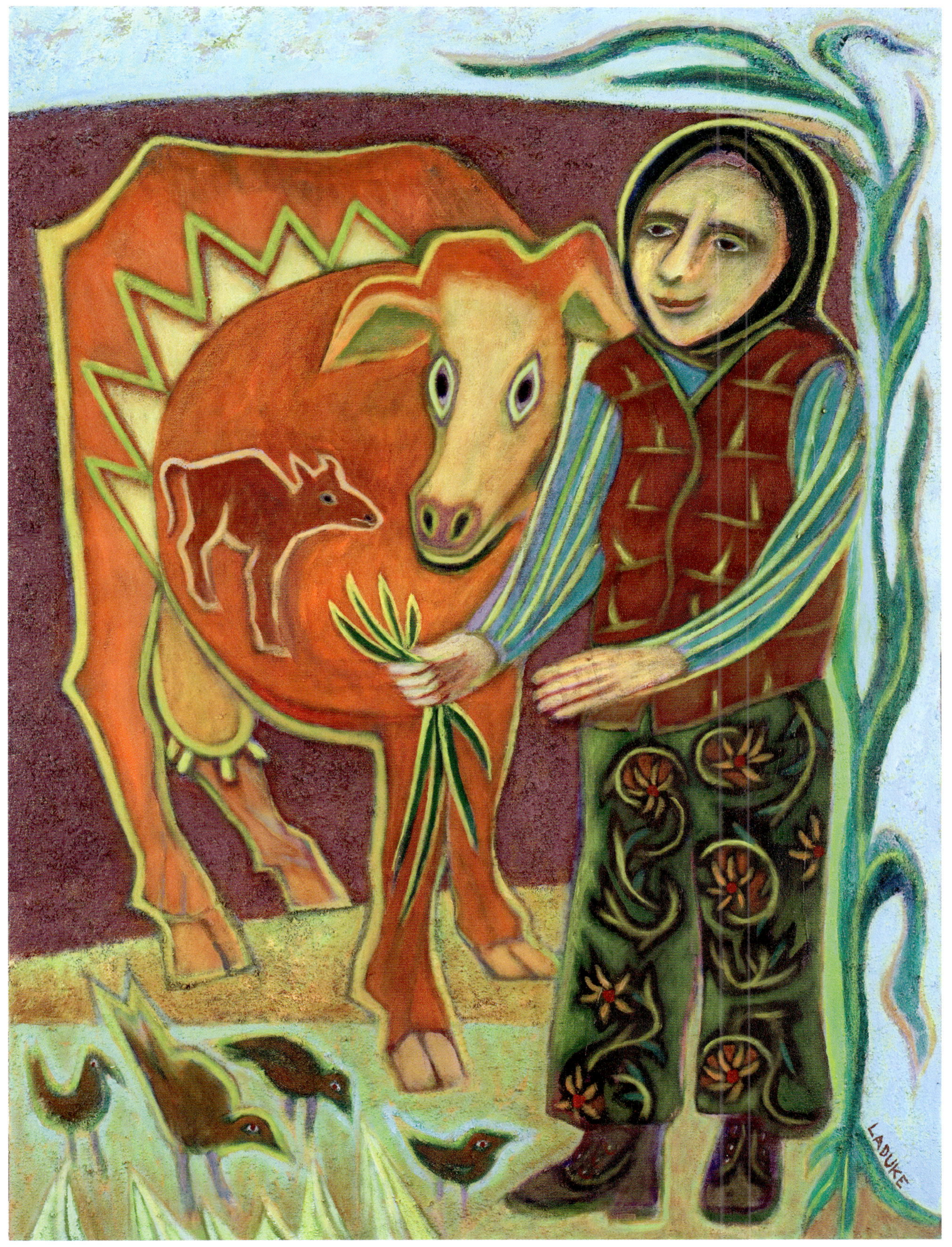

Kosovo: The Cow's Name is Nora • 44"x32" • 2006

Kosovo: Romani Goat Project p. 127

This painting is modeled after the family of Sadbere and Muharrem Tepeku and their granddaughter in the village of Gadime.

The family represents the often persecuted Romani culture, whose people are referred to as "gypsies" or Roma people. The community is composed of large families with little to no income who lack education and resources.

The Romani people have suffered at the hands of Serbs as well as ethnic Albanians. Paul Polansky, an American author specializing in books about the Romani people of Eastern Europe, stated that only 30,000 of the 150,000 who lived in Kosovo before the war remain in their homes. In 1999, he estimated that 14,000 gypsy homes had been burned down as part of a "systematic" cleansing of the community.[12]

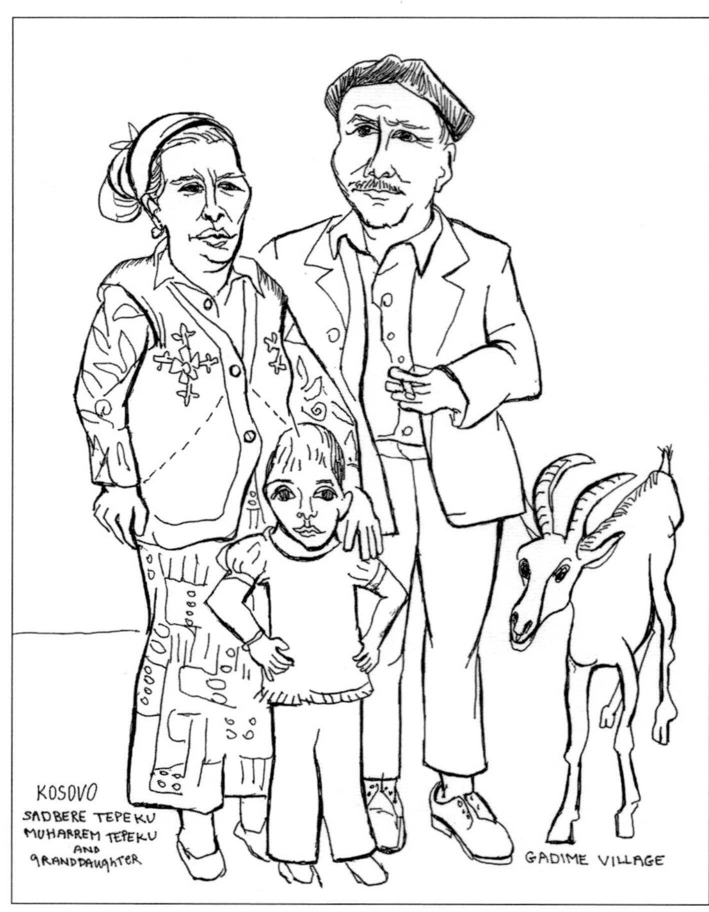

Kosovo: Sadbere Tepeku, Muharrem Tepeku and Granddaughter, 2006

Heifer's *Engagement of Roma People in Animal Breeding Project* began by providing goats to twenty-five Roma families. Trainings in goat breeding, milk hygiene, reproduction problems and other topics taught families not only practical lessons but also about the value of education. An increasing number of families participate and all are encouraged to send their children to school and to grow gardens.

The painting conveys the artist's warmth toward the many grandparents she encountered in Eastern Europe who, in contrast to more Westernized younger generations, carry on centuries-old cultural and lifestyle traditions. They have worked hard to support their families and they have endured very hard times. Their colorful clothes speak to their resilience; the materials blend in with and simultaneously complement the lush mountainous terrain that surrounds them. The community's goats have multiplied—many throughout the painting eat, cavort and rest. Grandfather proudly holds high a branch that carries a LaDuke signature—a bird of hope.

[12] Polansky, Paul; www.ess.uwe.ac.uk/kosovo/Kosovo; The Globe and Mail, Thursday, March 23, 2000.

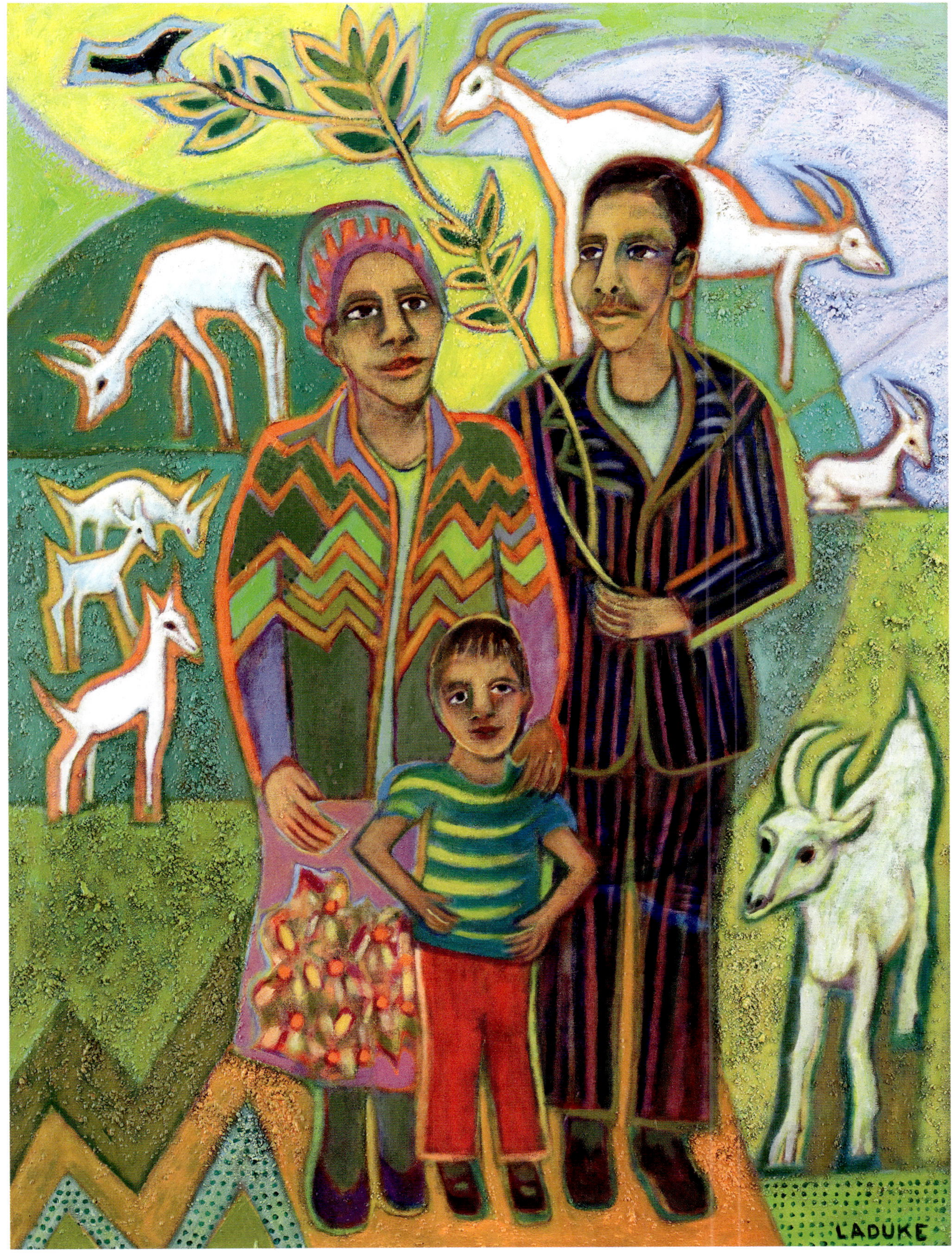

Kosovo: Romani Goat Project • 44"x32" • 2006

Eastern Europe: Hen Project p. 129

The images of this mural panel closely resemble those of the painting *Poland: Brzezowka Village Hen Project* although Betty has transformed the crosses on the skirt's Tree of Life pattern into birds with outspread wings. Where sadness was so powerfully portrayed in the painting, the face of this woman is lighter and more hopeful.

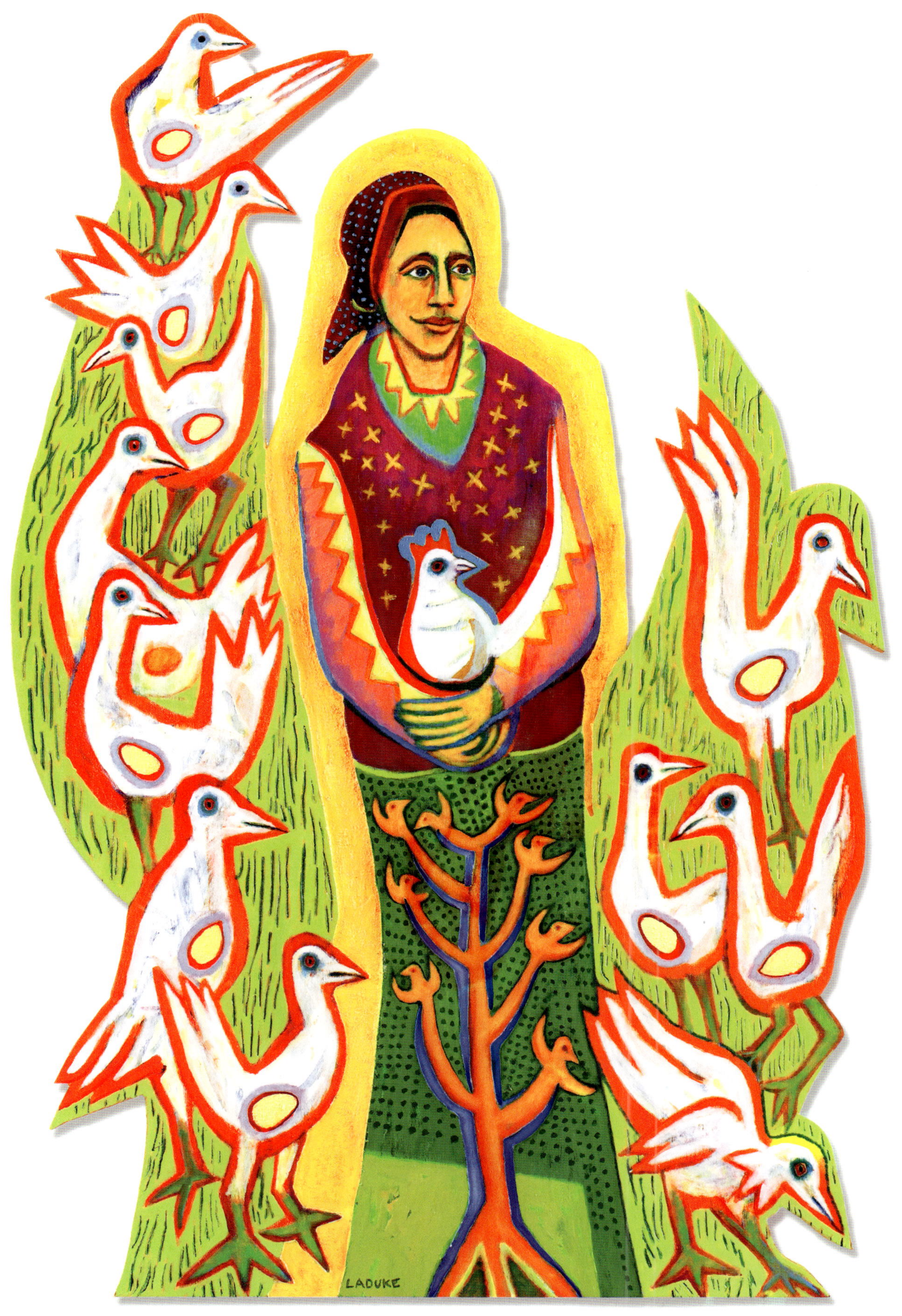

Eastern Europe: Hen Project • 64"x48" • 2007

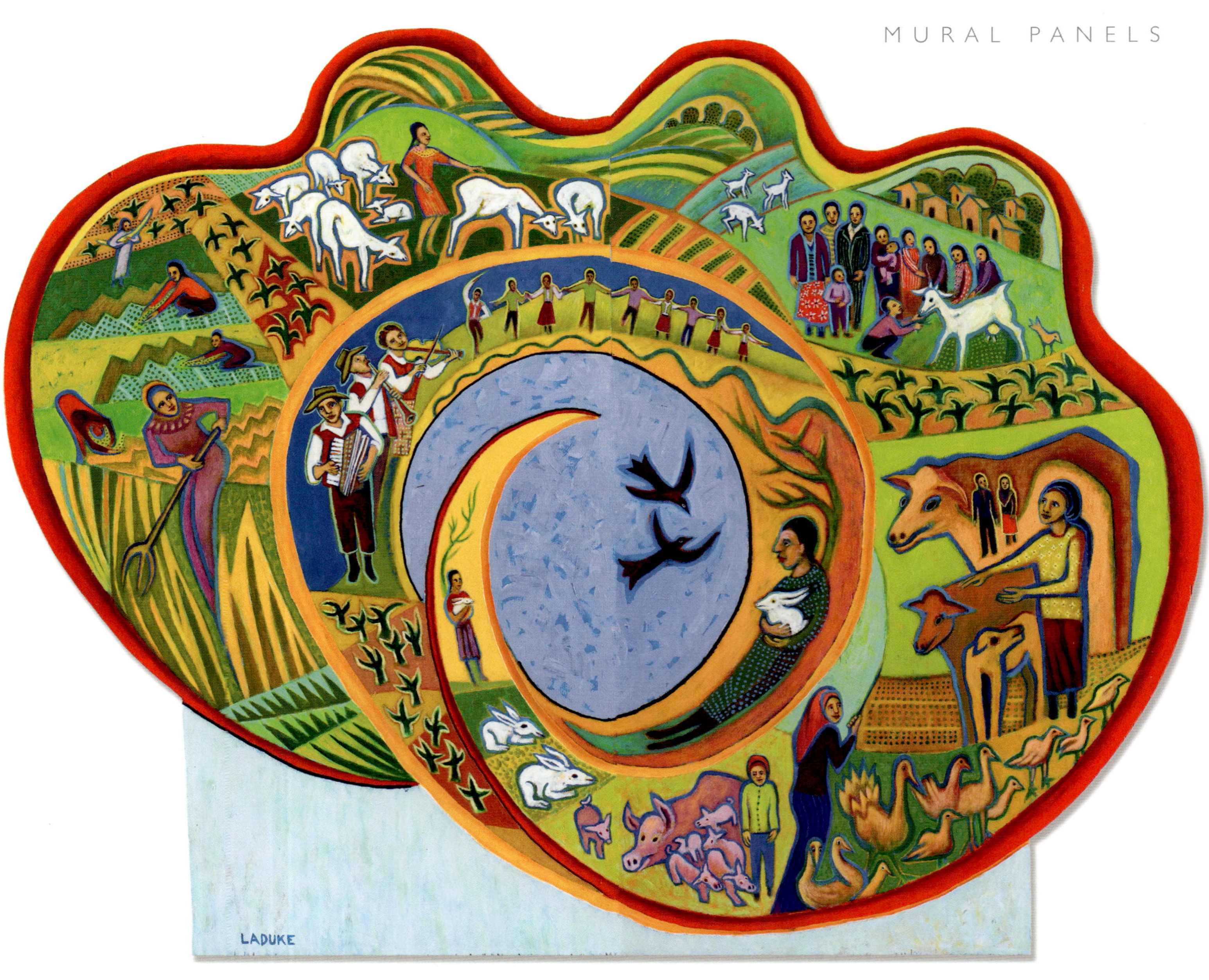

Eastern Europe: We may be Poor but our Culture is Rich • 96"x72" • 2007

Eastern Europe: We may be Poor but our Culture is Rich

The undulating border of this painting and the waves of activity portray a thriving community in which dance, music, animal care, farming and sense of community all play important parts. Derived from the painting *Albania: We may be Poor but our Culture is Rich*, this magnificent piece tells many stories.

Eastern Europe: The Cow's Name is Nora p. 131

The touching story of Nora the cow, whose owner—who had lost so much in her life—nursed its sick calf back to health, has been told in the painting *Kosovo: The Cow's Name is Nora*. In this mural panel, the design on the woman's shirt has evolved into a Tree of Life. The chickens are more substantive and the cow now carries signs of new growth in the form of seedlings. Most important, the green tinge of the woman's face in the painting has been replaced with a healthier glow.

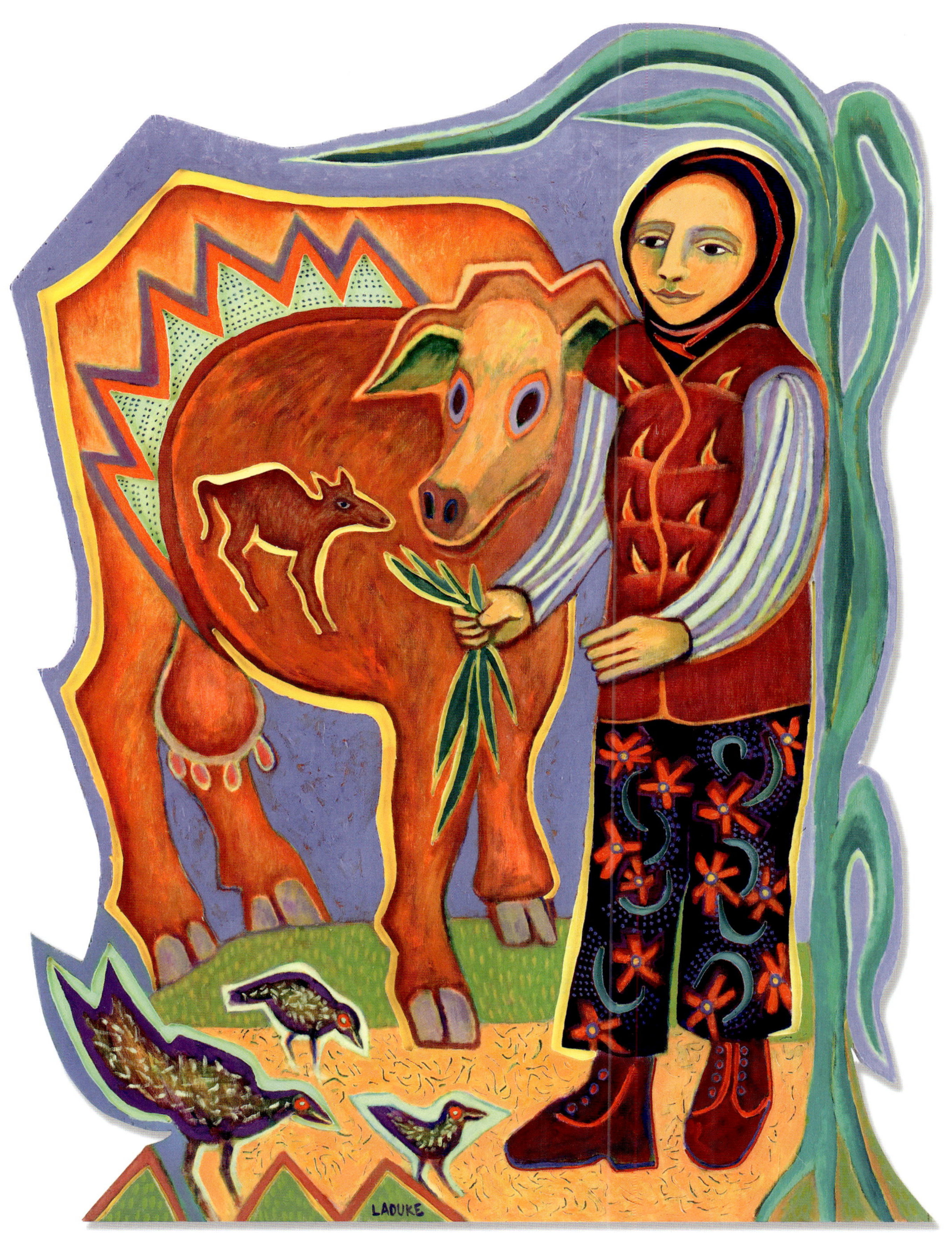

Eastern Europe: The Cow's Name is Nora • 62"x48" • 2007

THE AMERICAS

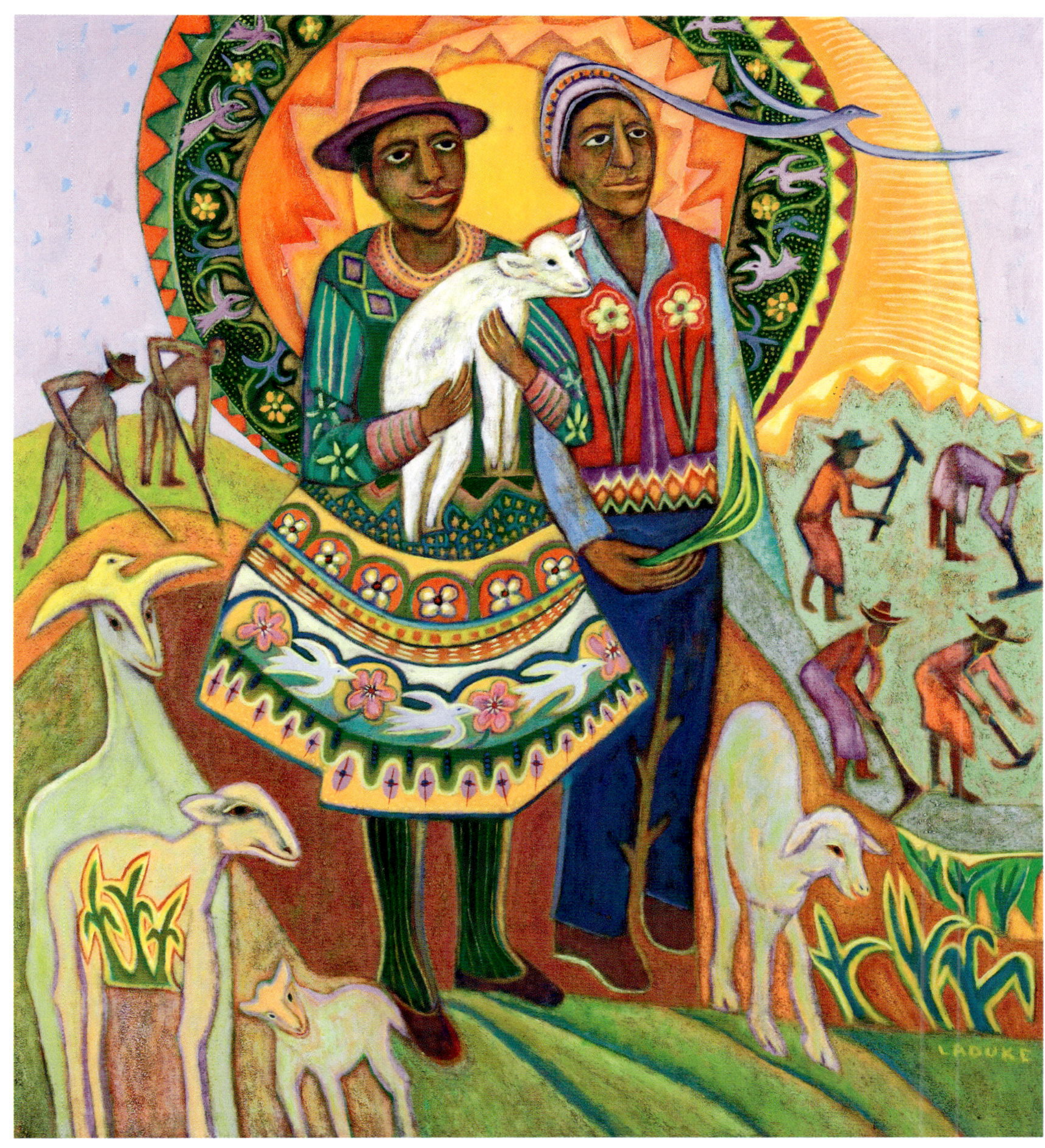

ECUADOR

PERU

USA

The Americas Murals

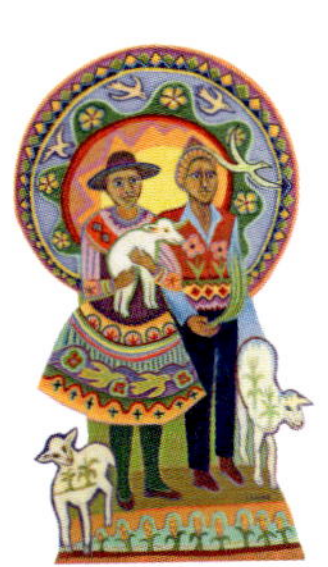
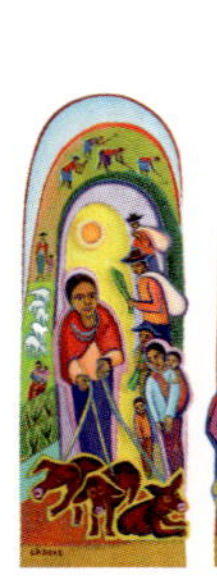
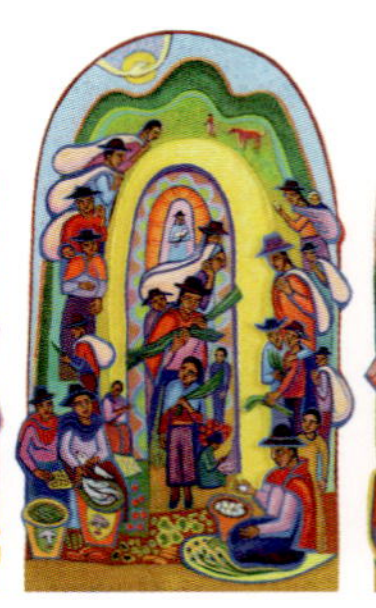
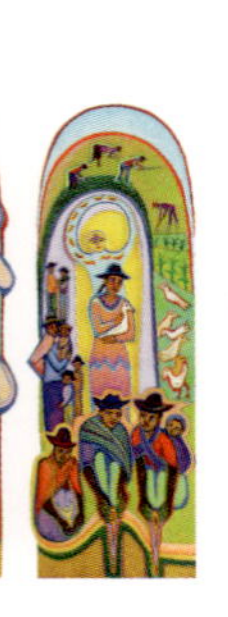
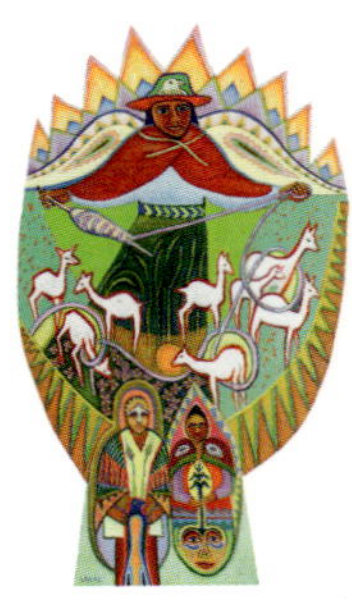
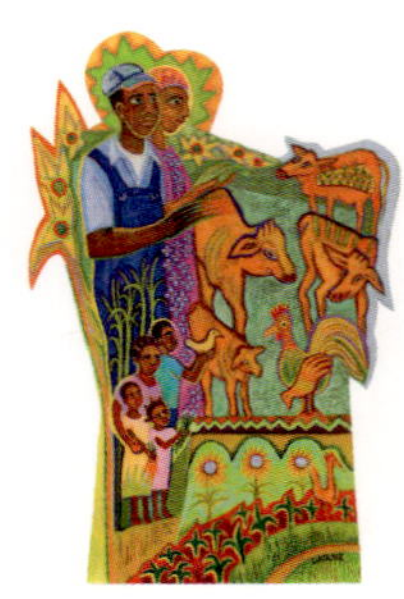
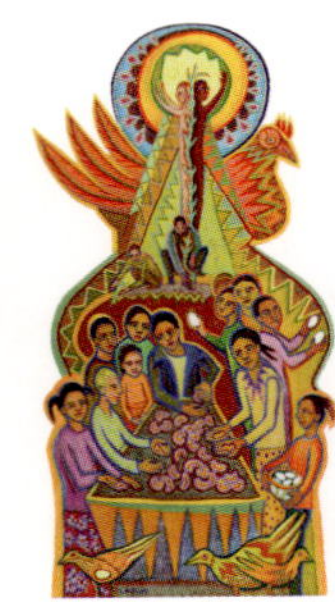
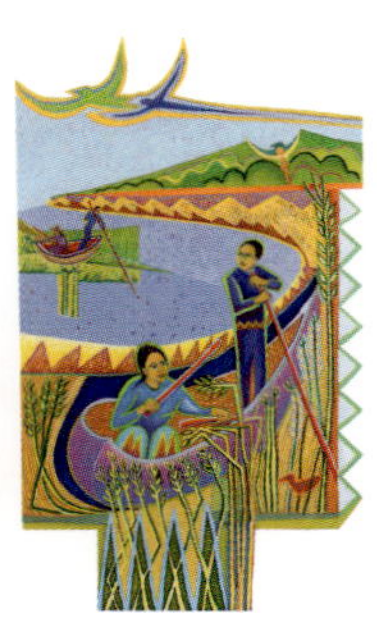

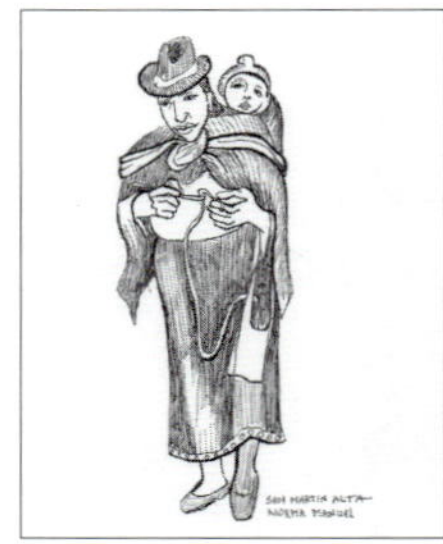
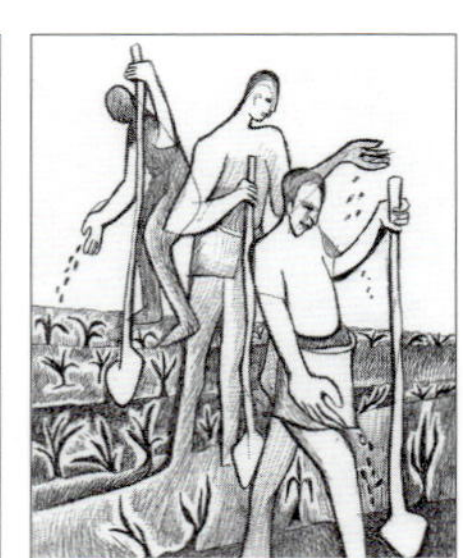
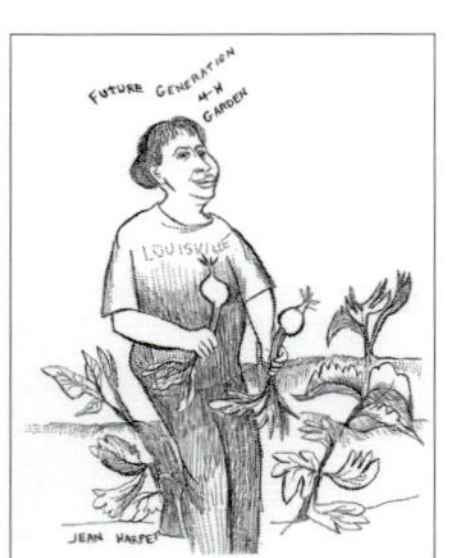

Left: Ecuador, San Martin Alta, Norma Manuel, 2004;
Center: Peru; 2004;
Right: USA, 4-H Garden, Jean Harper, 2007

Ecuador and Peru

Introduction

In 2004, Betty was invited by the United States Embassy in Ecuador to present art workshops and to exhibit her work in villages throughout the country. During this time, she visited a Heifer-supported program at the Indigenous Development Center in the Andean town of San Martin Alto in the Chimborazo Province. The following year, she went to Peru, this time as a participant in a 2005 Heifer Educational Study Tour.

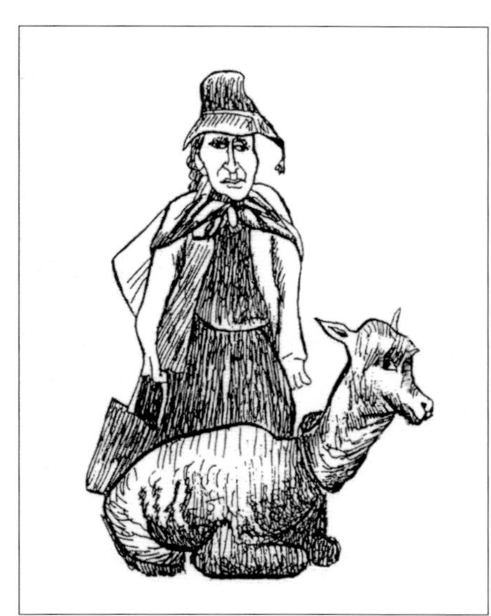

Pass-On Ceremony, 2004

Betty's Latin American sketches, paintings and mural panels honor "Pachamama" (Mother Earth), market day and the importance of weaving and spinning within indigenous Latin cultures. A Latin version of the Tree of Life entitled *Peru: Andean Tree of Life* contrasts with Betty's *Poland: Tree of Life* painting (on page 117) and an earlier *Eritrean Tree of Life*, although all highlight cultural pride. She shares the particular flavor of Latin American Passing on the Gift ceremonies

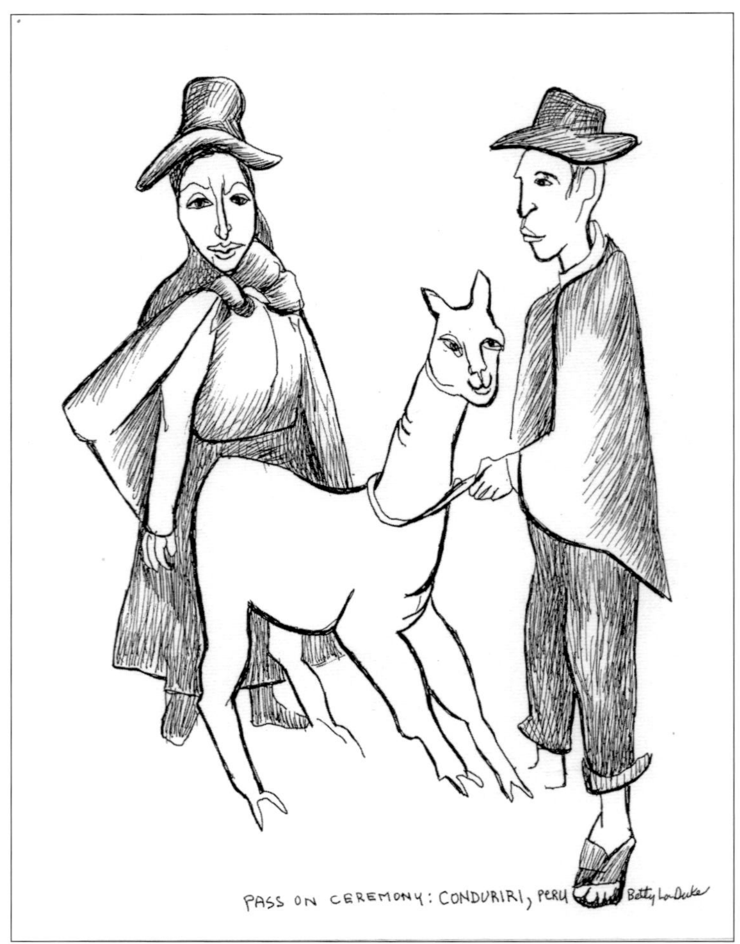

Pass-On Ceremony, Conduriri, Peru, 2004

where gifts are primarily alpacas, llamas, chickens, sheep and guinea pigs. Community efforts to improve the land and collectives that benefit many are beautifully illustrated.

In stark contrast to the warmth of Africa, Betty encountered dramatic climate changes on her trips to South America. But the cold weather was not the only thing that drew her to the intricate and colorful sweaters, shawls and mittens in the marketplaces. Women who spin and weave are powerful images in Betty's work: their folk art speaks of ancient customs and a proud cultural heritage. The Ecuadorian and Peruvian women she portrays are enveloped by warm, vivid colors and patterns of hand-woven cloth that tell stories about where they come from.

Betty visited rural communities in the Andes Mountains of Ecuador and Peru where she sketched people working together in the fields and sacrificial offerings to Mother Earth. Her work often included Andean camelids, namely alpacas and llamas, a common Heifer gift in these regions. Such livestock are healthier and less expensive to manage than imported breeds: they live naturally on mountainous terrain and will eat almost anything that grows in the area. One of the greatest benefits of alpacas is that their hooves don't damage the soil the way other large livestock can.

Ecuador

The Heifer program that Betty visited is situated in the Ecuadorian Andes in a region with the country's highest indigenous population. Family members are often separated for months at a time due to a need to earn income elsewhere. With the hope of stanching the flow of departures, Heifer contributes training and animals through a revolving fund. Its partner, the non-profit Indigenous Development Center (also known by the Spanish acronym CEDEIN) helps families maintain small, integrated farms in this high-altitude environment. Farmers learn to use integrated, organic farming methods to grow healthier food and medicinal herbs for their families and animals. They build terraces, plant trees, preserve grasslands and dig ditches to prevent further soil erosion on the steep, hilly terrain. Seeds and cuttings from native plants are gathered and planted—with the hope of returning the land to the condition of previous generations, when families could make a living in the region.[1]

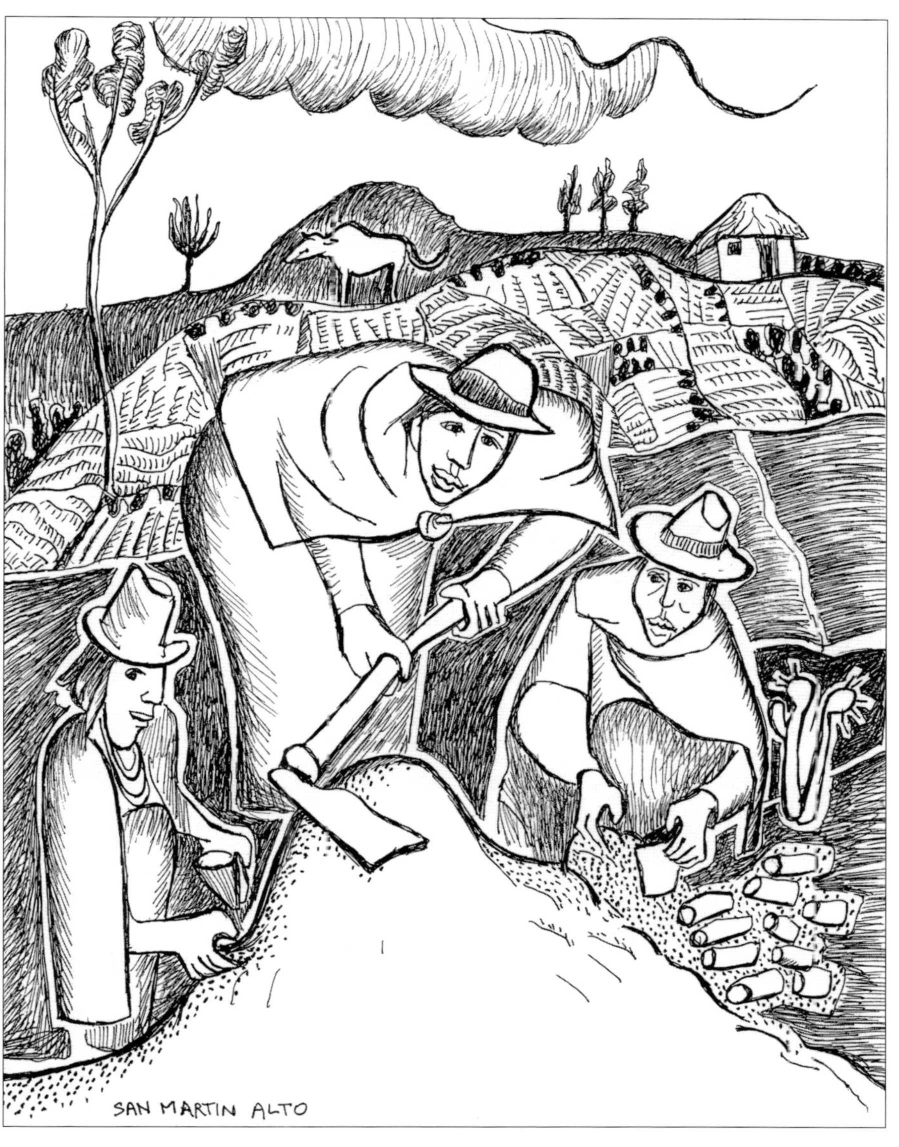

San Martin Alto, 2004

[1] www.heifer.org: Haddigan, Michael; "Preserving Their Land Through Integrated Farming;" 2003.

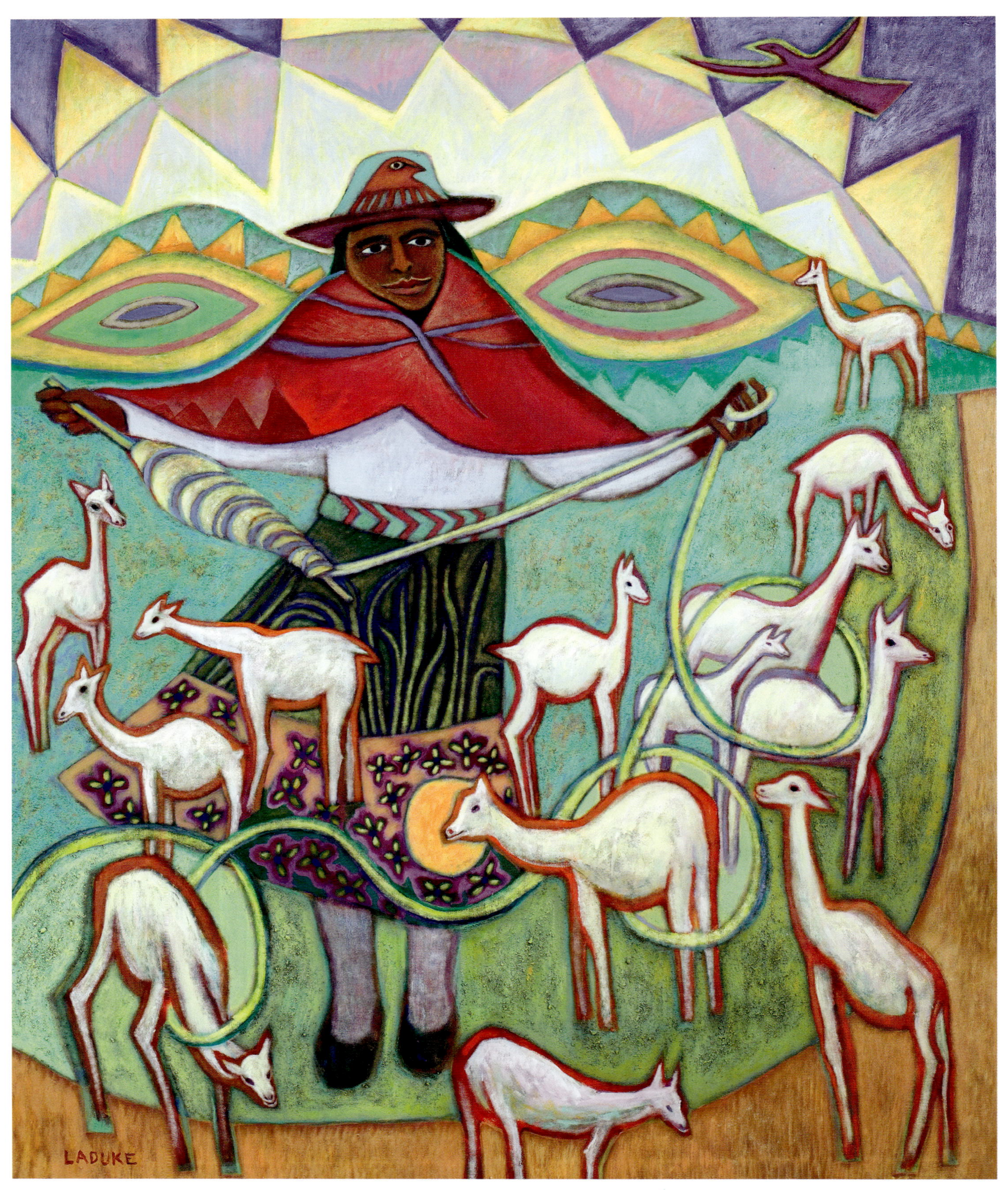

Ecuador: Spinning Dreams • 68"x54" • 2004

Ecuador: Spinning Dreams p. 138

"Experiencing the pride with which this woman was taking care of her alpacas was wonderful. I could barely keep up with her, running after her with my sketchbook to catch the essence of what she was doing. In my painting, I let the yarn envelop the alpacas as they were moving around and grazing. It became a sunrise image, one that seems prophetic of the future where the connection of people, their culture and their land has to remain."

—Betty LaDuke

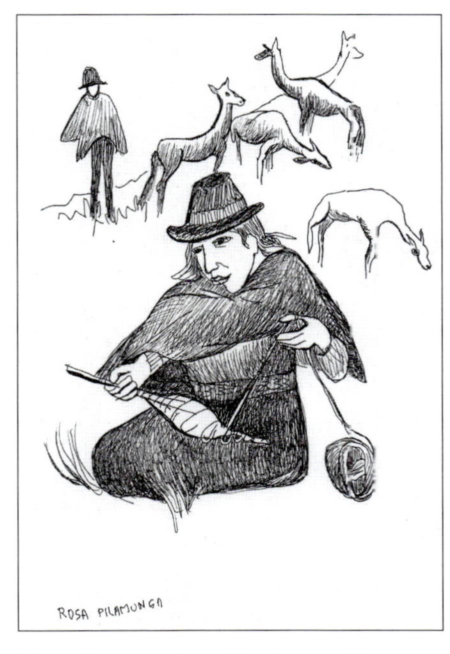

Rosa Pilamunga from San Martin Alto, spinning wool, 2004

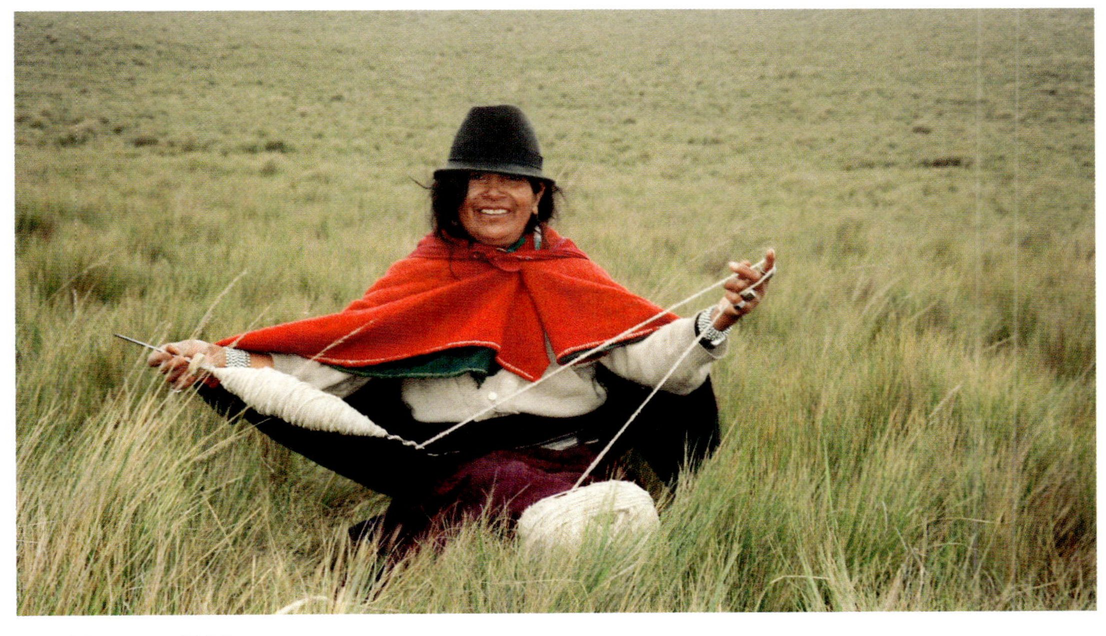
Rosa Pilamunga, 2004

"In Ecuador, I was so aware of the role of fiber and fabric in world cultures. It was a peak moment to view a part of a culture that has gone on for centuries—you can't believe the beauty!"

—Betty LaDuke

The photograph and sketch of Rosa Pilamunga from San Martin Alto personifies the integral nature of weaving, spinning and working with natural fibers to life in Ecuador and other Latin American countries.

Rosa is the model for the painting *Ecuador: Spinning Dreams*. She spins wool with a distaff (a stick holding wool that will be twisted into yarn) that is then fastened to another stick known as a spindle. But instead of attaching the yarn to a spindle, the woman lassos her foraging alpacas with the very yarn they have bestowed, illustrating the circular and integral nature of connection between woman, alpaca, yarn and land. The versatility of alpaca yarn reminds Betty of the maguey plant that she encountered during her student years in Mexico in the 1950s. This plant produced fiber that was spun into cloth; a nutritional fermented drink called pulque; and stalks for roof thatching. Here, the alpaca's adaptable yarn is used for a wide range of clothing, bedding and textiles. To Betty, these plants and animals represent the "staff of life"—a basic survival staple of the culture.

"Market Day is to me a real joy. I love market places all over the world!"

—Betty LaDuke

Volcanoes in the background carry primordial legends about life and death. The woman moves to the rhythms of the life cycle within a circle that is not quite complete. Standing between the eyes of the volcano, she is part of the story of creation. Her essence has moved far beyond the woman in the original photo to signify a timeless ancient drumbeat of myth, movement and growth.

Ecuador: Riobamba Market Day p. 141

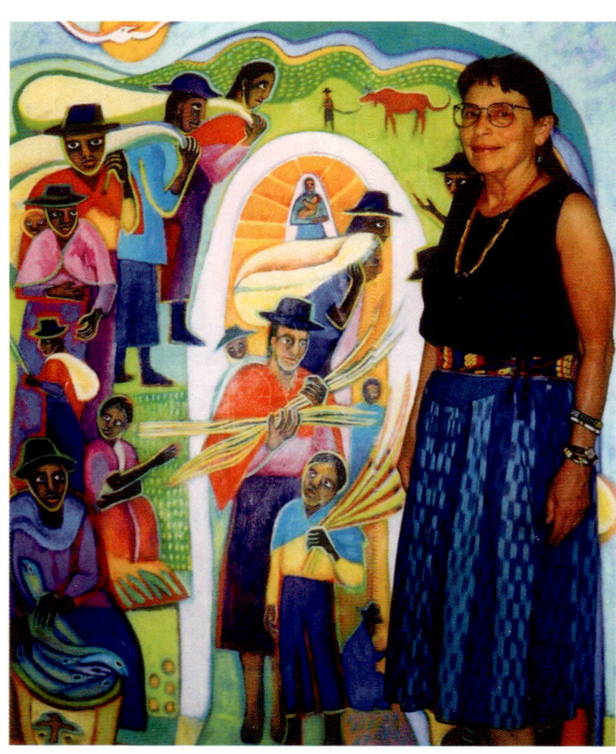

Betty stands before her painting, *Riobamba Market Day*, 2007

Market Day in Riobamba, the capital city of Chimborazo Province, is a kaleidoscope of constant movement. The rhythm of people and animals coming and going moves forward with lively conversation, hard won sales, intricately designed pottery, bright fabrics and other wares, aromatic smells, religious deities and more.

The energy and constant movement of *Ecuador: Riobamba Market Day* jumps off the painting. Even the baskets, with their decorative faces and spirit designs, have something to say as people carrying heavy loads talk, sell, bargain, hug and walk past each other throughout the day. Many carry heavy loads and children on their backs. They revel in the opportunity to meet up with friends from other villages on this special day.

The market is awash with the intense colors of indigenous cultures and elaborate designs that transform everyday objects such as pottery and baskets into folk art. In this predominantly Catholic society, a pink archway frames the image of a compassionate Virgin holding a child. In this place, spirituality co-exists with daily routine. In the background, people care for their animals and work the land.

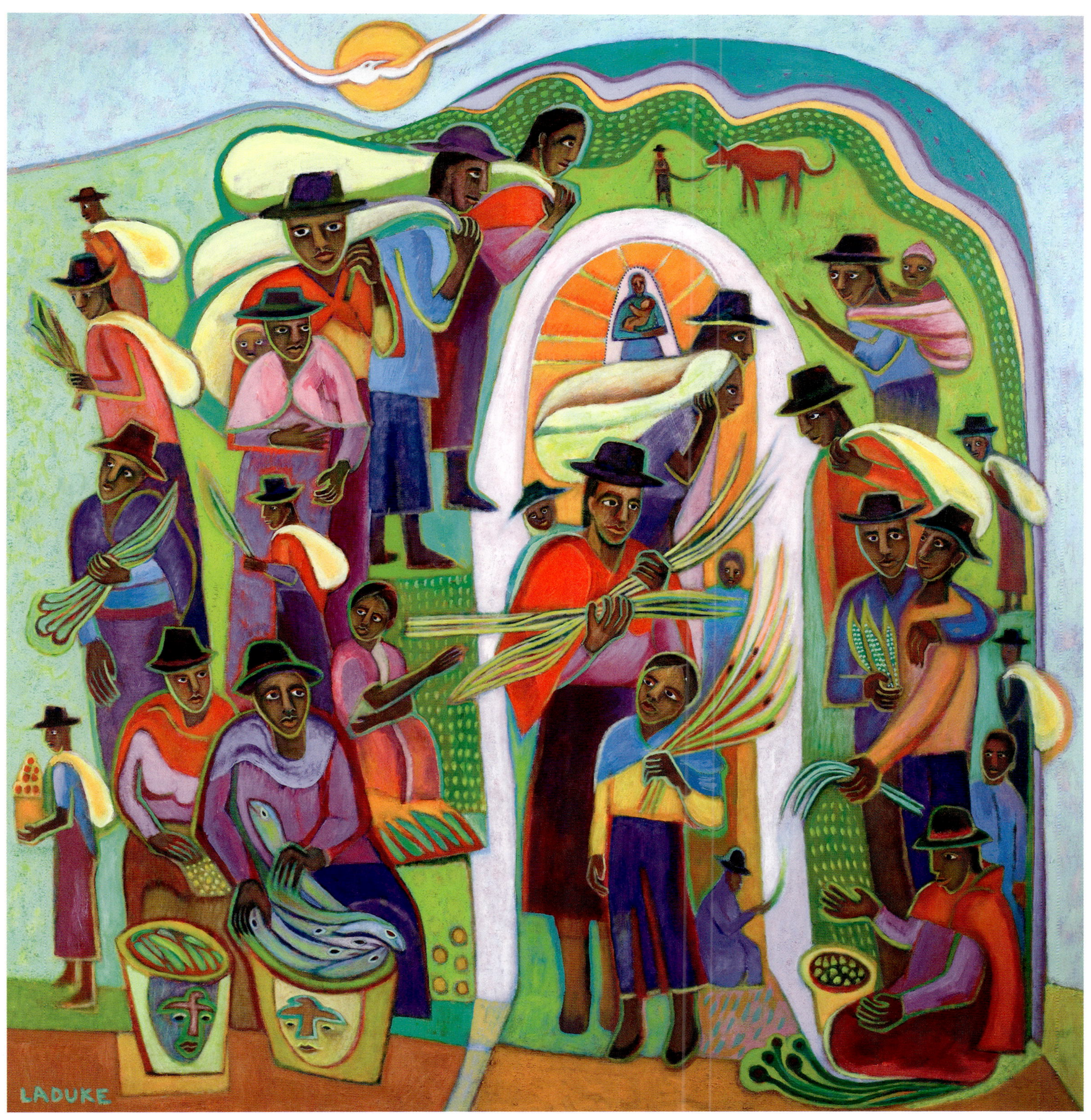

Ecuador: Riobamba Market Day • 72"x68" • 2004

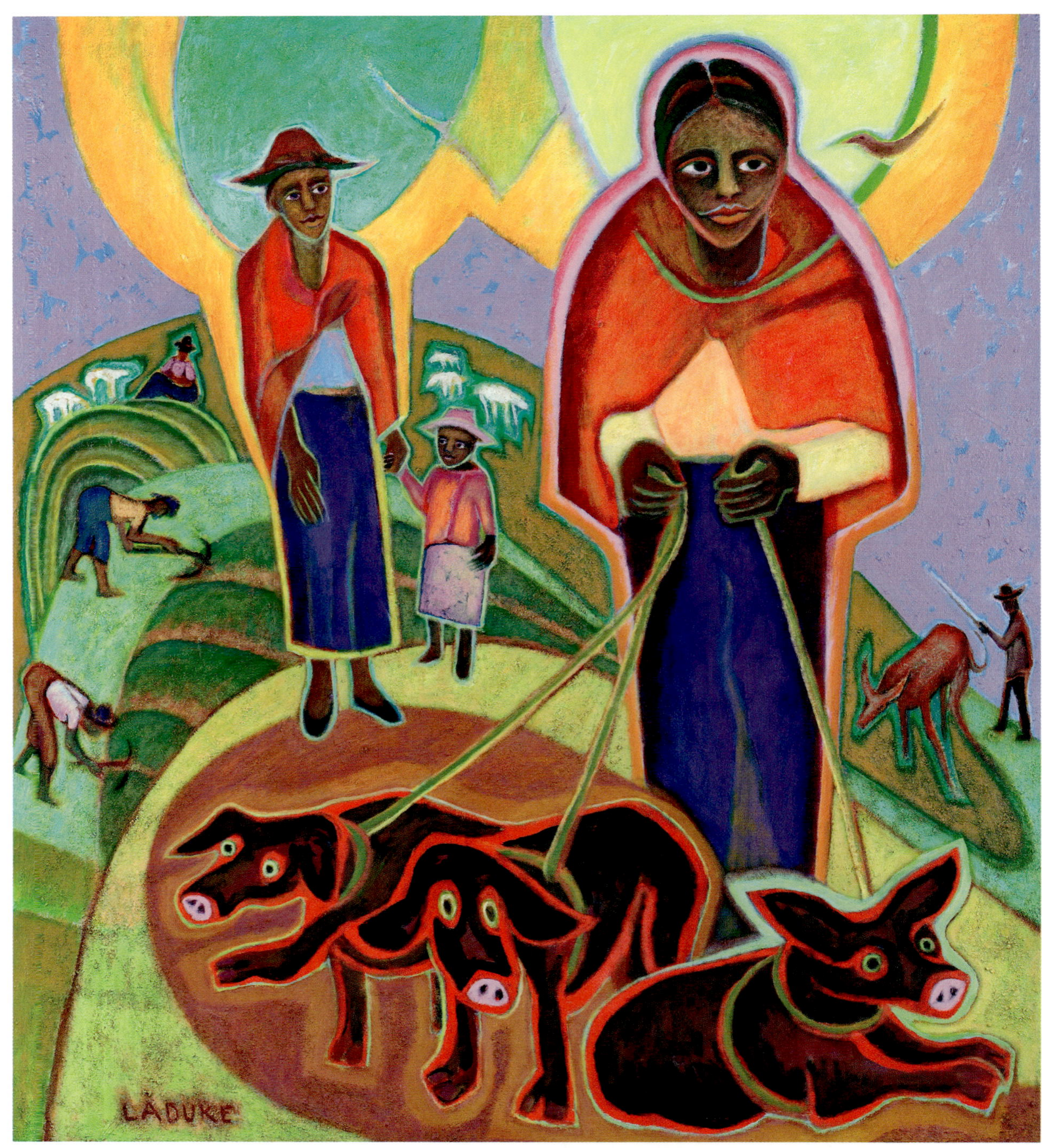

Ecuador: Riobamba, Three Pigs • 54"x50" • 2004

Ecuador: Riobamba, Three Pigs

Betty enjoyed watching this woman make her way to market with three leashed pigs. The animals have been raised with great care by their owner, who hopes to get a good price for them at the Animal Market. The sun and trees form a radiant circular aura around the people in the foreground. Industrious farmers work the hilly land in the background as others herd their sheep and cows.

Ecuador: Seeds of Hope

Men and women in the mountainous San Martin Alto community work together to prevent further soil erosion. Making good use of resources provided by Heifer for training and seedlings, villagers plant borders around small farm plots that capture rain water for the gardens.

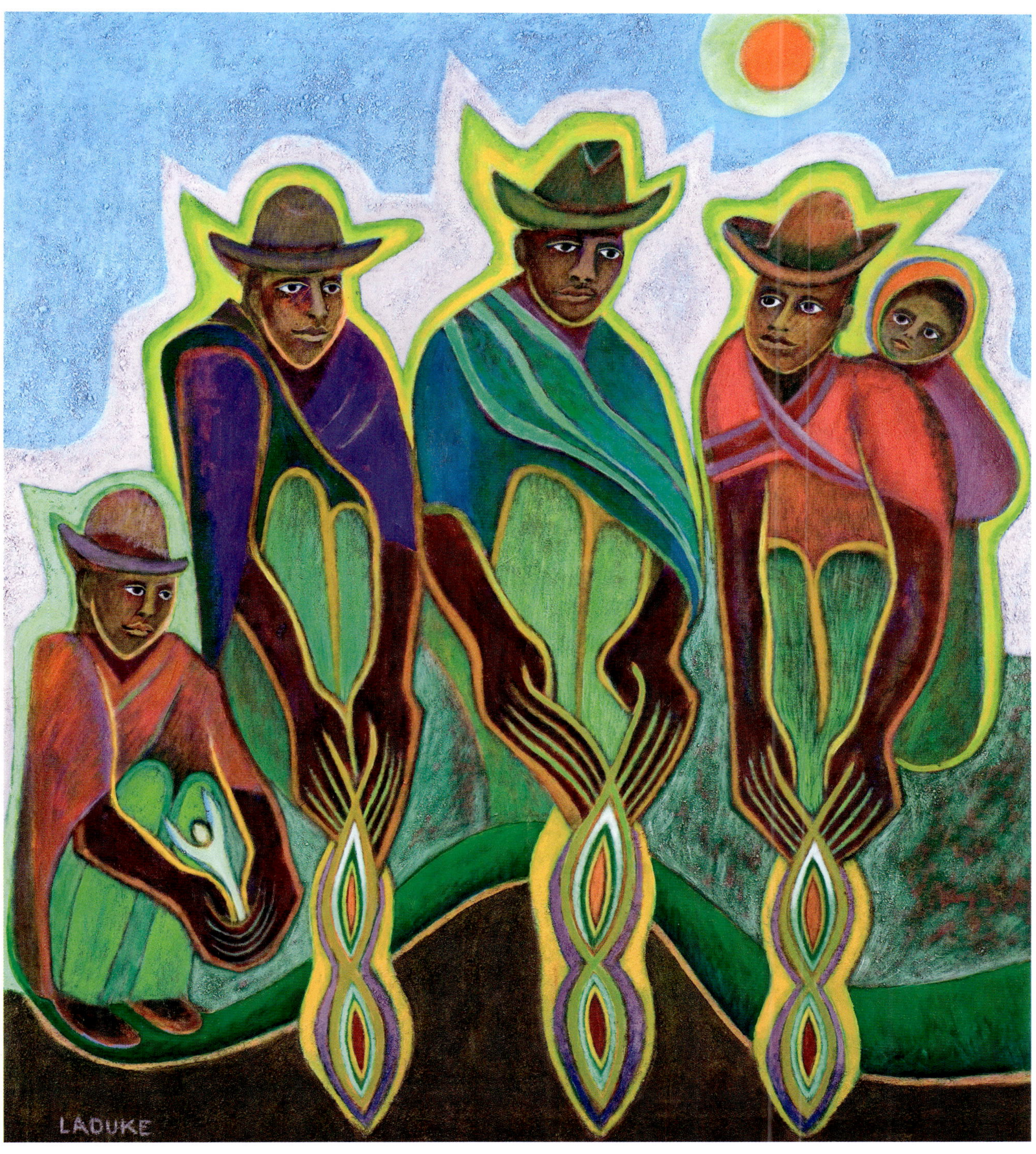

Ecuador: Seeds of Hope • 54"x50" • 2004

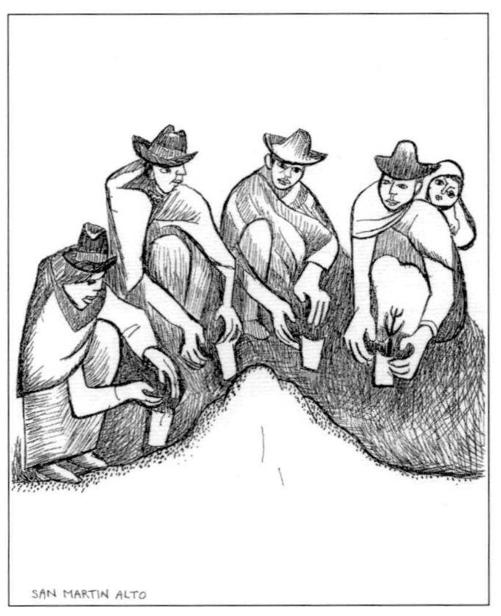

San Martin Alto, Plantings, 2004

In the painting, two men and a woman carrying a child place seedlings into plastic bags near a mound of earth that has been prepared with mulched soil. Bags of seedlings will be given to other villagers so they, too, can grow hedges to curb erosion on these steep slopes. The woman on the left holds a small symbolic person whose arms reach toward the skies, signifying life-giving qualities of working the soil and protecting the land. Workers are surrounded by the sun's yellow glow and the green of new growth. Though they look ahead rather than at each other, the rhythm of synchronous movement connects them.

"I was invited into this woman's home, which was a tiny thatched-roof hut. I sketched quickly as it was so smoky that I had to leave. Though she had little, she was roasting black lima beans on the grate to offer us some refreshment."

—Betty LaDuke

Ecuador: Riobamba Welcoming p. 145

In *Ecuador: Riobamba Welcoming*, Betty has moved the woman outdoors, where she is connected to the Earth and the fire. The roasting pan holds crackling lima beans and hands that surround them over a hot purple-red fire. The circular energy of the hands in the fire represents the welcome extended to Betty, who was greatly warmed by the woman's generosity.

The woman's bird hat is surrounded by a larger green and yellow bird that looks upon another bird hovering nearby. Each bird has distinct colors and shapes. The green bird, signifying growth, casts a bright glow upon the woman and the fire. People in these regions know a great deal about birds and what they convey: which ones come during which season; who will eat the crops; when the rains will come; and when planting season begins. Birds also carry spirit messages. Always, in Betty's paintings, they send a message of hope and possibility.

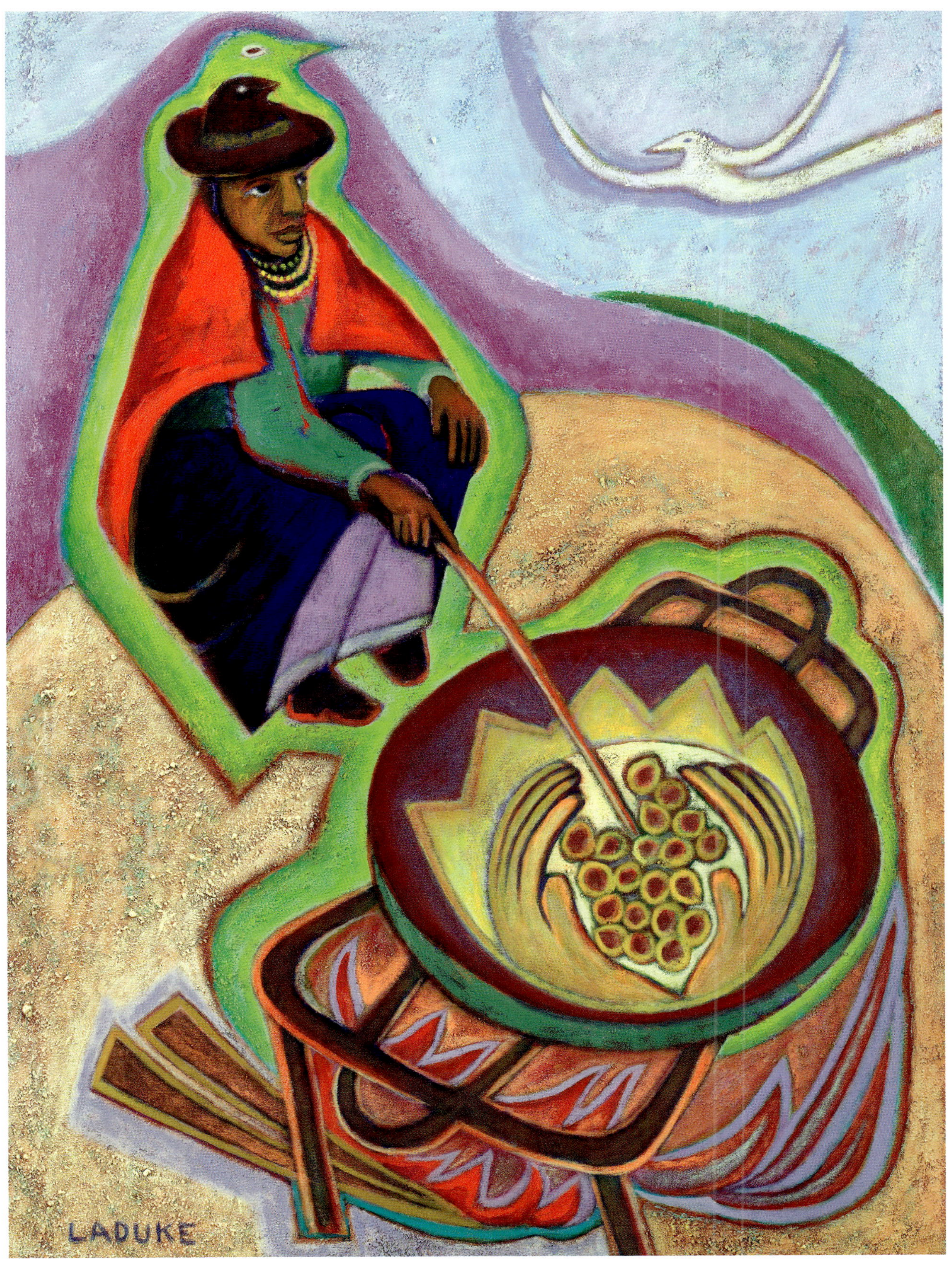

Ecuador: Riobamba Welcoming • 44"x32" • 2004

Peru

Peru is home to the Incan Civilization, believed to have been formed from various Andean cultures that trace back twenty thousand years. It is commonly believed that the Incas ruled from the thirteenth to sixteenth centuries. Around 1438, aggressive military expansion under Emperor Pachacutec turned the Incan domain into the most powerful nation in South America. After his death, civil war pitted the followers of the Emperor's two sons against each other. This division was not resolved until 1532, the same year that Spanish conquistadors arrived, destroyed the Empire and forbid the practice of the Inca religion.[2] Amazingly, Peruvians in the remote Andean village of Cuchuma that Betty visited in 2005 continue to identify with their ancestry and practice the Incan religion.[3]

Religion for the Incas is rooted in the worship of nature and its cycles. "Inti," the Sun God, was revered above all. Centuries ago, emperors and kings were thought to be Inti's children. "Pachamama" or Mother Earth and other lesser deities were also honored.[4]

With no written language, Incan history has been passed down orally and, as a result, much has been lost. However, some things remain: the amazing architecture of Machu Picchu and the tradition of colorfully woven tapestries, for example. At the height of Incan power, such tapestries were presented to solidify treaties between the Incan capital of Cusco and governing powers of outlying territories. These ties helped to keep the vast Empire united.[5] The woven cloth of today's Andean culture conveys the proud heritage of an ancient people struggling to keep their traditional ways of life. These exquisite fabrics are captured in Betty's Peruvian paintings and mural panels for she, too, appreciates the importance of this cloth as folk art that represents a rich history and culture.

Peru: Passing on the Gift p. 147

In the high plains of Peru's Conduriri District, Heifer partners with the Andean Camelids Producers Association to improve the genetic quality of the region's alpacas. Smaller than llamas, alpacas are valued for their fiber, which is used for weaving and knitting. These hardy animals are well-suited to the vicinity as they survive in arid, hilly areas.

Heifer provides training in animal health and nutrition as it promotes conservation of natural prairies and seeds temporary forests of oats and barley for times of drought. In cooperation with the government, farmers plant trees to prevent erosion. In addition, women of the area gather to talk about daily concerns. Such gatherings encourage leadership and an increased respect for the contribution of women by village members.

---

[2] www.about-peru-history.com/inca-civilization.html.

[3] Kingsolver, Barbara, "Following the Ancient Paths of Peru;" Work Ark Archives, 2005; www.heifer.org.

[4] philtar.ucsm.ac.uk/encyclopedia/latam/inca.html.

[5] www.about-peru-history.com/inca-civilization.html.

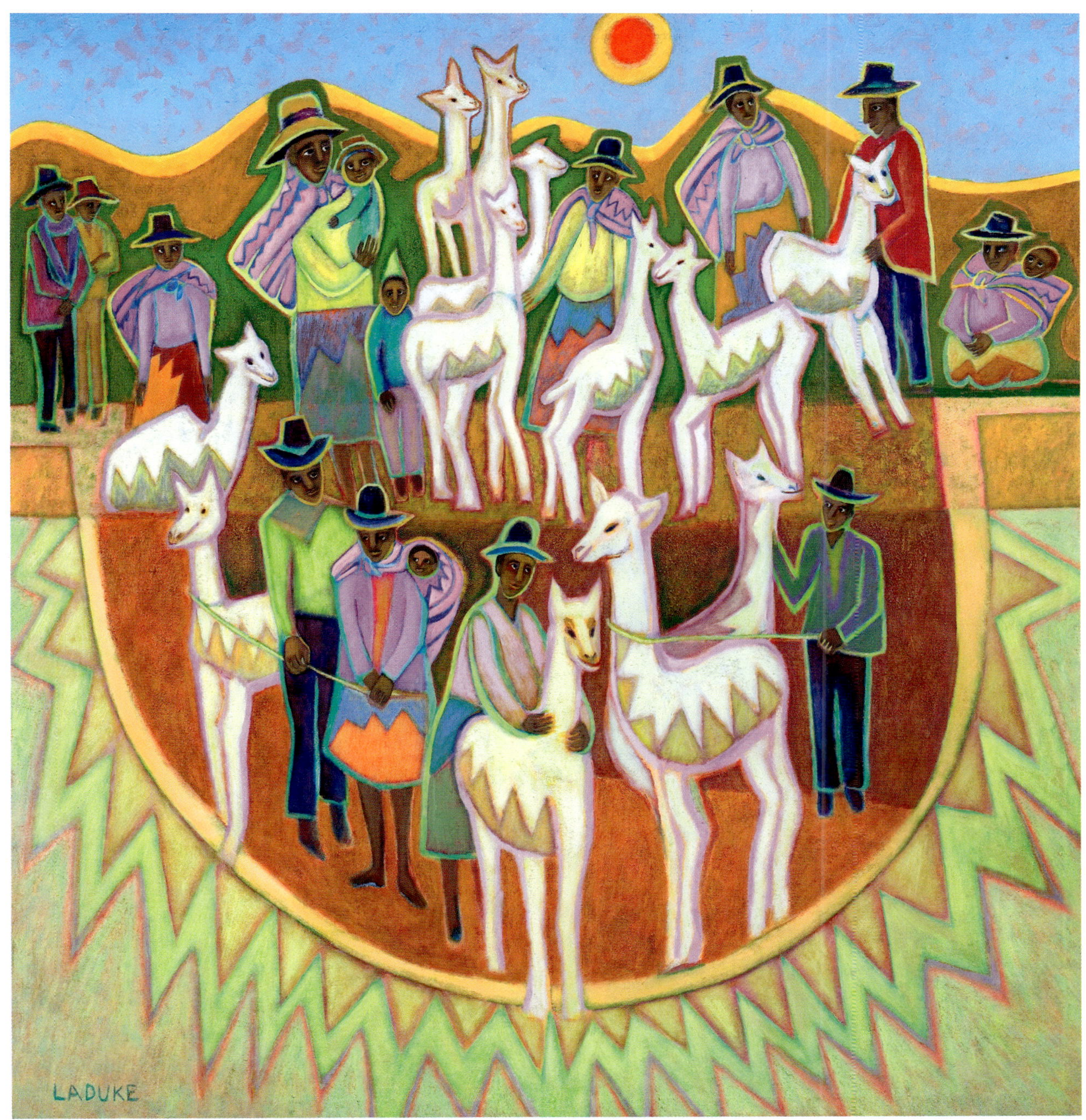

Peru: Passing on the Gift • 72"x68" • 2005

The Pass-On celebration was indeed festive. Community members had woven and hung a welcoming arch of blankets from bamboo poles. They threw confetti and served "chicha" (a popular Peruvian corn drink) as the children danced. During the ceremony, fifty-two families passed on 104 alpacas. The message that one Heifer recipient sent to another was compelling: "We all work and share what we get. It's a sign of how well we are doing as a community. I took care of all of these animals with much love. Now you have to do the same."

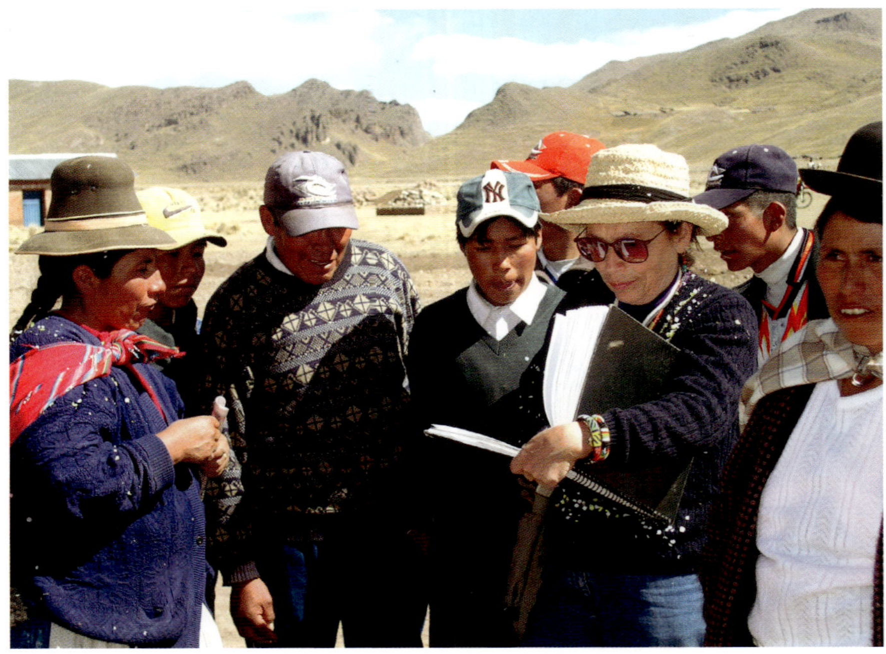

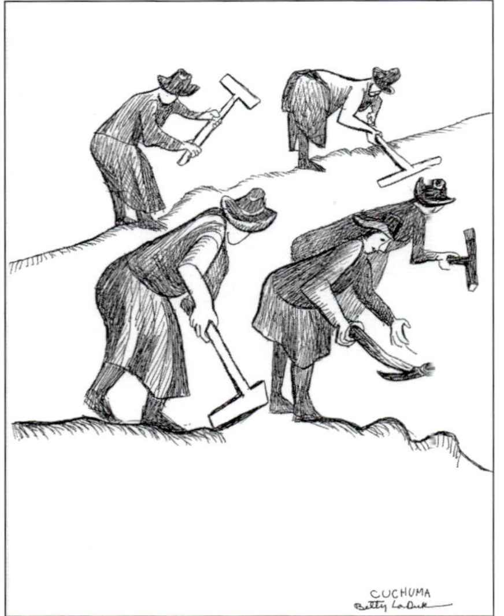

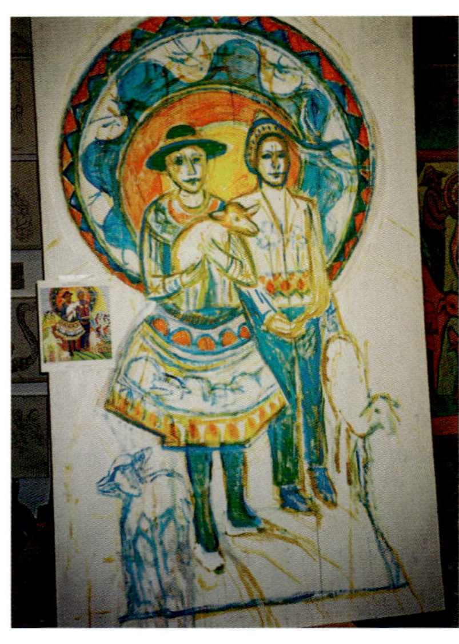

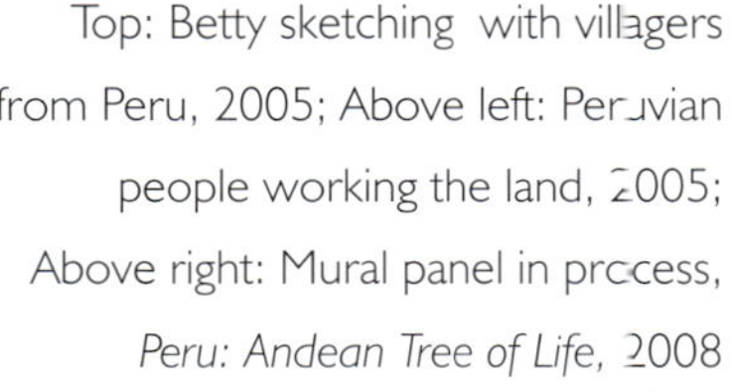

Top: Betty sketching with villagers from Peru, 2005; Above left: Peruvian people working the land, 2005; Above right: Mural panel in process, *Peru: Andean Tree of Life*, 2008

The heart of Betty's painting lies within a horseshoe that, like the Pass-On ceremony, brings people and alpacas together. The excitement is palpable—people are happy to share their good fortune. Brown earth tones of the ground and hills contrast with colorful clothing and the bright sun within a deep blue sky. Near the top of the painting, people are enveloped by a lush green border that is symbolic of hard-won gardens they have cultivated in the dry, mountainous region.

About Cuchuma

Betty's three other Peruvian paintings represent her experiences in the town of Cuchuma, a small and remote farming community high in the Andes Mountains, 110 kilometers south of Cusco in the valley of the San Pedro district. The area's natural resources have been greatly diminished by over-grazing, forest burnings that clear land for crop farming and uncontrolled tree felling and poaching. Many young people have left the area to find work in the city. Heifer is helping the community to improve its sheep production; protect wild fauna; recover genetic material of the potato, Peru's basic staple; and increase nutrition, health and the use of medicinal plants.

In conjunction with several other non-profit organizations, Heifer helped the community to build an ecolodge, which has increased rural tourism while providing young people with jobs. Because youth groups from the city are the lodge's most frequent visitors, cultural exchange between urban and rural adolescents is another benefit. Villagers share profits from this community-run endeavor, which are often used to diversify crops and build greenhouses. The lodge also serves as a community center that brings villagers together to discuss common concerns.[6]

[6] Schrock, Janet West, daughter of Heifer founder Dan West, "Project Visit Report" Andean Highlands of Cusco, Peru, January 2004 on www.heifer.org.

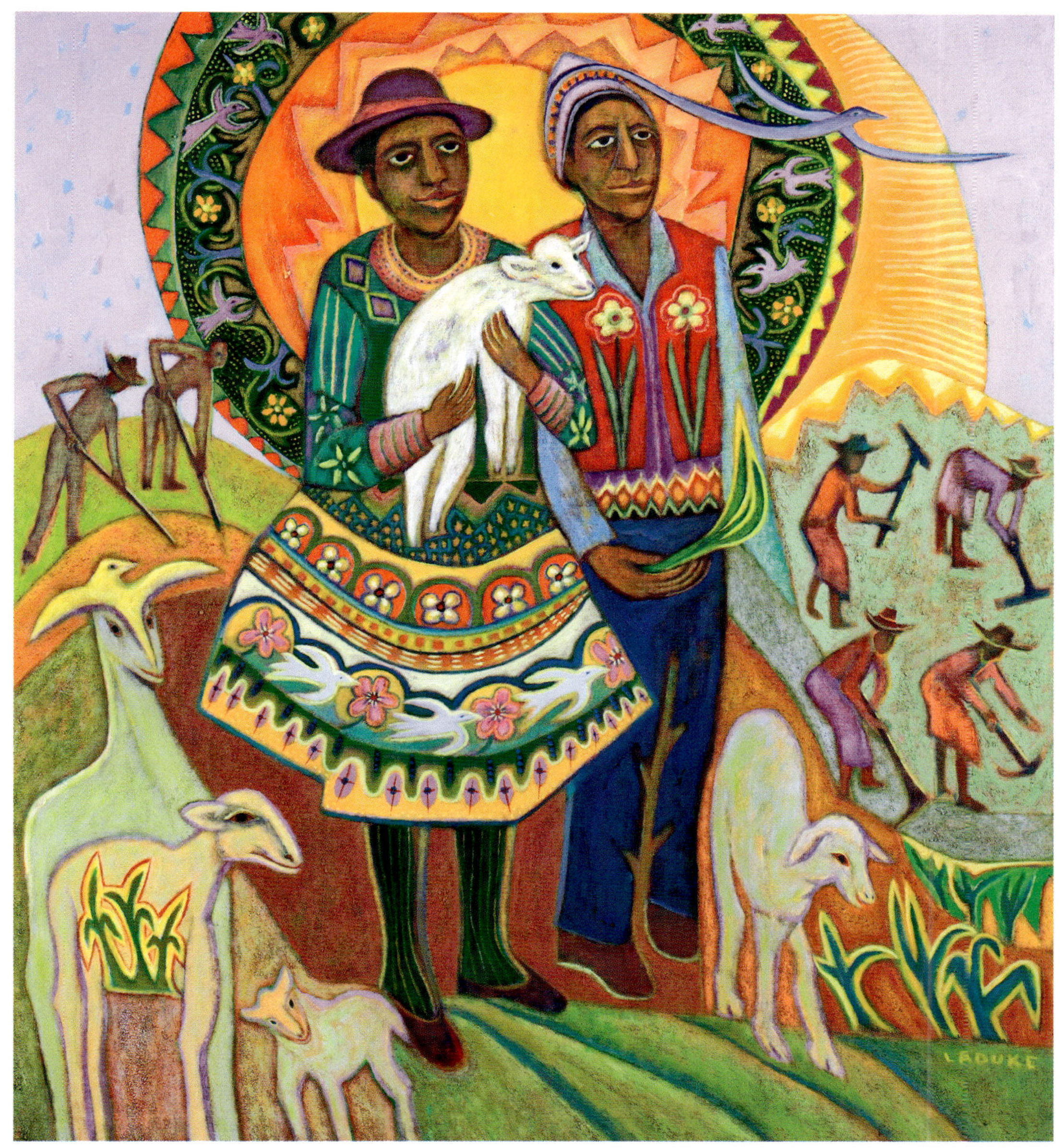

Peru: Andean Tree of Life • 54"x50" • 2005

Peru: Andean Tree of Life

"This husband and wife have been recipients of Heifer animals for a long time and they have passed on many animals. Now grandparents, they stand tall because they feel so good, so fulfilled and so connected to their community."

—Betty LaDuke

Initially, Betty was invited into this couple's home. "A few years before," they told her, "we had received a cow from Heifer. Now, we have rabbits, chickens, sheep and cows. We have improved our home and we wish for the same good fortune for other families."

The couple's world is rooted in nature and fertility. Their benevolence graces an environment that reflects growth and productivity. At closer glance, a beautiful bird unwinds the yarn from the man's "chollo," a traditional cap with ear flaps. The woman nurtures a baby sheep in her arms. Eye-catching flower and bird patterns of their clothing jump out at the viewer. Betty sees the pair—so integral to their community—as the base of her ever-symbolic Tree of Life. In Peru, the dynamic bird and flower patterns extend into the body of the tree, which holds the sun at its center. The landscape is composed of people working in the fields. Animals in the foreground thrive: some carry a modified rendition of plants and birds that complement the Tree of Life.

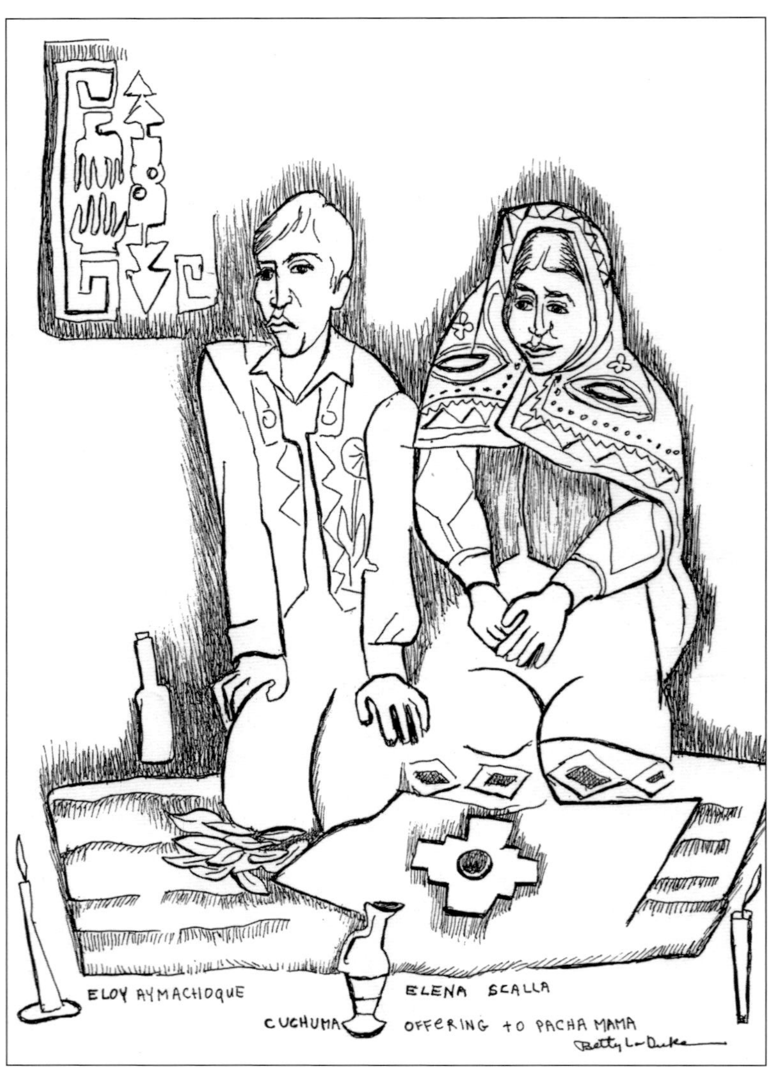

Eloy Aymachoque, Elena Scalla, Cuchuma Offering to Pachamama, 2005

Peru: Pachamama Awakening p. 151

Betty's sketch entitled *Eloy Aymachoque, Elena Scalla, Cuchuma Offering to Pachamama* inspired the *Peru: Pachamama Awakening* painting. It is evening and the community rests. Husband and wife chant as they make offerings to Mother Earth. They pour chicha into the ground at a ceremony outside the Community Center. The long ceremony of chanting and prayers is conducted in Quechua, the indigenous language of the Inca people. In his community, the man is a "curandero" or healer who uses medicinal plants to cure basic illnesses of people in his village. Heifer and its partner organizations work to preserve ancient medicinal knowledge of the curanderos.

In the painting, husband and wife represent the Earth's male/female energy and the balance that is needed to integrate these forces. The community understands the importance of respecting the Earth that nurtures them. The man's healing hands rest on a bird. He holds the artist's image of knowledge and curative powers within him. A face that forms the lower part of the woman's body symbolizes "Pachamama" (Mother Earth). Birds inhabit her visage and corn seedlings rise up from within her. We intuit the artist's meaning of "Pachamama" and her accompanying earth spirits: we are more than flesh and blood, we are spiritual beings.

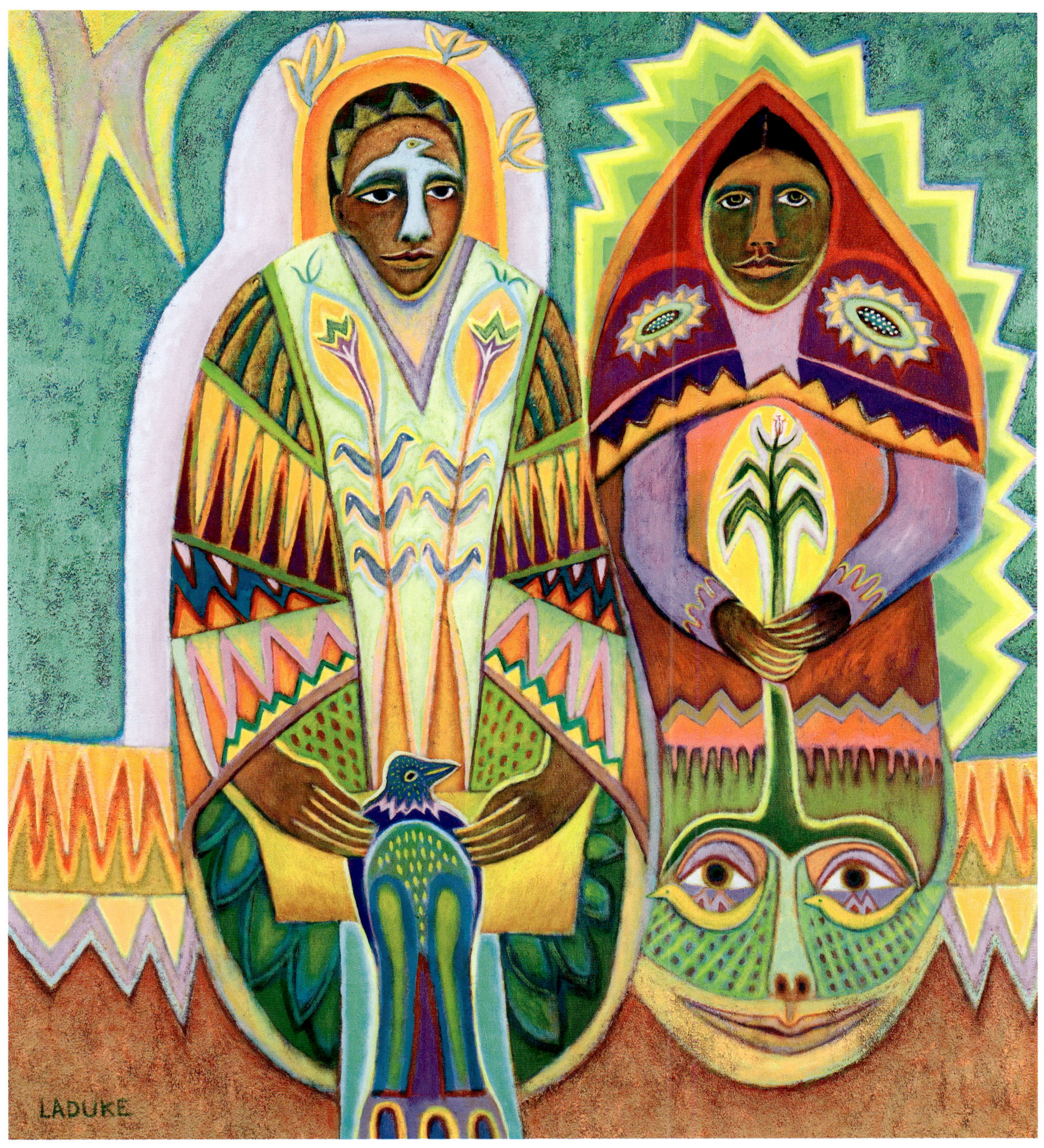

Peru: Pachamama Awakening • 54"x50" • 2005

The Cuchuma Women's Poultry Collective brings together struggling women of all ages to raise chickens and their incomes. In the process, their spirits are also raised by living in a caring and productive community that honors their contribution.

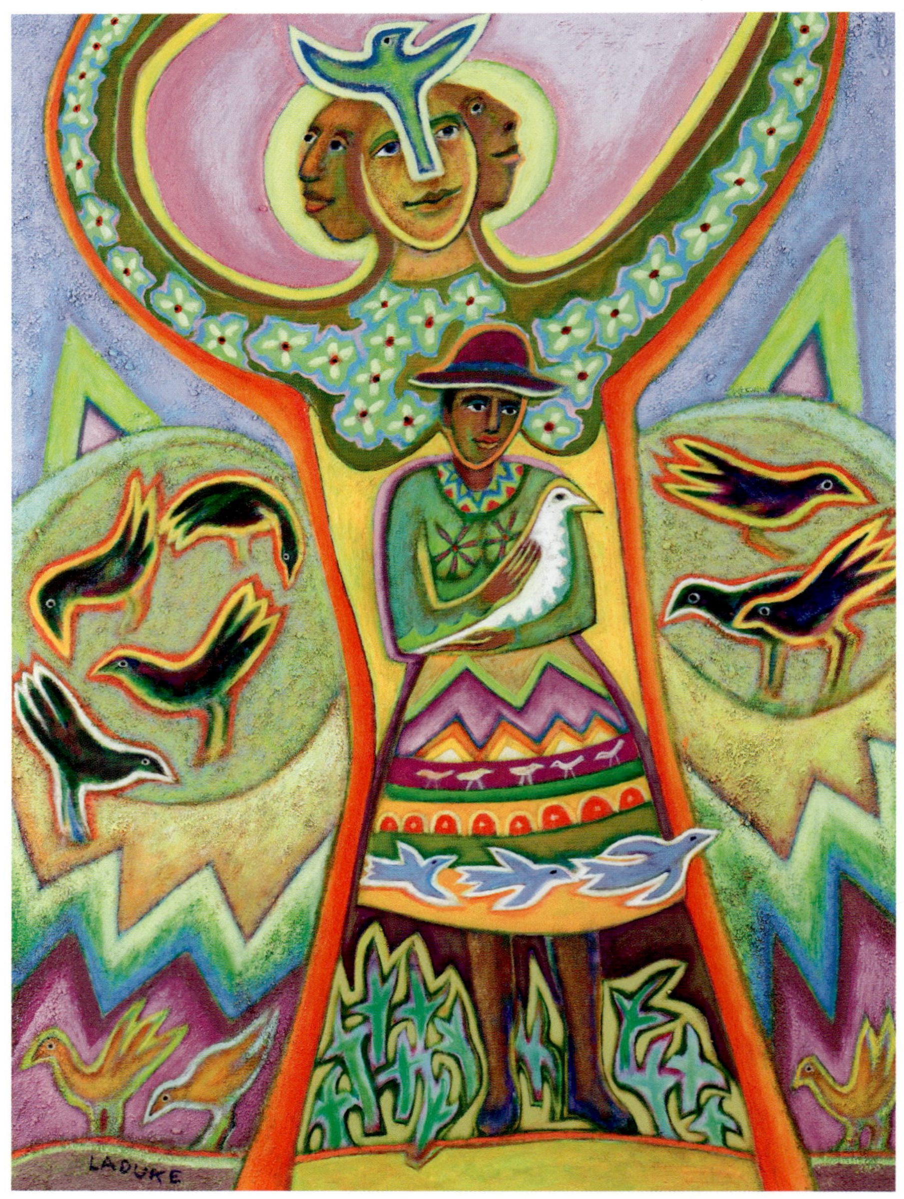

Peru: Cuchuma Women's Poultry Collective • 44"x32" • 2005

Peru: Cuchuma Women's Poultry Collective

In the painting, a huge female figure presides, whose shape reiterates a favorite LaDuke symbol, the Tree of Life. This tree goddess has three heads, which signify the unity and strength of women coming together. As is often the case, a bird of possibility is an integral part of the women's heads. It gently hovers over them in a protective manner. There is great power in the woman's huge arms that, laden with flowers, branch up toward the skies.

Within her "trunk," a smaller woman, wearing the region's short, richly decorated, traditional embroidered skirt, strokes a symbolic white chicken. In the background, clusters of dark-feathered chickens happily roam free within a fenced-in yard.

LATIN AMERICA MURAL PANELS

Latin America: Tree of Life

Taken from the painting *Peru: Andean Tree of Life*, husband and wife form the base of a Tree of Life. The man's left arm has morphed into a green tree branch that he gently clasps with his right hand. The woman holds a baby sheep while others prance nearby. Corn grows beneath their feet and within the thriving sheep. The tree and the couple's clothing are decorated with bright flowers, birds and patterns that speak of ancient traditions and joy. The sun shines brightly at the center of the tree. The bird that was part of the man's hat in the painting has flown with him to the mural panel.

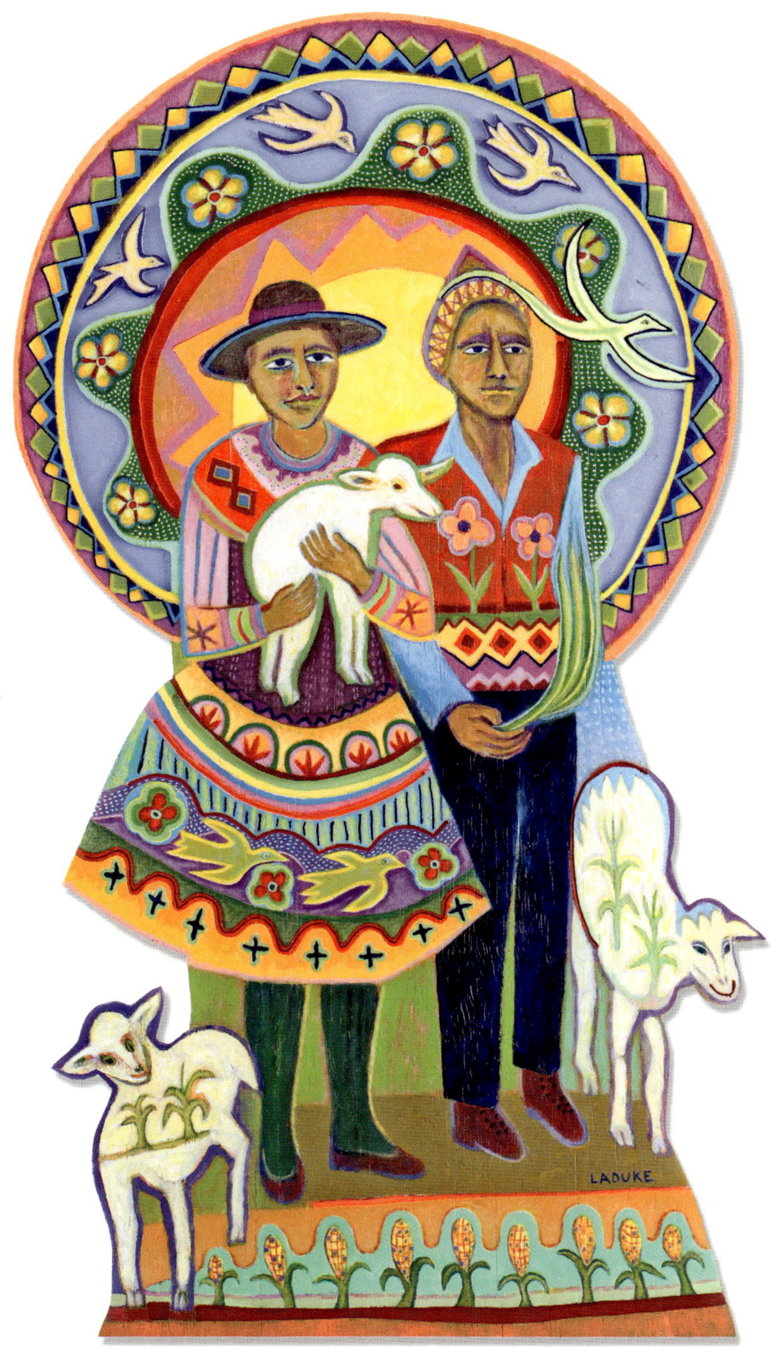

Latin America: Tree of Life • 76"x48" • 2007

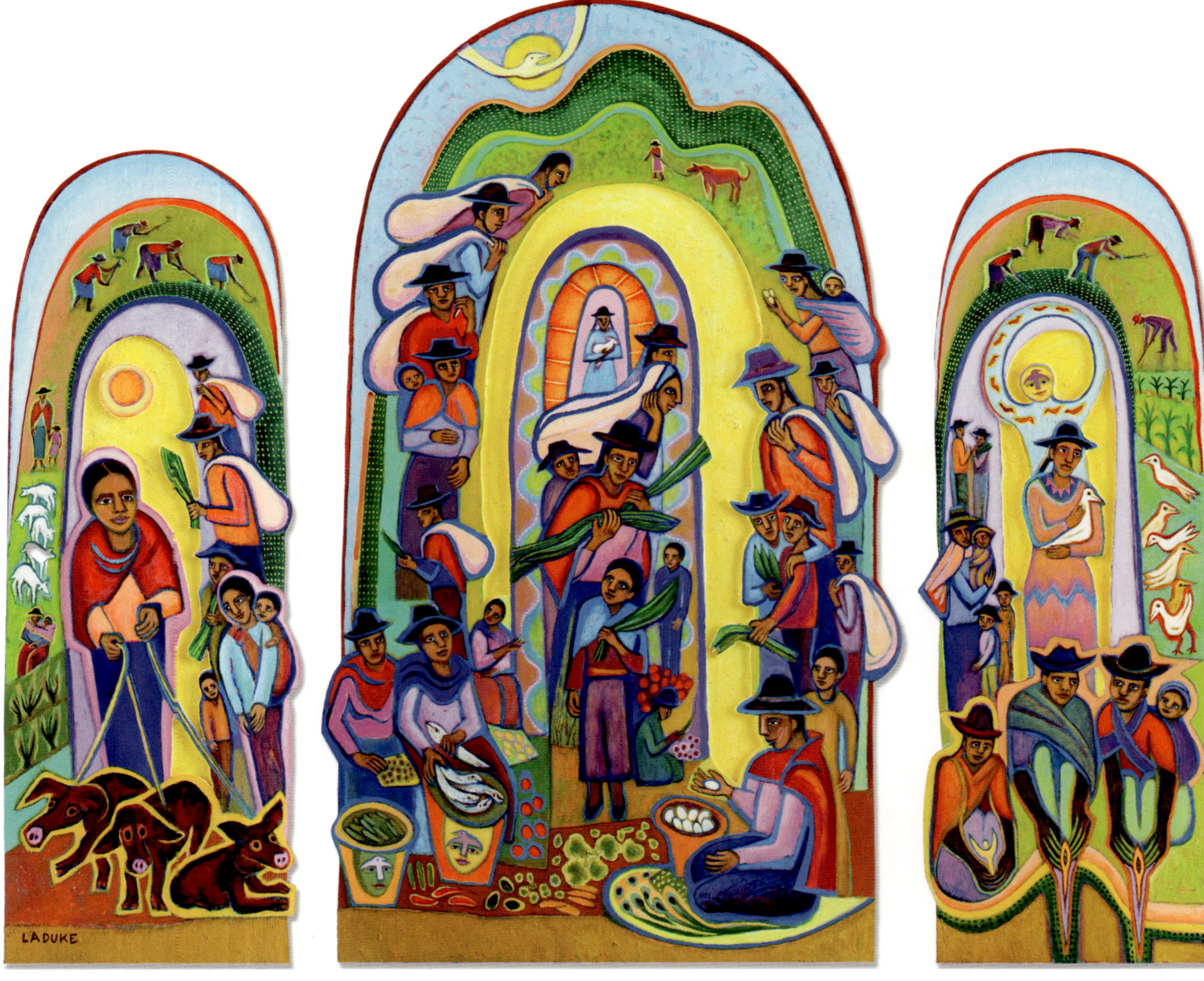

Latin America Market Day Landscape • 84"x92" • 2007

Latin America Market Day Landscape

This triptych (work of art divided into three sections) combines elements of four LaDuke paintings, including (from left to right): *Ecuador: Riobamba: Three Pigs; Ecuador: Riobamba Market Day; Ecuador: Seeds of Hope;* and *Peru: Cuchuma Women's Poultry Collective*. In this vivid landscape, Betty portrays a cycle that begins with farmers plowing the land and planting seedlings and ends with people bearing the fruits of their labor to the marketplace. Villagers often walk long distances to bring their animals, eggs, fruits and vegetables to sell at the market.

Latin America: Pachamama p. 155

The mural panel *Latin America: Pachamama* uses images from Betty's *Ecuador: Spinning Dreams* and *Peru: Pachamama Awakening* paintings. Alpacas are lovingly lassoed as before but here, the background contains giant wings that belong to the bird in the woman's hat

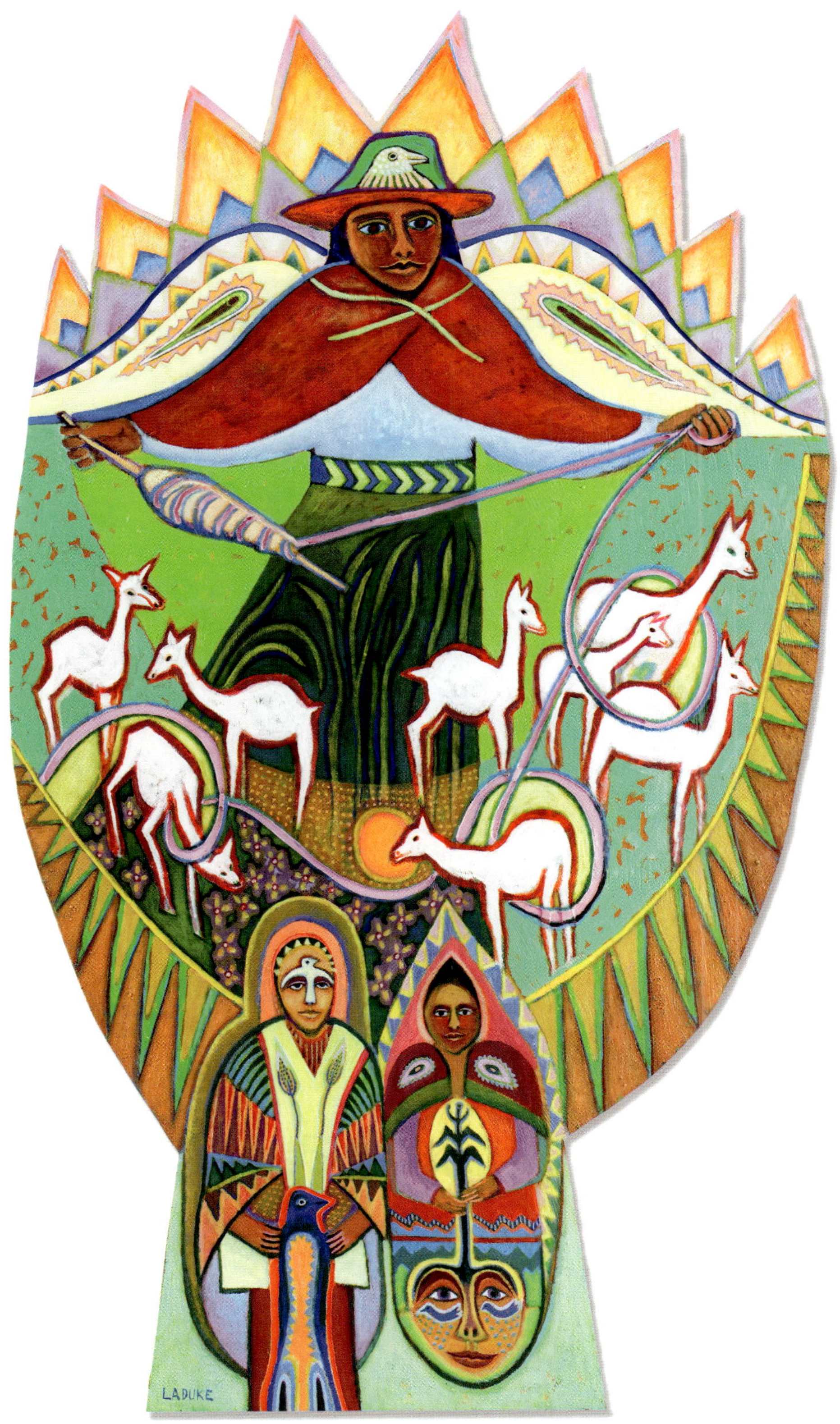

Latin America: Pachamama • 84"x48" • 2007

or to the woman herself. In either case, they intimate a freedom from survival worries that the alpacas provide. Village spiritual leaders, a husband and wife who honor Pachamama, sit below with their offerings. In turn, Mother Earth sends gifts to these village representatives in the form of corn plants that grow from her head into the woman's hands and that climb up the center of the man's body.

Introduction to United States Mural Panels

The North America mural panels were not extracted from paintings as were most of the other Heifer mural panels. Reflecting Betty's direct experience with her subjects, these pieces posed different challenges. How, for example, could little red worms be made to stand out in the murals' routed wood? As Betty explains it, "I had to feel my way into how to organize the sketches as ideas took shape. The first panels were rough sketches of forms and shapes. I gradually pared them down, filled in the details, and developed the story lines."

The history and impact of racism in the United States permeates the stories of Betty's North America mural panels. She presents the struggles of African American farmers in rural Mississippi; multiracial children in Little Rock, Arkansas; and Native Americans on White Earth Reservation in Minnesota.

Mississippi

In an American RadioWorks public radio story (November 2001), Smith, Ellis and Aslanian reported that:

Below: evolution of the *Worm Story* Mural Panel, from early stages to nearly finished piece, 2008

> "Life in the Jim Crow South was often dangerous for African Americans. Lynchings and white mob violence provoked real fear in black communities. For many Southern blacks, other hazards menaced their daily lives. A white

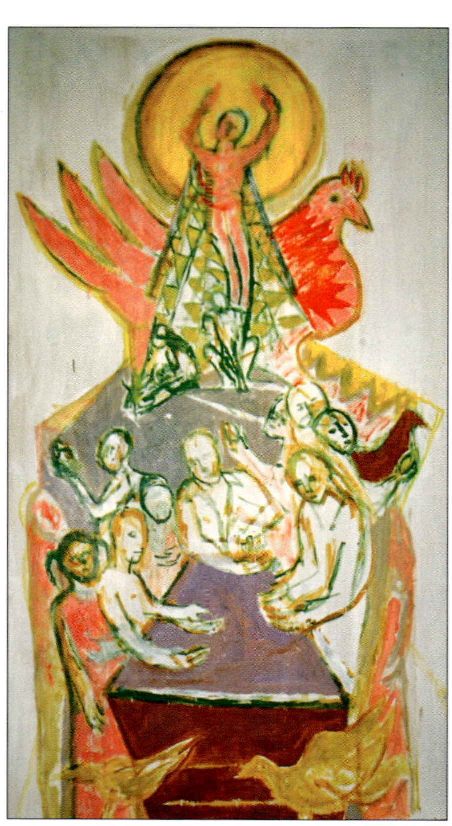

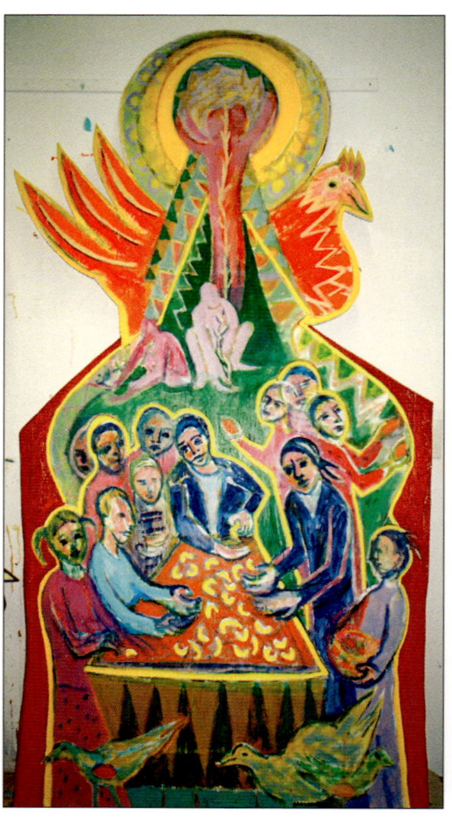

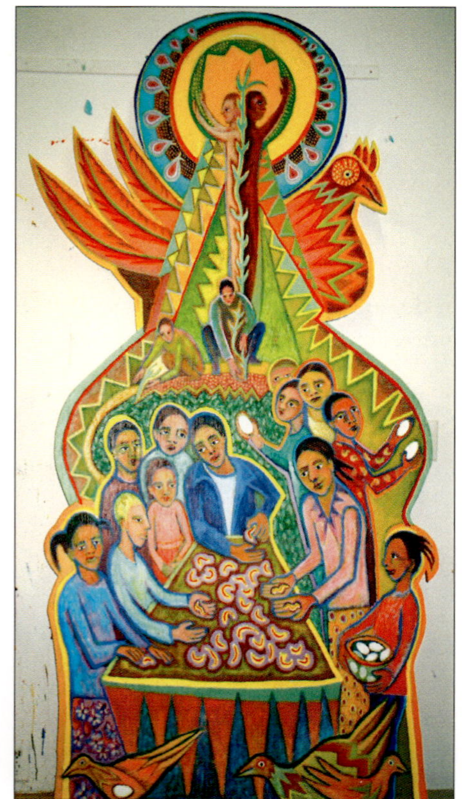

> employer might try to take sexual advantage of his black maid, a white landowner might cheat his or her black tenant farmers, a white shopkeeper might insult a black customer in front of others. The prospect of humiliation by whites was a constant source of anxiety. It was meant to be: white Southerners reacted swiftly against blacks they perceived were 'getting uppity'—that is, actively trying to get ahead in life, or asserting themselves in front of whites."[7]

In another part of the American RadioWorks series, John Blewen described a horrifying story that took place in Winston Country, Mississippi, the site of Betty's *USA: Saving Rural America* mural panel:

> Like any black Mississippian who grew up in the Jim Crow years, MacArthur Cotton can tell you stories. The story of his grandfather, who, Cotton says, was fatally beaten by whites for teaching other blacks to read. Or the story of the black sharecropper in Winston County in the 1950s, who took the day off to go to a church gathering—without his white boss's permission. Cotton was there—about fifteen years old at the time, he says.
>
> "He [the sharecropper] didn't go to plow that day but his boss man wanted him to plow. So . . . he came up to church with the rest of the people, and, [the boss came and said] 'I thought I told you to go to the field.' And [the sharecropper] got ready to walk away and [his boss] just kinda grabbed him and shot him six times. You know, right there, he fell and laid out there."[8]

Little Rock, Arkansas

Little Rock, Arkansas, is the locale of Betty's second North America mural panel and the home of Heifer International Headquarters. Historically, it was also the home of the "Little Rock Nine"—nine African American students who were denied entry to Central High School in 1957 by the Arkansas National Guard (called in by then-governor Orval Faubus in defiance of a federal court order). That court order had come from the now famous 1954 U.S. Supreme Court ruling *Brown v. Board of Education of Topeka, Kansas,* which labeled racial segregation in public education a violation of Fourteenth Amendment rights. Overnight, Little Rock became an international symbol of resistance to desegregation. President Dwight D. Eisenhower responded by federalizing the National Guard. He sent units of the U.S. Army to escort the nine harassed and terrified students into the school on September 25, 1957. Military presence remained for the duration of the school year.[9]

---

[7] Smith, Stephen; Ellis, Kate; Aslanian, Sasha, "Remembering Jim Crow;" American RadioWorks, Nov. 2001: americanradioworks.publicradio.org/features/remembering.

[8] Blewen, John, "Oh Freedom Over Me;" American RadioWorks, Feb. 2001: origin-americanradioworks.publicradio.org/features/oh_freedom/story2.html.

[9] Encyclopedia of Arkansas History and Culture: encyclopediaofarkansas.net.

White Earth Reservation Callaway, Minnesota

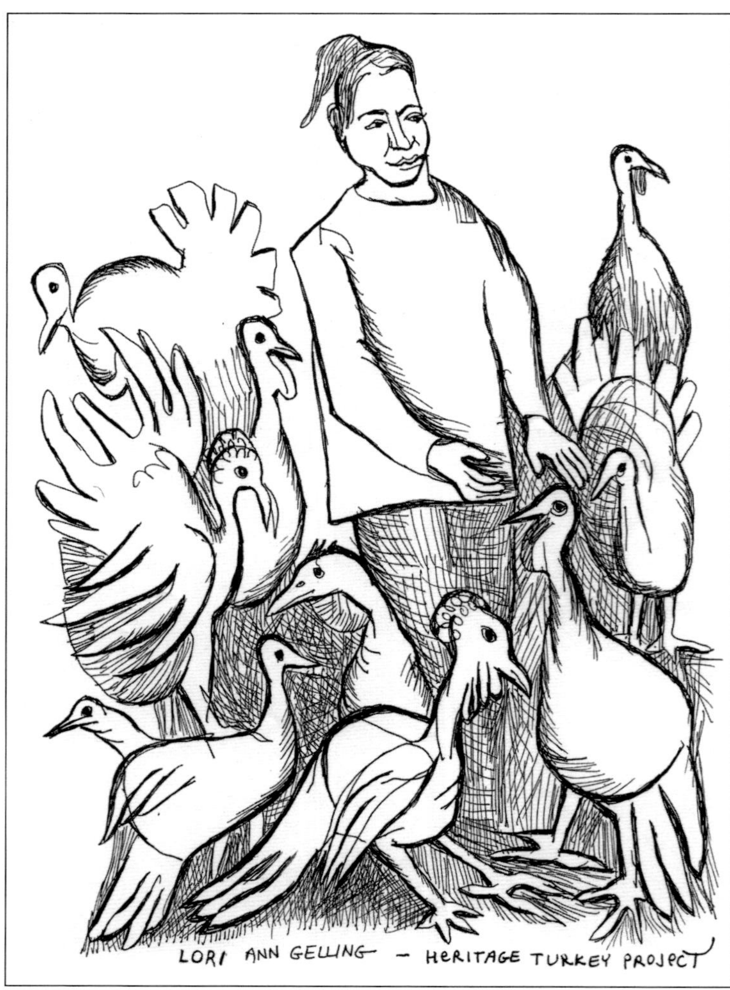

Lori Ann Gelling, Turkey Heritage Project, 2007

Unbeknown to Betty, Heifer began partnering with the White Earth Land Recovery Project (WELRP) on the White Earth Reservation in northwestern Minnesota in 2004. This is the home of the third largest Indian tribe in North America, the Anishinaabeg, also known as the Ojibwa or Chippewa.[10]

WELRP was founded in 1989 as a separate entity from the tribal government by Betty's daughter, Winona LaDuke. Since then, this non-profit organization has worked to recover the Reservation's original land base and to restore and preserve traditional Ojibwa ways. *Native Harvest* was conceived in 1995 as an income-generating enterprise. Its catalogue mail order and internet business offers the public naturally harvested foods and native crafts.

Efforts are underway to restore the much healthier traditional Native American diet to Native American communities throughout the United States in order to curb the high incidence of diabetes[11] and other diseases such as tooth decay, tuberculosis and arthritis associated with processed foods.[12] On White Earth Reservation, Heifer has supported efforts to strengthen local food systems such as community gardens and greenhouses; process wild rice and maple syrup; and restore heritage turkeys to the area.

Winona is passionate about preserving the Anishinaabe's cultural heritage, especially wild rice gathering, a sacred centuries-old tradition that plays a critical part in preserving the ecosystem of Northern Minnesota. Within the Tribe's oral history, wild rice is revered as a special gift:

> "... given to the Anishinaabeg from the Creator, (it) is a centerpiece of the nutrition and sustenance for our community. In the earliest of teachings of Anishinaabeg history, there is a reference to wild rice, known as the food that

[10] www.mnsu.edu/emuseum/history/mncultures/anishinabe.html.

[11] In 1995, while the national prevalence of diabetes in adults was 7.4%, it was 22-72% among Native American adults under twenty. The American Journal of Public Health (2002) stated that the incidence of diabetes is increasing in the general U.S. population by 14% in contrast to 46% in some Native American populations) DiabetesSite.Net, taken from American Journal of Public Health 2002 September; 92(9):1485-90.

[12] The Weston A. Price Foundation for Wise Traditions in Food, Farming and the Healing Arts: Fallon, Sally, and Enig, Mary G., Ph.D., "Guts and Grease: The Diet of Native Americans;" www.westonaprice.org/traditional_diets/native_americans.html.

> grows upon the water, the food, the ancestors were told to find, then we would know when to end our migration to the west. It is this profound and historic relationship that is remembered in the wild rice harvest on the White Earth and other reservations—a food that is uniquely ours and a food that is used in our daily lives, our ceremonies and our thanksgiving feasts." [13]

An ongoing campaign to protect wild rice from genetic manipulation and contamination began in 2002. Since then, Winona has assumed a leadership role in voicing opposition to the paddy rice industry's attempts to expand production of genetically modified cultivated "wild" rice:

> "Winona LaDuke of the White Earth Land Recovery Project told legislators that wild rice is sacred to the Chippewa culture. American Indians worry if a test plot is issued for genetically engineered wild rice, the modified variety will spread to stands of the native crop." [14]

Supported by Native American tribes, religious organizations, and others, Winona's efforts also focus on promoting fair trade for hand-harvested natural lake wild rice and on educating others about the traditions and culture of those who gather and process it. In 2003, the White Earth Land Recovery Project received one of ten International Slow Food Awards for the Defense of Biodiversity.

---

[13] http://savewildrice.com; 2005.

[14] "Legislative proposal seeks to protect native wild rice;" Scott Wente Bemidji Pioneer; Published Friday, March 31, 2006; www.savewildrice.org.

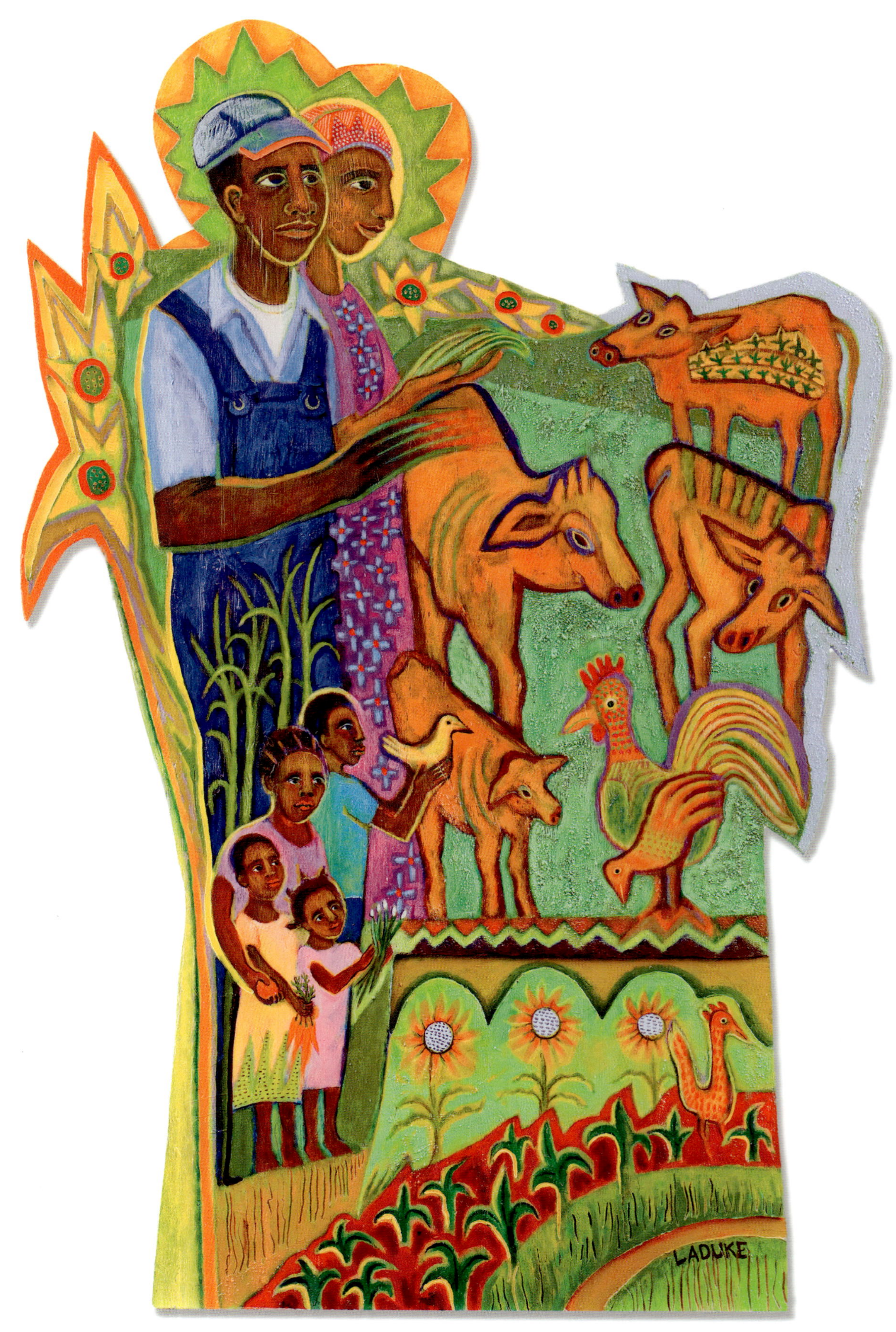

USA: Saving Rural America • 84"x48" • 2008

USA: Saving Rural America p. 160

Mississippi's Winston County was first settled by the Choctaw Indians 1500 years ago. Centuries later, slavery ruled, with almost one black slave for every two white people in the area (e.g., in 1837, the county population was 2,193 Caucasians and 959 African American slaves)[15] In 1999, almost a quarter of the population of close to 20,000 people lived below the poverty line and 2004 saw unemployment rates of 7.7%.[16] When in the 1980s, an economic downturn pushed large timber companies to leave the area, a group of African American citizens began to talk about ways to address the growing struggles of the farming community and rising unemployment. They formed the Winston County Self-Help Cooperative (WCSHC) in 1988, which initially focused on helping farmers increase their buying power through cooperative purchasing agreements. Fortunately, they caught the attention of the Mississippi Association of Cooperatives (MAC),[17] which provided them with technical assistance in areas such as sustainable production, marketing and community food security.[18]

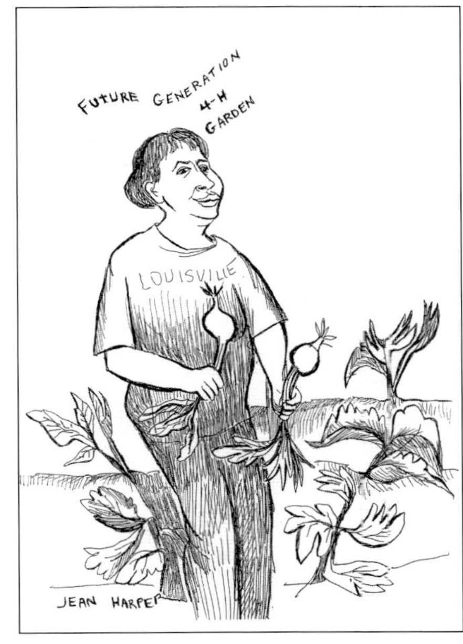

Jean Harper, *Future Generation, 4-H Garden*, 2008

Today, the organization has a broad mission—"to help save rural America."[19] Expanded programs include areas such as: leadership development; financial literacy; home buying; animal husbandry; business planning; computer training; and a youth component that incorporates a community garden. In 2006, WCSHC held its first Youth Agricultural and Training Conference, which highlighted rural opportunities for young people interested in agriculture. WCSHC has received awards from the NAACP, the Federation of Southern Cooperatives and Heifer International. WCSHC partners with the Extension Programs of Mississippi State University and Alcorn State University.[20] Since 2001, Heifer has supported the Association's work by providing training in a wide range of areas: community development; loan applications; land retention, soil management and other environmental concerns; housing; livestock production and care; home and market gardening; field crop and forage production; and forestry. In addition, Heifer donates livestock and seeds to WCSHC's youth program, enabling young people to sell vegetables from their garden project and to compete in livestock shows.

Frank Taylor, WCSHC's president of twenty years, is the grandson of a sharecropper. He is proud of the organization's part in the area's improved tax base, cleaner air and water; increased wildlife habitat and reduced erosion. Most especially, he says, "we want our children to inherit something good."[21]

---

[15] Bauer, Lisa, Center for Rural Entrepreneurship, September 2007.

[16] City-data.com: www.city-data.com/county/Winston_County-MS.html.

[17] An affiliate of the Federation of Southern Cooperatives, whose primary goal was to help black farmers retain their land.

[18] "Community food security is defined as a set of circumstances that enable community residents to obtain a safe, culturally acceptable, nutritionally adequate diet through a sustainable food system that maximizes community self-reliance and social justice." Source: Community Food Security Coalition: www.foodsecurity.org.

[19] Bauer, Lisa, Center for Rural Entrepreneurship, September 2007.

[20] Alcorn State University was the first state-sponsored institution for blacks set up under Congress' 1862 Morrill Act as a land grant institution; source: Bauer, Lisa, Center for Rural Entrepreneurship, Sept. 2007.

[21] Bauer, Lisa, Center for Rural Entrepreneurship, September 2007.

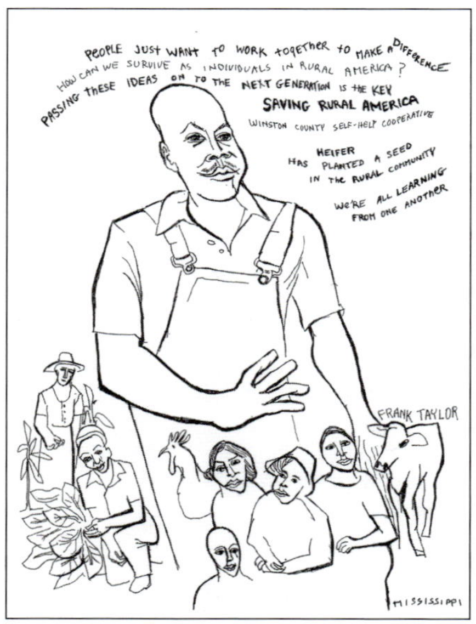

Frank Taylor, "People just want to work together . . . ," 2008

The mural panel on page 160 was inspired by a young couple, Derek and Cylesha Hardin, ages 29 and 25 respectively. As rancher members of WCHSC, they received five calves from Heifer with the understanding that they would contribute five heifers to other cooperative members. The panel portrays the magic of hands digging deep into the garden, where green meets the dark pigment of Derek's hands. Within him, plants flourish. He and his wife look out upon cows, roosters, chickens, sunflowers and gardens that they have nurtured. Cylesha's vivid pink dress is filled with flowers.

Below them, a family of four (modeled after the Hardin family of five) appreciates the lush surroundings created by members of WCSHC. The parents appreciate the opportunity their children have to learn about responsibility as they help care for the cows. The father is posed to send a message of hope to his community in the form of a bird. The mother holds her children as they, in turn, clutch carrots and scallions from the garden. One daughter's dress is decorated with seeds. Beautiful flowers and garden patches dot the internal (cow) and external landscapes. Without words, much contact is made between the animals and people. There are many ways to communicate gratitude.

USA: Gibbs Elementary School: The Worm Story p. 163

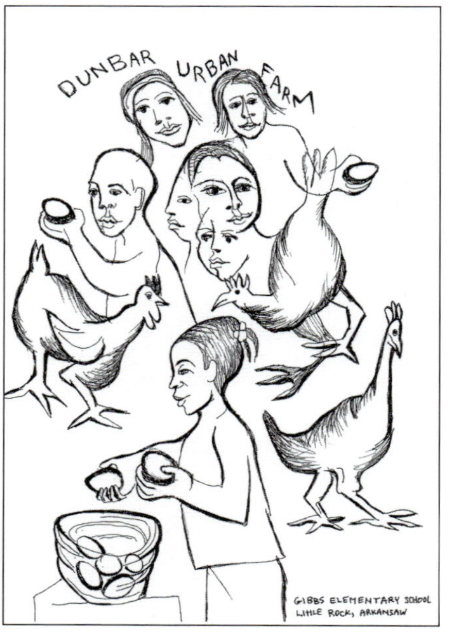

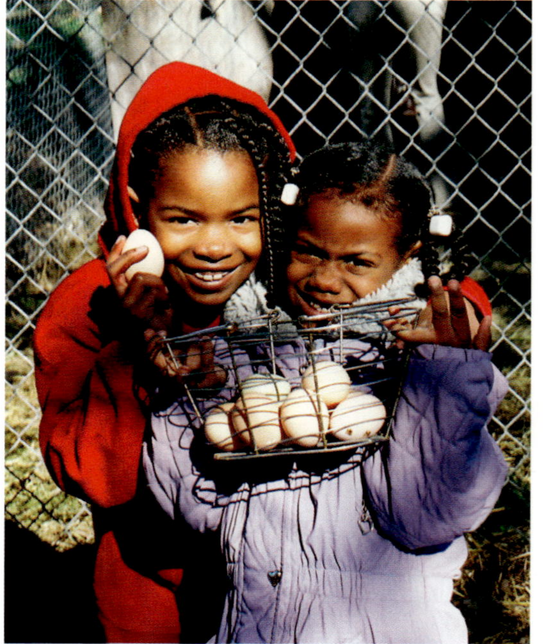

Above: *Dunbar Urban Farm* in Little Rock, Arkansas, 2008; Right: Students at Dunbar Elementary School gathering eggs, 2008

Based in an economically depressed multiracial community of South Little Rock, Arkansas, the Vermiculture Project at Gibbs Elementary School is part of Heifer's Dunbar Garden Project. Students at the Dunbar Middle School benefit from a skills-based, entrepreneurial gardening project that teaches them about organic farming, the environment and leadership. The beauty of the Dunbar Garden Project is that it can be replicated in urban schools throughout the country. In addition, children can take what they learn home to encourage their parents to grow a "kitchen garden" in the backyard.

At Gibbs Elementary School, fourth graders participate in a vermicomposting (worm compost) project. The children cultivate red earthworms, a species that prefers rotting vegetation, compost and manure. Their nutrient-rich worm castings fertilize and condition the soil of the program's gardens. In addition, a hen house and fenced-in roaming area

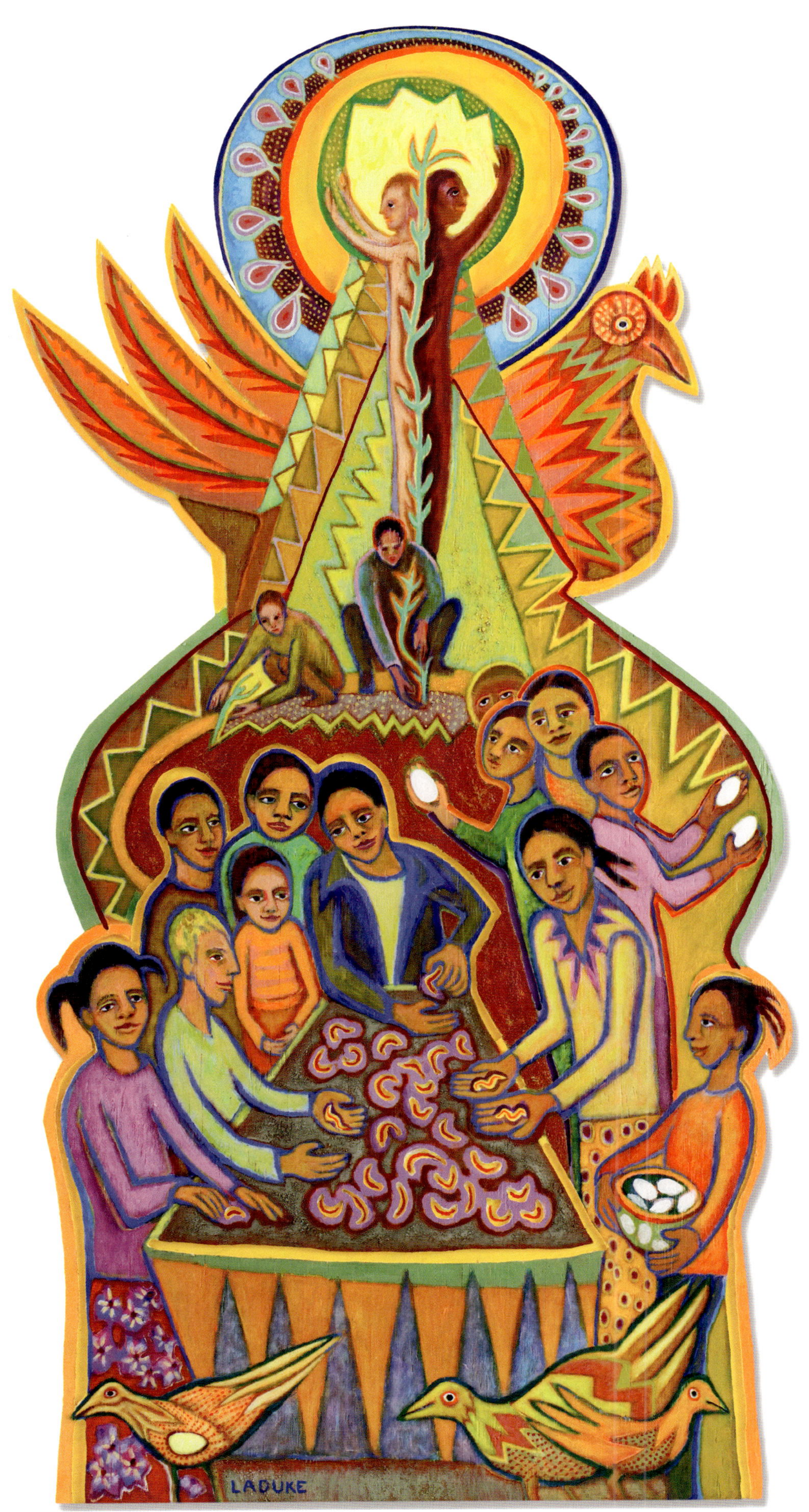

USA: Gibbs Elementary School: The Worm Story • 84"x48" • 2008

have been constructed on school grounds. Third graders gather and count eggs, which are used for the school lunch program along with garden produce such as pumpkin, melons and greens. Composted chicken manure and eggshells are added to the worms' bedding material.

On her visit to the school, Betty expected the children to shy away from the squiggly, slimy worms in big aerated bins. Rather, she found that they enjoyed creating mulch from decomposing garbage such as lunch scraps, shredded paper, decayed leaves and composted animal manure and eggshells. They formed alphabet letters with the fat squirmy bodies in the palms of their hands. In fact, they loved digging into the warm soil in search of worms. Betty was delighted to note that "they were interested and curious about science and biology, gathering around these worms to see the mystery of life at work." A tactile person herself, Betty loved watching the children smell, feel and touch the worms. She was fascinated by the idea that the worm's waste could create something so good for the soil.

In the mural panel, she strove to capture the children's delight. The multicultural mix of children—Latin, Asian, white, black—was "a nice coming together in America," especially in light of Little Rock's segregationist history.

Also portrayed is Betty's image of growth in the form of a beanstalk with a young person on each side, one black and the other white. A giant chicken forms the background landscape, representing the children's delight in "seeing life create life." Within the sun, the children throw seeds upward in a circular motion, ensuring that each child will receive seeds from the other. Symbolically and in contrast to the past, the children now work together. The sun has an aura of vegetation and growth. Below, children work in the garden and chickens roam freely. One child embraces a basket of eggs and others proudly carry individual eggs. The central image portrays a racially-mixed cluster of children who happily handle the plump red, purple and yellow worms in the mulch-filled bin.

Betty says, "I had already had four years of Heifer Education Study Tours but this was my country. It meant a lot to see an urban area with diverse people from around the world living and working together. I enjoyed reorganizing the sketches to tell a larger story about integration and working together."

USA: White Earth Reservation Wild Rice Harvest p. 167

"It is exciting to come full circle. I can now make visible to others things that I did way back when. I first experienced a wild rice harvest with Winona's father in 1958. My second time took place in the fall of 2007, only this time, I watched my grown daughter fulfill her father's dream of protecting this sacred staple of her Tribe."

—Betty LaDuke

Known as "manoomin," wild rice is a sacred hand-gathered food that grows naturally on the edges of the many lakes and rivers of the Great Lakes region. Rice collection calls for a two-person team: at the back of a canoe, one person pushes the boat forward with a pole while the person in front uses two sticks to gently whack ripened rice from the top of the plants into the boat. In this mural panel, the pole pusher is Betty's seventeen year old grandson, Ajuawak. His rice gathering partner is his mother, Winona LaDuke. In the background, another duo carries out the same tradition – an indication of the communal nature of this ancient process. Unique to this area, this "soul" food is collected by teams of Anishinaabe Tribe members who are assigned to different lakes.

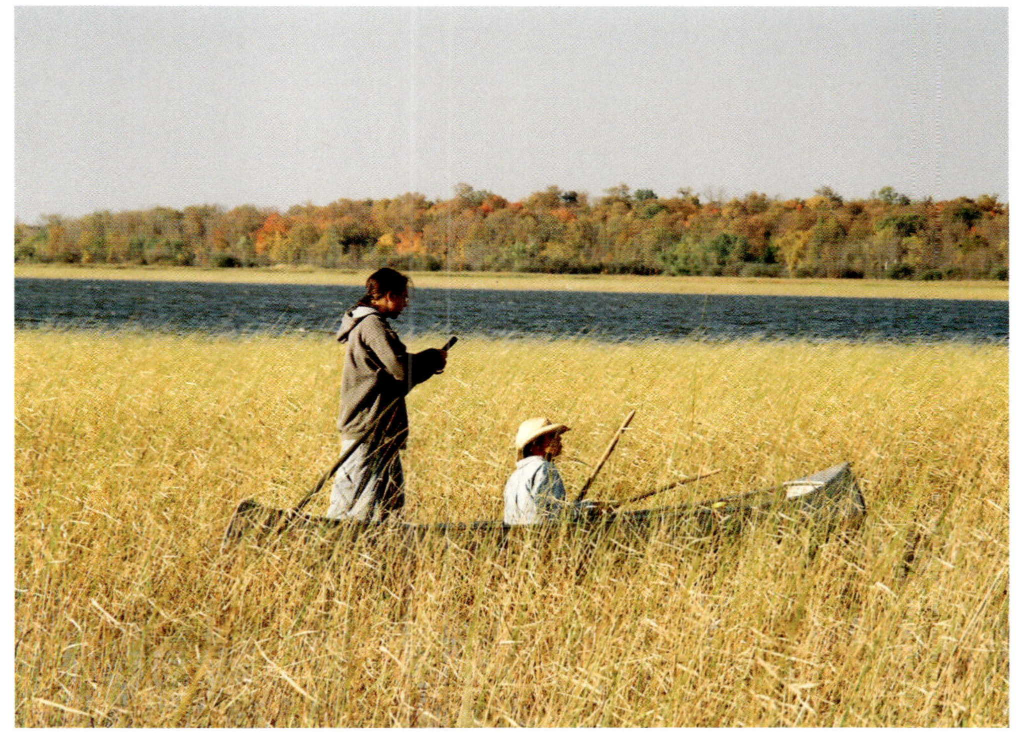

Winona and her son, Ajuawak, collecting rice, 2007

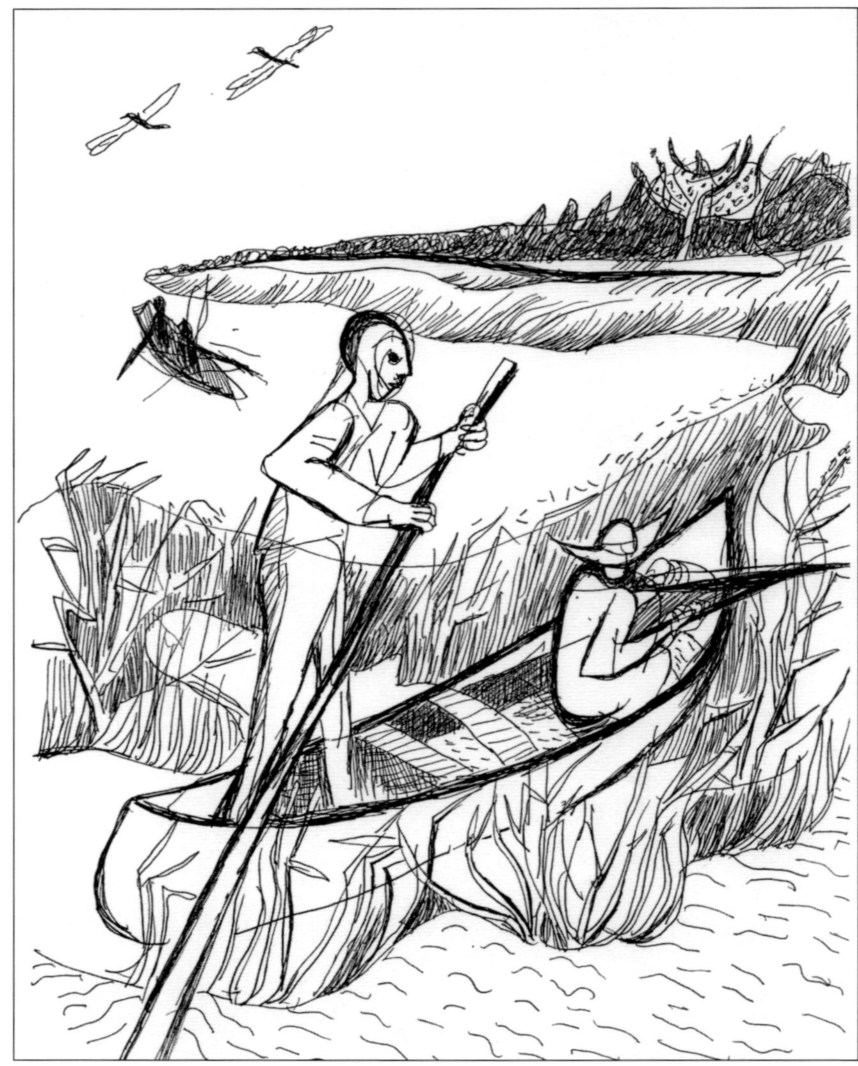

Ajuawak and Winona LaDuke collecting rice, 2007

Many spirits honor the Earth: a bird at the top of the mural panel holds a female form within it while its traveling partner carries seeds of growth ensconced in bright green. Below them, a person reaches to the skies and in the process, becomes one with the mythical bird above him. A duck at the bottom right watches the rice gathering process from his place in the stalks. He is fascinated but unafraid. Native American design patterns and symbolic rice surround the lake. In all, it is a serene and beautiful setting that is at one with nature. The mural panel captures a spiritual relationship that has to do with more than wild rice gathering—it honors the special bond that Native American people have with the land.

Once gathered, the wet rice must be parched or dried before the grain can be separated from the chaff. Heifer's contribution to the process—updated machinery that parches the rice—benefits the entire community. Families sell a portion of the rice and keep some for their families. The tribe also contributes rice to support the work of Winona's organization, the White Earth Land Recovery Project.

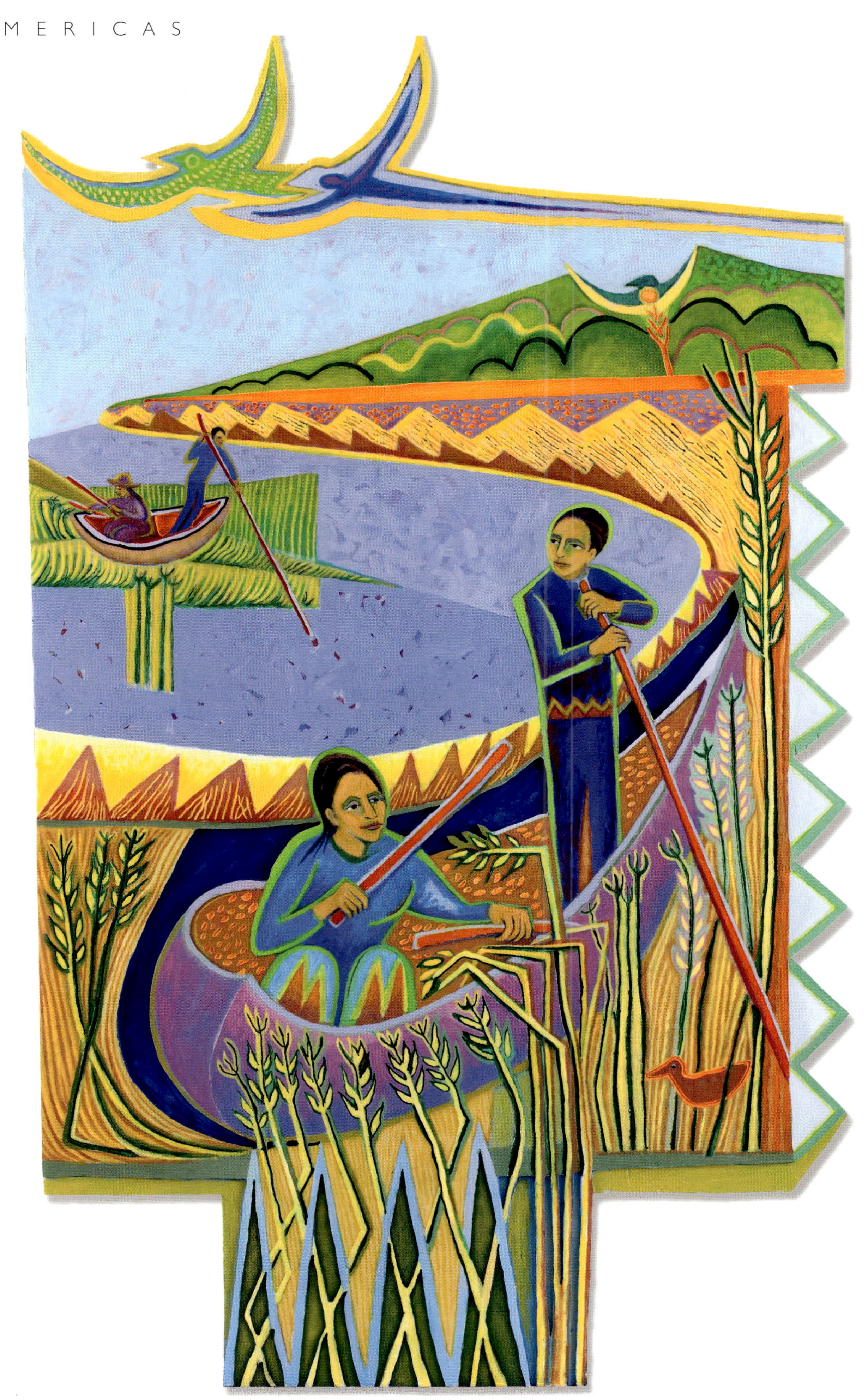

USA: White Earth Reservation Wild Rice Harvest • 84"x48" • 2007

"Across the African continent from Timbuktu in Mali to Asmara in Eritrea, women work creatively—weaving; working with leather, straw, beads or clay; painting with mud, sadza, oil or acrylic; sewing fabric appliqué; or sculpting monumental stone. Their art incorporates myth and reality as expressions of their joy, frustration, humor and hope."[1]

—Betty LaDuke

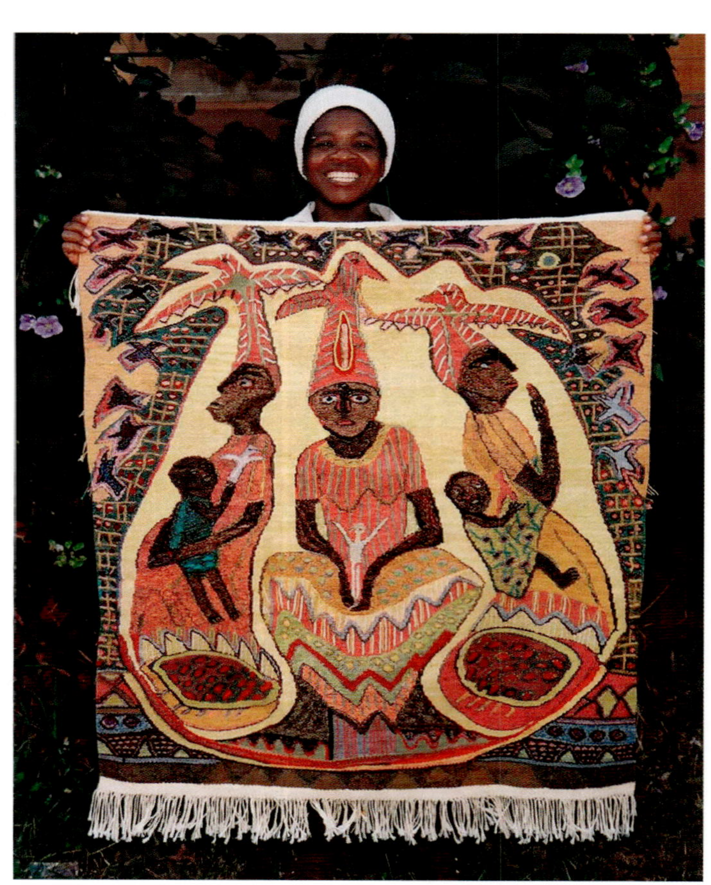

Harare, Zimbabwe, Cold Comfort Farm Weaving Collective, 2005. Reproduction tapestry design taken from Betty's painting, *Nigeria: Bird Women, Keepers of the Peace*, 1986

[1] LaDuke, Betty; *Africa: Women's Art, Women's Lives*, Africa World Press, Inc., 1996; p. ix [introduction].

Celebrating Women's Creative Hands and Spirits

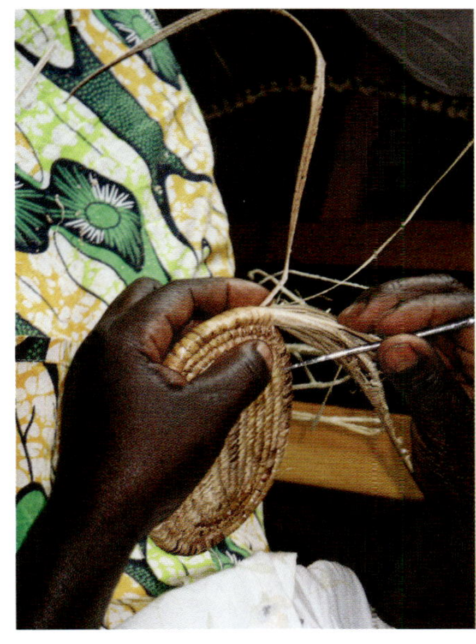
Basket weaving, Rwanda, 2006

It is fitting to describe Betty's mural panel entitled *Celebrating Women's Creative Hands and Spirits* in this final chapter because it represents a culmination of her life's work. Betty's focus through the years has been on the power and strength of women. They care for and find inventive ways to support their families; they create beauty within the often stark reality of their lives; and they speak out against injustice and violence. Their voices grow louder as they achieve some success with entrepreneurial endeavors that benefit their communities. In Betty's eyes, women are the anchor in an often troubled, multicultural world. She honors their powerful life force, which as mentioned previously, is connected to fertility, transformation, and symbolically, to multiple images of Mother Earth.

The mural panel has the archetypical Tree of Life at its center. Representing nature, it connects to the Earth below and to the sun and sky above. Betty believes that we are all a part of the Tree of Life, which, mirroring the cycle of life, is rooted in the ground to the past, connected by the trunk to the present and linked by the branches to the future. On each side of the tree is an arched panel. The right arch holds an Otomi woman who characterizes indigenous women throughout the world. On her loom, she weaves corn cobs that represent the food chain and the Earth. The eyes of the woven faces above guard the relationship between the symbolic corn and the people. In the left arch, women weave baskets with materials that transform into LaDuke birds. The baskets are as vibrant and round as the sun, which benevolently graces the scene from above. The spiral of life flickers brightly over their heads. These women epitomize what Betty means by creative hands and spirits: they weave to generate utilitarian items, to sustain their families, to express themselves, to enhance their environments with bambolse[2] and to honor the spirits.

Weaving is important to the mural panel and to Betty in her life. She has great respect for the intricacies of this craft, whether on cloth or baskets. The Cold Comfort Farm Weaving Collective outside of Harare, Zimbabwe, has honored her work by creating twenty woven renditions of the painting, *Africa: Bird Women, Keepers of the Peace* (1986). These pieces have been sold to support the Collective with the exception of one that was given to Betty in appreciation of their use of her design.

Baskets have special meaning. When she was in high school, she could not understand why her teacher was so excited about some Native American baskets that she showed to the class. But several years later when she moved to New Mexico, Betty began to

---

[2] refer to page 25 for definition of bambolse, in Chapter entitled Spiritual and Symbolic Imagery.

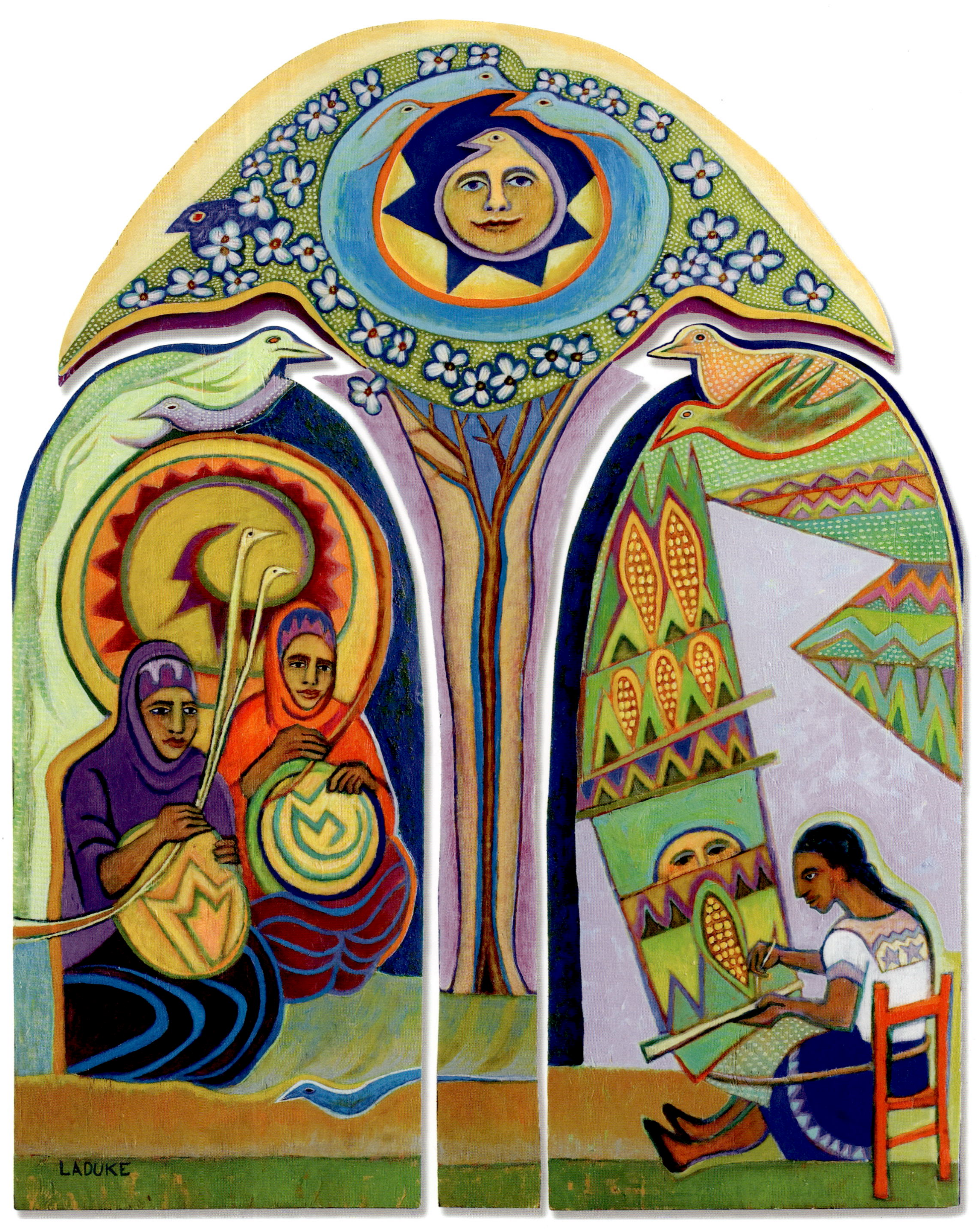

Celebrating Women's Creative Hands and Spirits • 80"x58" • 2008

appreciate the link between this ancient craft and survival. Made from renewable sources, baskets fulfill a variety of practical purposes: they hold goods to be sold at market and they function as storage bins. Design elements, some of which carry spiritual messages, identify particular regions, tribes or cultures.

Whether women are making pots, baskets, clothing, pouches, jewelry or other traditional art forms, creativity flows from their fingers. When their hearts sing and their spirits soar, this is indeed cause for celebration.

Like the women she so admires, Betty personifies the creative spirit. She is open, she is interested and she is able to translate her experience into universal truths. Her work is an affirmation of life. In Heifer International, she has found the perfect partner in that they share the same message: care for yourself, your family and your community; and care for the Earth. Whatever you give will come back to you and, much like the Heifer cows, multiply. Pass on the gift.

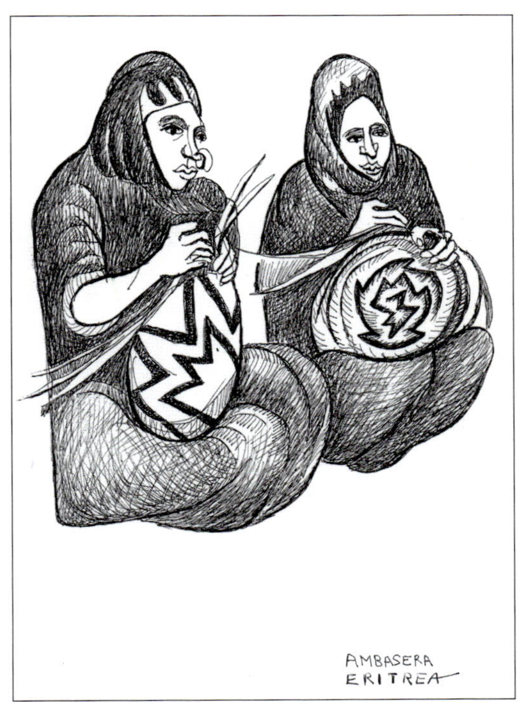

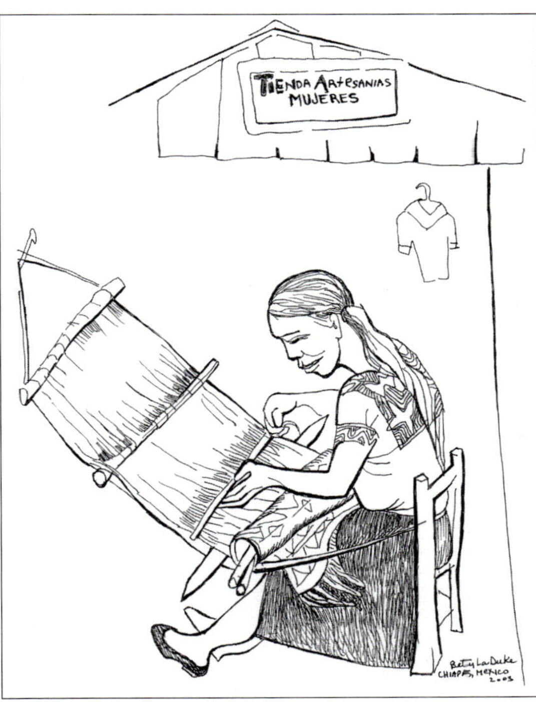

Left: Ambasera, Eritrea basket weavers, 1995; Right: Chiapas, Mexico, woman weaving on hand loom, 2003

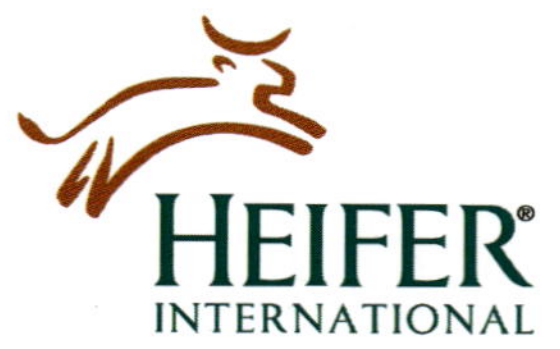
HEIFER®
INTERNATIONAL